Counsel for the Damned

Counsel
For the Damned

A BIOGRAPHY OF
GEORGE FRANCIS VANDERVEER

BY

Lowell S. Hawley

AND

Ralph Bushnell Potts

J. B. LIPPINCOTT COMPANY
PHILADELPHIA AND NEW YORK

PRINTED IN THE UNITED STATES OF AMERICA

LIBRARY OF CONGRESS CATALOG CARD NUMBER 53-8926

TO AVIS AND LUCILLE

ACKNOWLEDGMENT

POSSIBLY the most difficult task in the world is to disinter memories of a nearly forgotten day and to wipe the mind free of prejudices that have built up in the intervening years; to recall yesterday's dreams as they were dreamt, free from the distortion of retrospect. Inevitably, the dreams of youth must lose a little of their first breathless fascination when reviewed in the light of later years and greater wisdom.

However, in order to preserve the life story of George Francis Vanderveer, a conscientious effort was made by Mrs. Ellinor Vanderveer not only to recall the incidents of their life together as they must naturally appear to a mature woman looking back on life, but also to recall how they appeared to a young couple looking ahead. This she has contributed in order that the story might be told; and that there might be some belated understanding of a man who was almost universally misunderstood.

The names of two authors appear upon this work. Actually, the story that follows has been compiled from the contributions of persons too numerous to mention here. But, certainly, in addition to Mrs. Ellinor Vanderveer, some special acknowledgment should be extended to Alfred H. Lundin, Samuel B. Bassett, Will G. Beardslee and Leslie Sulgrove, who have given so liberally of their time, and to:

Lewis Abraham	Paul P. Ashley
Howard A. Adams	Dave Beck

8

ACKNOWLEDGMENTACKNOWLEDGMENT

Stephen V. Carey
Nat Carle
Stephen F. Chadwick
Ralph Chaplin
Cornelius C. Chavelle
Paul Coughlin
George H. Crandell
Miss Mary Cunningham
John F. Dore
Honorable Malcolm Douglas
Alec Duff
James A. Duncan
Frank J. Eberharter
William G. Fargher
Honorable Howard M. Findley
Mary E. Frear
Miller Freeman
H. Sylvester Garvin
John Geisness
H. Otto Giese
Warren Hardy
John S. Harlow
Benjamin T. Hart

Edward E. Henry
Honorable James W. Hodson
Tyre H. Hollander
Drayton F. Howe
Charles T. Hutson
Sam L. Levinson
Mark M. Litchman
Honorable Roger J. Meakim
John A. Milot
Charles P. Moriarty
John N. Rupp
John E. Savage
Bruce Shorts
Ford E. Smith
H. Orley Solomon
Oscar Strobel
George R. Stuntz
John N. Sylvester
Millard Thomas, Clerk of the
    U.S. District Court
Elmer E. Todd
Robert B. Walkinshaw

Counsel for the Damned

CHAPTER ONE

*Tribe follows tribe, and nation follows nation, like the waves of
the sea. Your time of decay may be distant but it will surely
come, for even the white man, whose god walks with him as
friend with friend, cannot be exempt from the common destiny.*—CHIEF SEATTLE

O<small>N THE SEVENTEENTH</small> of July, 1897, the Alaska steamer
Portland, with more than a ton of gold aboard, nudged
its way through the waters of Puget Sound toward Schawa-
bacher's Wharf in Seattle. She saluted with a long low blast
from her whistle that echoed amid the cheers of men and
women jammed tightly together clear back to the foot of
Union Street, for rumors of the Klondike gold strike already
had swept across the nation.

By the time the *Portland* was tied up at the wharf and her
gangplank lowered, a new era had begun in the history of
the Pacific Northwest. Two days earlier Seattle had been a
modestly growing metropolis off in the far corner of a
nation, the northernmost major city accessible by the trans-
continental railways. Now it was on the main line of Opportunity, in a strategic spot to sell outfits and supplies and
steamship tickets to men bound for the Yukon. Also, it was
in a strategic spot to greet the returning sourdough with his
poke full of gold, and to offer him everything that his gold
could buy; and particularly the things he had missed most

during the long and lonely months—the glory of human companionship and the touch of a feminine hand.

Reservations for the return trip north aboard the *Portland* had been sold out while the ship was still wallowing through the swells of the Strait on her southbound journey, and while rumors about the extent of the great gold strike were still unconfirmed. The demand for steamship tickets had kept pace with the rumors, and vacationing tourists who had booked passage for the trip now found themselves holding reservations as valuable as the winning tickets of a sweepstakes.

Loggers swarmed in from the hills to pool their wealth and bid for tickets. Farmers offered title to their land in exchange for reservations. Businessmen and civic leaders left their jobs and traded their savings for passage north to that fabulous land where, according to reports, gold nuggets could be dug from the earth almost as easily as clams could be dug from the shores of Puget Sound.

Owners of small fishing boats, cannery tenders, river boats, and inter-Sound stern-wheelers studied maps and charts of the Inland Passage, and the great migration was under way. Potential passengers offered to pay fantastic prices and they were not demanding about accommodations. They swarmed aboard everything that would float, and aboard a few things that wouldn't. They pitched tents on barges to be towed by heavy-laden tug boats, and before long a pilot could almost chart his course by skirting the bleached and broken bones of other ships that had foundered on the way.

Seattle streets leading down to the waterfront sparkled with the newly painted signs of Northern outfitters as merchants scrambled for the profits to be made on boots and shoes and kerosene lanterns, pickaxes and bedrolls. Horses and pack-mules sold at incredible prices, and some of the more ingenious citizens discovered that a profit could be made from the mongrel dogs rounded up from the city's streets. Yukon-bound fortune hunters had heard that they might need sled

dogs, and even fox terriers were purchased at high prices by
the more desperate and the more gullible.

Recognizing a good thing, Seattle businessmen and the
Chamber of Commerce got behind a promotional campaign
to tell the world about the fortunes being made in the Yukon
and in Alaska and to mention, not incidentally, that Seattle
was the gateway to Alaska—"The Queen City of Puget
Sound—Where Rail Meets Sail." Press releases poured out in
a steady stream. Special editions of Seattle newspapers were
sent out in wholesale numbers, and local citizens were urged
to send copies to the folks back home. Yukon gold reacted as
a growth-hormone for the area, and each day more people
came.

There were hard-bitten men who had begged or borrowed
a grubstake, determined to reach the gold fields; victims of
gold fever—desperate men with desperate dreams, spending
their last dollars at the outfitting stores in Seattle. There were
tight-lipped men who came but didn't say much; who put up
at the best hotels and walked around the city in silent meditation; and then left as quietly as they had come. There were
professional men from all parts of the country: physicians,
surgeons, dentists, lawyers, teachers, clergymen.

There were bartenders and blacksmiths, undertakers and
prostitutes. There were those who came without knowing
why they came; irresistibly drawn by a golden magnet. Seattle was booming, while the rest of the country was still struggling to pull itself out of the depression of 1893. There were
those who drifted in because they had to be on the move;
because there was no other place to stop. And they jammed
up in the Pacific Northwest like tumbleweeds in the corner
of a prairie fence.

Grubstakes dwindled as the impatient newcomers awaited
their chance for passage north and, meanwhile, tried to keep
abreast of hotel and boardinghouse prices which were creeping ever upward in the face of increasing demand. Many of
the fortune seekers were obliged to lower their sights. Their

interest shifted away from gold nuggets to bread and butter.
They moved out to the logging camps and to the shingle
mills, to the wheat fields and to the orchards, looking for
work . . . begging for work:

"Christ Almighty, mister—a man has got to eat! What do
you expect me to do? Just keep walkin' and starve to death?"

The farms and the mills and the factories and the canneries
and the logging camps absorbed many of them; whistle punks
and harvest hands, berry pickers and apple knockers, fish-
scalers, tie-cutters and roustabouts. Some of them worked
hard but they didn't always accomplish much because it was
all new and all different, and they had to learn the ropes.
They worked cheap, however, and usually they didn't demand much. Many of them brought along their bedrolls, still
bearing the bright new tags of the Northern outfitters, and
all they needed was a place to spread them out. Three square
meals a day, and a little tobacco money. That was enough—
to start with. Collectively, competing with one another for
jobs, they helped to establish a basis of cheap labor to be in-
corporated into a new industrial economy.

In the city things were still booming. New arrivals were
waiting to take the hotel rooms vacated by those who had
gone broke and departed, and the new arrivals had dreams in
their eyes and dollars in their pockets. They headed straight
for the outfitting stores and then they, too, took their turn at
waiting.

Seattle prospered, and as it grew, its streets were extended
and new districts were opened. New and better buildings
rose where once had stood the outskirts, and the more prosperous citizens moved to the better homes and to the better
buildings, leaving behind the cradle of their civic birth:
dreary, aging buildings with tall dark windows; pawnshops
and cheap stores; flophouses and second-hand emporiums;
streetwalkers, human derelicts, and soapbox orators. This was
Old Town, spread out near the waterfront; clustered about
Pioneer Place, First and Second Avenues South, and creeping

upward along Yesler Way—an angling street tracing the
course of an ancient skid road where Henry Yesler's oxen once
had skidded the giant logs of a virgin forest to his waterfront
mill.

It was Mark Matthews, a tall, thin, dynamic minister of the
Gospel, who thundered from his Presbyterian pulpit that human souls were being skidded down the same old road to per-
dition. Thus did Seattle get the name of its Skid Road district,
and thus did a nation add a new definition to its lexicon . . .
although Eastern journalists changed the term to skid *row*
when giving it local application, and the error has been
perpetuated.

To the Skid Road district of Seattle came the itinerant
workers, the bindlestiffs, the underpaid and the overexploited;
the uneducated and the uncultured; the pimps and the prostitutes and the pickpockets; the unshaved, the unwashed, and
the unwanted. Like the Puget Sound Indians before them, they
were pushed back to their reservation, and they shared membership in a legion of the damned. However, the Skid Road
district rendered a remarkable service in heading off Northern
gold before it could leave Seattle.

Many a sourdough returning from the North dissipated his
hard-won fortune within a few blocks of the docks where his
ship had landed, as he was goaded into buying drinks for the
house and silk stockings for the ladies of the evening. More
than one grizzled old prospector who had withstood the hazards of a Yukon winter failed to survive his first night back in
the States, and was found the next morning floating in the
waters of Puget Sound, face down, and pockets emptied.

By the dawn of the twentieth century, Seattle was a booming, sweating, sprawling, expanding metropolis of more than
eighty thousand population. It stood in the heart of one of the
greatest stands of virgin timber the world has ever known.
From the waters of Puget Sound came salmon in seemingly
endless numbers. And from the Klondike in the year 1900
came twenty-two million dollars' worth of gold.

Everywhere was a vast frenzy to get a share of the abundant but elusive wealth. Great fishtraps fringed the edges of the Sound and the silvery hordes of salmon approximated in value all the gold of the Klondike. Swarms of men moved through the forest armed with axe and saw, and the great trees crashed to earth to scream their protest as they passed through the giant saws of the lumber mills. Their discarded branches withered and dried, and fires raced across the logged-off land and licked at the standing timber until the hills were black and ugly. Seattle had become the boom town of the nation. Klondike gold had robbed it of its chance for normal growth and, like a child in a fairy story who is touched by a golden wand, it grew up almost overnight.

Not the least of those who helped to bring about the miracle of transformation were the men who wrote and revised and interpreted the rules of the struggle as it progressed—the referees and the ringside judges who attempted to enforce some semblance of the Marquis of Queensbury rules upon a rough-and-tumble battle for a multi-million-dollar purse. These were the men who wrote the laws of a new territory and the constitution of a new state—the men who established the courts, and struggled to trace the elusive threads of justice.

For the most part, they left no monuments except for the long rows of dusty volumes to be found in the law libraries of a later generation. They leveled no hills and they erased no forests. And yet they were a part of all of it, and apart from all of it.

Perhaps the most colorful and certainly the most controversial legal figure of the Pacific Northwest during its most dramatic era was George Francis Vanderveer. Judges who presided at his trials and lawyers who opposed him in the courtroom readily acknowledged him to be the outstanding trial lawyer of the Northwest, and there were many who rated him above Clarence Darrow in the national scale. He saved dozens of men from the hangman's noose, and he pitied them for the stupidity that got them into trouble. He defended men intent upon revolution and told them, at the same time, that their plans were ridiculous. He was a man goaded by restless passions which drove him, always, to seek the path of greatest resistance—to throw his weight upon the short side of an uneven struggle and to glory in the excitement of the battle.

George Vanderveer arrived in Seattle in 1901, when he was twenty-six. He held degrees from Stanford and Columbia Universities and he had begun his law practice in New York City before succumbing to the lure that was drawing men from all walks of life to the turbulent arena of the Pacific Northwest. He was admitted to the practice of law in the State of Washington, and he solemnly repeated the oath required at that time—at least one sentence of which was destined to shape the pattern of his life:

"I solemnly promise and swear that I will never reject from any consideration personal to myself, the cause of the defenseless or oppressed. . . ."

No man who took that oath ever lived up to it more unflinchingly, or paid a higher price for his unyielding integrity. It lead him to refuse positions and retainers that would have made him wealthy; and through much of his life it denied him membership in the society to which his intellect and his tastes aspired. It drove him from the inner circles of respectability to the fringes of Skid Road, and it deeply scarred the polish of his early training until he became a brawling, blasphemous, but ever-brilliant lawyer stalking through the courtrooms of the nation and hammering out legal victories wherein the decisions were to become the precedents of a later day and age.

There is hardly a man or woman in the United States today whose conception of justice or whose rights and privileges before the court have not been affected in some measure by the precedents established by the legal battles of George Francis Vanderveer. In the State of Washington, particularly, the criminal code of the present day is largely an out-

growth of his personal efforts. And while the name of
George Vanderveer still lingers as a legend down around Skid
Road, and while that name is frequently mentioned when
attorneys get together to talk about the good old days, still
there are many in Seattle today who have not heard the name
at all. By flouting the orthodox in nearly every respect—political, marital, moral, social and civic—George Vanderveer
did little to enshrine his name as that of a respected leading
citizen.

He died in 1942, and he left no monument except that
which is inscribed within the long rows of law books in the
modern law library. In his own way, he helped to shape the
dramatic history of the Pacific Northwest during its most
colorful era; but to an even greater extent, the history of the
Pacific Northwest helped to shape the pattern of his life. He
was the product of unusual times.

Among the very few men of the legal profession who did
leave an enduring monument was Judge Thomas Burke, recognized as Seattle's leading citizen during the closing years of
the nineteenth century and the beginning of the twentieth,
and George Vanderveer's first employer in Seattle.

Not only had Judge Burke erected one of the more imposing office buildings of the city to perpetuate his name, but he
operated and owned controlling interest in the West Street
and North End Railway. Actually, it was but one of thirty-
two separate and privately owned street railways serving the
young city and operating over two hundred and twenty-one
miles of track. The W.S. & N.E., however, had a proud distinction: it was one of the few companies that had not gone
into receivership. This was due, in large measure, to the
Judge's astute management. He had recognized early in the
game that the high price of tailor-made electricity with its
expensive power installations was enough to drive a young
company to the wall; and he had shrewdly determined to roll
his own.

Thus, in the basement of the Burke Building at Second and

Marion Streets, he had installed his own private light plant. It supplied power for the Judge's street railway system, and it supplied light for the Judge's office building in downtown Seattle. It worked remarkably well except for those intermittent occasions when one of the two cars of the railway system neared the end of the long winding track which led clear to Ballard; but then, because of resistance and distance from the source of supply, the car would sap the power from the lines. All of the electric lights in the Burke Building would fade under the strain until their filaments glowed dull red, and the distant streetcar would creep ahead at a snail's pace while passengers leaned forward in their seats as if determined to help resolve the crisis by the combined strength of their will power. Somehow the crisis was always met and conquered.

By the turn of the century, the Judge had advanced to the point where his thoughts concerned the welfare of his city rather than the welfare of his own personal empire, and he welcomed the proposal by Stone and Webster that all of the independent street railway companies be bought and consolidated into one city-wide system. Despite the fact that the West Street and North End Railway had remained solvent, it was offered as a part of the over-all package, along with all of the companies that had gone into receivership, and the Judge was happy in the belief that his city would soon have a coordinated and adequate public transportation system.

It was Judge Burke who, in 1896, led the great civic fight before the Seattle City Council to prevent the Northern Pacific Railway from erecting a half-million-dollar station across the face of Seattle's waterfront. It was Judge Burke who warned the city fathers not to vacate public streets leading down to the waterfront in exchange for getting a railroad depot that might look pretty on picture postcards. Those streets leading down to the waterfront, he warned, were the veins and arteries that would handle the life blood of a great city of the future. And while it might be pertinent to note

that the Judge, at the time, was western counsel for the Great
Northern, a competing railway, and was the personal representative of James J. Hill, still the city was not long in
conceding that his arguments were valid and that the best interests of the city were being served by his efforts—either pur-
posefully or coincidentally. Even the transient population of
Skid Road, which claimed no abiding interest in Seattle's future,
nevertheless hailed the Judge's triumph in blocking the proposal. They were opposed to the idea of donating public
streets to a railway company, just as a matter of principle.
But their cheers were mostly for the Judge's victory, and not
for the Judge himself.

For it was the same Judge Burke who, a decade earlier,
had opposed the will of a disorganized mob intent upon running all of the Chinese out of Seattle, as a part of the general
anti-Chinese revolt sweeping the Pacific Coast. He had stood
up at a mass meeting and appealed to the workingmen to uphold the authority of the law. In an impassioned and dramatic speech before a hostile audience, he had pointed out
that tyranny begins when law and order end, and that the
workingmen become slaves under tyranny. Seattle ultimately
had pulled through its period of disturbance with the best
record of any major city on the Pacific Coast for upholding
the rights of its minority, but Judge Burke had not come out
of the struggle unscathed. Previously popular with the working classes, he had emerged from the anti-Chinese riots with
the contemptuous cognomen of "Chink-lover." The laboring
men who had revolted against the influx of cheap Chinese
labor showed little inclination to forgive and forget, even as
they cheered his victory over the Northern Pacific Railway.

By the time George Vanderveer arrived in Seattle, an air
of prosperous serenity had settled over the Judge's private
domain. His law clients included some of the largest and
most prosperous corporations of the Northwest; and while
the lights of the Burke Building still dimmed each time a
car of the street railway system neared the end of the line,

the Judge hastened to explain that it was only temporary. Already he was toying with the idea of erecting a new office building across the street—larger, more imposing, and a more enduring monument.

It was Kenneth Mackintosh, Vanderveer's former classmate at Stanford and at Columbia, who arranged the meeting between young Vanderveer and the aging Judge Burke. Mackintosh was well established in the Judge's office, and his enthusiastic recommendation no doubt had a great deal to do with the Judge's prompt offer to give young Vanderveer a job.

It was a happy combination, bringing together the careers of two of the outstanding attorneys of the Northwest; one nearing the end of his career and the other just starting out. For a while they moved quietly along like two of the Judge's streetcars on parallel tracks, with one headed toward the carbarns and the other just beginning its long careening trip toward the far horizon. And yet, while they were close together, there was little evidence of the driving power which each, in his own right, was capable of producing. Possibly the magnetic poles of two great personalities so close together served to neutralize each other.

The Judge's respect and admiration for young Vanderveer was not long in the making. The Judge, by his own admission, had just taken one hell of a beating in court. It had been a routine case, he confided. His client, the scion of a wealthy family, was accused of sneaking up the back steps of the family home and sleeping with a servant girl, who charged that he was the father of her illegitimate son. She demanded money for the child's support.

There were no corroborating witnesses. She accused and he denied. It was her word against his, and the shadow of a reasonable doubt was as big as all outdoors.

The boy, a college student, told a straightforward story that was not shaken in any way on cross-examination. Although the lad had a nervous habit of running his tongue

over his dry lips, the Judge felt positive that the jury had
believed him. The girl, on the other hand, appeared a little
too glib to be convincing.

The case was already won, the Judge felt. However, in his
final argument to the jury, the girl's attorney unleashed a blis-
tering attack against the defendant. "What manner of man is
this, who will seduce a poor, innocent working girl, profess
his love for her, and then lack the manhood and the decency
to acknowledge his own son?"

The college boy sat and blushed through the tirade, looking self-conscious and licking nervously at his dry lips.

"There are laws of man and laws of God!" the attorney
shouted. "And one of God's immutable laws is—like father,
like son. Now look at the father. Observe his facial manner-
isms. And now look at his son."

The attorney whirled and pointed to the spot where the
tiny infant sat in his mother's arms. Every eye in the courtroom turned to look. There sat the baby, running his little
spike of a tongue around his lips in exact imitation of the
defendant. The jury was out less than a half hour, and
brought in a verdict for twenty-five thousand dollars against
the Judge's client.

Judge Burke laughed as he recited the facts of the case, but
it was not a happy laugh; and George Vanderveer undertook
to do a little investigating on his own.

Being unfamiliar with the habits of infants, he took his
problem first to a physician and inquired as to what would
cause such behavior. He received the off-hand conjecture
that it might be something sweet; candy, maybe. More likely
syrup. Something sticky that couldn't be wiped away by the
first lick of the tongue.

A few afternoons later, young Vanderveer had the complete explanation ready for the Judge: "What they used on
the baby's lips was molasses. I've located the store where
they bought it—a little grocery store not far from the Courthouse. The man who runs the place described the girl and

the attorney perfectly. It was on the last afternoon of the trial. They came in and bought the molasses, and they had the baby with them; and they stood right there in the store and debated whether or not it would show on the baby's face. The old man remembers it because it struck him as an odd kind of discussion at the time."

The Judge was highly pleased and he assigned Vanderveer the task of interviewing jurors on the case, seeking affidavits from them to support a motion for a new trial. Many of the former jurors agreed that they had been impressed by the baby's odd behavior and that this might have affected their decision. The decision and judgment were set aside and the case was never renoted for trial.

"You're going to go a long way in this business," the Judge predicted. "Too many young lawyers nowadays want to sit in the library and use their eyes looking up precedents, instead of getting out and using their feet to run down the facts in the case. In the successful practice of law, you have to use your feet as well as your head."

Vanderveer's admiration for Judge Burke was immediate and overwhelming. He liked the disarming informality of the man, the Irish twinkle of his eyes, the erectness of the squat figure, the dynamic vitality which had not burned itself out even yet. He admired the Judge's vast knowledge of the law and his ability to use that knowledge. But most of all he admired Judge Burke because he saw in him a man of dauntless courage who would enter a fight without asking the odds, and give to that fight every last ounce of his energy and his capacity for struggle.

During his first week in the Judge's office, Vanderveer heard an account of the part the Judge had played during the anti-Chinese revolt and it fascinated him. From that day forward he eyed the Judge with even greater respect.

Sometimes in the evenings he would give voice to his admiration during the course of discussions with his new-found attorney friends in Seattle, Ira Campbell, Bud Cummings, Herman Frye, or Bruce Shorts:

"I tell you, you've got to respect the old boy. It takes a lot of courage to stand up in front of a howling mob and stick up for a minority like the Chinese. You can't help admiring a man for that."

On one occasion, in the midst of a rare confidential mood, Vanderveer told Bruce Shorts: "Actually, when you come right down to it, there's only one real way you can measure a man. He can inherit money, or brains, or good looks, and he's not responsible for that. Whether he's a Methodist minister or a Skid Road pimp may depend a lot on how he's raised and what kind of a start he got in life. But I tell you, you have to admire a man who has the courage to go ahead and do what he starts out to do—what he thinks needs to be done. You can say whatever else you want to about him; but, by God, you've got to admit that he's a man."

CHAPTER TWO

Next to knowing when to seize an opportunity, the most important thing in life is knowing when to forego an advantage.
—DISRAELI

DAVID VANDERVEER, successful Iowa grain broker and former blacksmith, had realized for many years that his son, George, was a restless and an unregimented soul. And as a man who knew and loved and understood horses, he felt that he also understood people. It wasn't that George was ever a bad boy, he pointed out. It was merely that he was high spirited, and had an inborn rebellion against the harness.

Young George represented the "second crop" in David's paternal life, born after many fallow years, and after his other children had grown and married and moved away; and after David had lost his first wife and had married the much younger Mary Atwood Francis. To many of the neighbors and to some of David's own family, this second marriage appeared to be an example of an old man's foolishness, for he was already past fifty and had daughters older than his bride.

For a time David and Mary lived at Grinnell, Iowa, and here George Francis Vanderveer was born on August 2, 1875. He was the only child of the second marriage, and the only child within the home. Almost from the start there appeared to be an unusually strong attachment between the mother and the son.

Mary Vanderveer was a young woman of striking beauty,

with luxurious hair that hung to her waist and with a glowing complexion that belied her none-too-robust health. She
possessed a love of beauty and of culture, an admiration for
good books and good music, and a complete lack of interest
in her neighbors and in her surroundings in Grinnell. Her
home was her castle, and she seldom ventured beyond the
castle gates.

David Vanderveer remained the patient husband and the
indulgent father, proud of his home and proud of his family.
But much of his interest remained in another world where he
was engaged in buying and selling grain, studying market
conditions and crop forecasts, keeping one eye upon the
weather and remaining prayerfully hopeful that he might not
displease the gods in charge of early frosts, late rains, and
droughts. He spent more and more time away from home,
and after a few years he moved his wife and young son to
Ames, where he could be at home more regularly.

In the year 1889, when George was fourteen years of age
and halfway through high school, tragedy struck the Vanderveer household. Having suffered with varicose veins since the
birth of her son, Mary Vanderveer died as the result of sudden and severe hemorrhage while her husband and her son
stood at her bedside; and from that day forward, David Vanderveer attempted to fill an obvious void in his son's life.

Fourteen was just the wrong age for a boy to lose his
mother, he conceded later. "Younger children are better able
to forget, and older children are better able to understand."
But he did the best he could.

George returned from his mother's funeral with grave mis-
givings about a God who was a jealous God and who had
loved Mary Vanderveer so much that He had taken her for
His own, with apparent disregard of the fact that George had
loved her, too. Years later George Vanderveer confessed to
his wife that his mother's death had destroyed his previous
conception of a just and benevolent world, that he had rebelled against it; and had seethed at the futility of his own

rebellion. The trite and perhaps foolish phrases of a nine-teenth century funeral oration undoubtedly left their scars upon his restless soul.

David Vanderveer, ex-blacksmith and anxious parent, ap-plied the only remedy he knew how to apply. He tightened up on the check-reins and began his patient vigil to keep his high-spirited son from kicking over the traces.

Almost from the day of her son's birth, Mary Vanderveer had planned for him to attend college; and shortly after her passing, David turned his thoughts to the problem of selecting a proper university. One problem concerned him deeply: George had developed a fiery and spontaneous temper and he seemed hardly the type to submit to the customary hazing of Freshmen at the larger Eastern schools. Surely he would fight back, and fight viciously. The sting of a paddle against his posterior would undoubtedly set off that wild flailing of fists, and David could envision a crisis with possible expulsion during the first week. You couldn't rightfully expect a high-spirited boy like George to submit to that sort of thing any more than you could expect to apply a whip to a high-spirited horse without having the box stall become a shambles.

Sensational stories about the hazings at Eastern and Mid-western colleges were frequently in the news, and from vari-ous friends who had attended such schools he received detailed descriptions of the hazing programs—none of which set his mind at rest.

At about this time he became interested in another possibil-ity. Senator Stanford had endowed a new university at Palo Alto, California, scheduled to open on October first, 1891—a new university that would have no entrenched upperclass-men and therefore no organized hazing program. No initia-tion. No traditions to uphold. Possibly if George could move in here on the ground floor and get adjusted to his new en-vironment without any great crisis at the start, he might be able to move on through the four-year college course without complications.

David Vanderveer made inquiries and wrote for literature. He was particularly impressed by the reputation of Stanford University's President, David Starr Jordan. He talked it over with his son, and was pleased to find almost equal enthusiasm. There was something challenging in the idea of starting off at a new school and helping to form its traditions. Also, there was something particularly appealing to sixteen-year-old George in the idea of making a trip to California.

They moved out West the following September—father and son, together. At the start of George's Freshman year, David Vanderveer remained in Palo Alto in order to keep a little cautious pressure on the parental check-rein, and to do what he could to see that his son got the right kind of start. The distinguished-looking father with his strong face and neatly trimmed white beard and with his erect and powerful body became a familiar figure on the campus. He even attempted to help select George's friends, and to bolster his son's popularity among members of his class by inviting various students to join the two of them at supper.

His well-meant efforts failed to inspire any true appreciation on the part of his son. George demanded the right to select his own friends and to live his own life, pointing out that other students were able to attend school without such close parental supervision.

Years later Vanderveer recalled an incident wherein his father had attempted to interest him in another Stanford classmate who had lived in Iowa—Herbert Clark Hoover—but George would have nothing of it. So far as Vanderveer was concerned, the fact that Hoover had lived in West Branch, Iowa, was not much of a recommendation. Vanderveer expressed an unfavorable opinion of Hoover to which he clung even after the latter had been elected President of the United States.

Because of his son's rebellion against such close parental guidance, David Vanderveer left Palo Alto and took up his residence at the Coronado Hotel near San Diego. Before leaving the campus, however, he demanded and received the boy's reluctant promise not to turn out for football.

David Vanderveer had strong feelings on the subject of football. He argued vehemently that it should be abolished as a college sport. The old man insisted that it was too rough, too brutal, capable of inflicting permanent injury upon the players. Oddly enough, he did not offer any opposition to his son's participation in the school's boxing and wrestling programs and in succeeding years he offered encouragement by correspondence as George disposed of all of the opposition in his own weight division and climbed well upward into the heavier ranks.

An excellent student, pushed ahead in the early grades because of his mother's tutelage at home, George Vanderveer had entered Stanford as one of the youngest members of his class; and not until his Junior year, did he reach his full stature—approximately five feet, nine inches. In his Senior year he weighed one hundred and sixty pounds.

Left on his own at school, George quickly found his own circle of friends and he adjusted himself readily. He was popular with students and faculty members alike; pledged Beta Theta Pi and, to his father's surprise, accepted his initiation in good grace.

By coincidence, several of his closest friends at Stanford had come from the recently admitted State of Washington. There was Kenneth Mackintosh, an exceptionally handsome young man, widely conceded to have the most brilliant mind of any man in his class. He was a member of a pioneer family in Seattle and, like George Vanderveer, he had skipped rapidly through his preparatory schooling. The two men found common cause as the youngest members of their class.

There was Nat Carl, Vanderveer's roommate, who played guard on the Stanford football team and who invested his idle moments in a running tribute to God's country and the Pacific Northwest.

There was big Bill Campbell, star tackle of the Stanford

varsity and one of Vanderveer's idols and closest friends. Bill
Campbell hailed from Grays Harbor County in Washington,
and while he spent less time acting the part of a self-ordained
press-agent for the Pacific Northwest, he generally could be
counted upon to verify the boasts of the others. "That's the
absolute truth, Van. It's great country up there."

If young George Vanderveer was in any way impressed by
all the propaganda, he avoided giving any indication of it.
He claimed no attachment to his own home state of Iowa, and
he accused his friends of juvenile sentimentality. Jubilantly
he recited every news item and every batch of statistics
he could find which tended to discredit the State of Washington, and he offered involved theories about the harmful effects
of living in a damp climate. It was a game, but at times it
became heated under the pressure of youthful debate.

Those who knew George Vanderveer well during his college days shared the opinion that he was a young man with
one overwhelming sorrow. Despite his many honors won in
the boxing ring, he obviously regretted the fact that he could
not be on the football team. Football was a major sport and
boxing was a minor sport. Football offered the close companionship of team cooperation and squad spirit, while boxing
was mostly a solo enterprise, and the term "boxing team" a
misnomer. Through all of his years at Stanford, George Vanderveer watched and cheered and admired and apparently
envied the men who played on the team.

Each afternoon when the team came off the practice field
he would be waiting in the gymnasium for his roommate, Nat
Carl, and each afternoon he would challenge Carl to put on
the gloves with him.

"I'm dog-tired," Carl would usually protest. "All I want
to do is get out of this suit and take a shower. Let's just skip it
today, shall we?" But George Vanderveer would insist, and
usually the other members of the squad would gather around
to watch the battle.

Vanderveer lacked the height and the reach of his roommate, and he was outweighed by more than fifty pounds; but he packed tremendous power in either hand and was as clever and as fast as a professional fighter. Big Nat Carl, tired and slow, would usually take quite a beating at the outset. However, there were no rounds or rest periods, and sooner or later he would land a wild-swinging blow that would send the lighter man to the canvas. Then, over Vanderveer's protests as he scrambled to his feet, the big guard would pull off his gloves and call it quits for the day—and promise to try it again tomorrow.

There was no sparring and there were no pulled punches in the daily battle. It was as vicious and as savage as two contenders fighting for a championship; and yet they were roommates, fraternity brothers, and the very best of friends. No doubt it was Vanderveer's method of demonstrating that he was just as rough and tough and durable as any man on the squad. He relished the cheers and the words of encouragement and the friendly back-slapping from all of the players on the team. It was almost like being one of them. But not quite.

Big Bill Campbell, who later became Judge William Campbell of Grays Harbor County, Washington, recalled a particularly embittered outburst from Vanderveer just a few days before graduation. The two men were strolling side by side across the campus when Vanderveer confided that his one great regret was that he had not been able to play football for his alma mater. "And it's too late now to change it," he concluded. "That's the part that gets you—realizing that it's all over, and your last chance is gone. I can imagine that's what it's like when you get old and you're about ready to die, and you look back over your life and realize that you never did the things you really wanted to do . . . and there's not a thing in the world you can do about it."

Big Bill Campbell stopped in his tracks, and stood with his hands on his hips while he gazed at his companion and slowly shook his head. "You're working yourself into a lather over nothing at all," he protested. "Football isn't that important."

Vanderveer stared at him. "You big dumb ox!" he sighed. "You don't even know what I'm talking about, do you? It's not playing football that's important—it's the satisfaction of knowing that you did what you wanted to do, while you had the chance! Or it's that damn empty feeling in the pit of your stomach when you realize that you've let your last chance slip past, and now it's too late to change it! It's the— aw hell! You wouldn't understand!"

However, Judge Campbell felt that he did understand when he recalled the incident years later. He felt that he had a personal insight into the peculiar, restless driving force which made George Vanderveer one of the most colorful and controversial figures of the Pacific Northwest—a man with an insatiable lust for life and the full living of it—a man with a virtual mania for throwing himself into the midst of a struggle where he could fight shoulder-to-shoulder with other men toward a contested goal, and whose interest in the goal itself was never greater than his love of playing the game.

After graduation from Stanford, George Vanderveer joined Kenneth Mackintosh and Bill Campbell in moving on to the Law School of Columbia University in New York. He had completed his four years of study and received his Bachelor of Arts degree without so much as being placed upon probation, and David Vanderveer readily admitted that his pride and his pleasure were surpassed only by his amazement. He felt quite certain that George, by now, had completely found himself, and he never seriously considered moving along with him to New York. Instead, he made his plans to return to Iowa and turn his attention once again to the grain brokerage business.

During the years that immediately followed, David Vanderveer had reason to be satisfied with the quality of his horse-sense. The intricacies of the legal profession seemed to offer a challenge to his son's ever-restless intellect. Somewhere amid the involved history of common law and man's long struggle to establish human dignity, George Vanderveer apparently found a new conception of the principles of justice and a new foundation for the illusions which had been so completely shattered at the time of his mother's death.

With a generosity that was typical of him, David Vanderveer wrote to his son about a week before his graduation from Law School and explained that the monthly checks would continue to be sent until such time as George had found a position in New York and felt that his own income was adequate. His parental pride almost overwhelmed him when he received a letter in return, in which George insisted that he would accept no more financial help.

David Vanderveer was satisfied, then, that his long parental vigil was ended. Mary, he felt sure, would have shared in his boundless pride.

In New York City George Vanderveer was starting out without financial support for the first time in his life, and he discovered that it wasn't easy. He and Bill Campbell had agreed between them that New York was the logical place for a young lawyer to build his career, but they soon discovered that the city was densely populated with law firms which had no interest in a couple of young men just out of law school. Campbell was the first to land a job; it was not particularly to his liking and it gave him little opportunity to use his newly acquired education, but he accepted it readily and explained to Vanderveer that he would keep on looking for something better.

Vanderveer, growing increasingly discouraged, accepted a position as a law clerk with a large firm—a position which did not require a law degree, and which he described to Campbell as not much more than a messenger boy. However, he learned that the firm had been trying unsuccessfully for many months to serve papers on a wealthy defendant who lived on Long Island, and Vanderveer goaded the office manager into promising him a better position if he could serve the papers.

Many attempts had been made and one of the city's larger

detective agencies had kept some of its best operators on the assignment but they had failed. The man to be served lived on a large estate. He never left the house, and his butler permitted no one to enter; and yet the law required that the papers had to be served upon him personally—delivered directly into his hands. The nature of the case did not permit substitute service.

During his first day on the assignment, Vanderveer rode out to Long Island and appraised the estate from the street. Not far away he located a painter who was painting a barn, and he made arrangements to rent the man's complete outfit for the following day.

Early the next morning, Vanderveer drove into the estate with the painter's horse and wagon. He was dressed in the painter's smeared overalls and he wore the painter's cap. With businesslike efficiency, he halted the wagon near the house, placed a paint-smeared ladder against the white façade of the well-kept mansion, and then sat down and began stirring a bucket of red paint.

The butler came storming out of the house and ordered him off the property. Vanderveer shook his head.

"I been hired to paint this house and I aim to do it, so just keep out of my way."

"You must have the wrong place," the butler protested. He had come close enough now to glimpse the color of the paint within the bucket, and he appeared on the verge of collapse. "Not red! Not red! You're not going to put that on this house!"

Vanderveer grinned. "Ain't it horrible? But if that's what the man wants, who am I to argue with him? He ordered it; all I do is put it on." He picked up a large brush from the wagon and headed toward the house.

"Don't do it! Don't do it!" the butler gasped. "It's all a mistake! Nobody ordered this house painted red!"

Vanderveer looked annoyed. "Listen, you! I don't take

orders from butlers! When a man orders his house painted, I don't let his butler tell me not to do it! See what I mean?"

The butler began retreating toward the front door, pleading with Vanderveer to do nothing until he could get the matter straightened out. He was back within a couple of minutes, with his irate employer beside him.

In the face of Vanderveer's apparent confusion, the man identified himself as the owner of the estate, and he insisted that he had not ordered the house painted.

"Then why did you sign the contract?" Vanderveer demanded. He reached inside the overalls and pulled out a folded document and handed it to the man.

"I never signed any contract!" the man protested; and only after he had spread out the papers and adjusted his glasses did he realize that he had been served the papers he had been avoiding for many months.

In approximately twenty-four hours, Vanderveer had succeeded in doing what a number of private detectives had been unable to do in months of endeavor. He was rewarded with a promotion, and he began his practice of law.

Intelligent, resourceful, dependable, endowed with a dynamic personality and inspired by a love for his work, Vanderveer quickly won the respect and the confidence of his employers. Within two years he was being called into meetings with many of the firm's most important clients. On several occasions he attended conferences with J. Pierpont Morgan, and he made sufficient impression so that Mr. Morgan recognized him on sight and called him by name a number of years later. He drew up briefs, wills, contracts, legal documents of all kinds—but he was never permitted to represent the firm in court. There were older lawyers with years of courtroom experience; and the important cases handled by a large legal firm were not to be entrusted to a young man just out of college.

Bill Campbell and George Vanderveer saw each other less frequently now, for each had his own circle of professional acquaintances, and their hours of leisure were few. However, on a spring day in 1901, Campbell called on Vanderveer and the two men agreed to meet for lunch.

"This is something in the nature of a farewell luncheon," Campbell explained as soon as they were seated. "I've given my notice, Van. I'm packing up and going back home."

Vanderveer looked shocked. "Good lord, what's the matter?"

Campbell shrugged. "I'm just fed up, that's all. I'm tired of being nothing but a glorified office boy—a little toad in a big puddle."

They discussed Campbell's proposed move through most of the meal, and the big ex-tackle painted a glowing picture of the Pacific Northwest where history was being written with bold strokes. He insisted that it was the place for a young lawyer to get in on the ground floor, where there wouldn't always be older lawyers living out their seniority and consigning younger men to several decades of drudgery before getting a chance to establish their own practice.

"I'll tell you why I really wanted to see you," Campbell announced at last. "I want you to come with me, Van. I've known you for quite a few years now, and I know you're not cut out for this sort of thing. You can't take it any more than I can."

Once again Vanderveer looked shocked. "Are you crazy?" he gasped. "Do you think I've put in all this work to get a niche for myself, and then just walk off and leave it?" He reminded Campbell that the two of them had agreed at the outset that New York offered the greatest potential opportunity to a lawyer, and he insisted that he was going to stick it out and climb to the very top. Subtly he suggested that Campbell was becoming a quitter, and he urged him to change his mind about leaving.

The big man shook his head. "I remember once at Stanford, just a few days before graduation, when you told me you knew what it must be like to be old and waiting to die, and to realize that you'd never done the things you wanted to do. Do you remember that?"

Vanderveer grinned. "You're not that old, Bill; you just feel that old."

"How does anybody know how long he's going to live?" Campbell inquired earnestly. "Six months from now, either one of us might be dead; but at least I'll have spent a few months doing what I wanted to do." He announced emphatically that he had spent his last winter in New York, and once again he urged Vanderveer to join him in the trip west.

"I'll stay here now just to prove you're wrong," Vanderveer taunted. "Some day I'll have a nice big office and the best practice in New York, and you'll always wonder if you couldn't have done just as well if you'd stuck it out."

Bill Campbell left shortly after that. He returned to his home in Grays Harbor County, was admitted to the practice of law in the State of Washington, and before settling down to his legal career he made a trip to Seattle to see Kenneth Mackintosh who had left New York ahead of him, and who was employed in the office of Judge Burke.

It was late when Campbell reached Seattle and he checked in at the Butler Hotel. On the following morning, early, he stepped out onto the street, paused for a moment to breathe deeply of the crisp morning air with its salt water tang, and then he stared in amazement. Not a half block away, striding resolutely toward him, was George Vanderveer!

Even under Campbell's persistent questioning, Vanderveer would offer no explanation for his sudden change in plans, but to Bill Campbell there was no mystery. Seattle was the boom town of the nation, and Vanderveer's continued absence from such a scene would have constituted a real mystery, for his whole personality seemed always to drive him toward the center of the greatest activity.

Vanderveer explained that Mackintosh had helped him secure a position in Judge Burke's office, and while he disclaimed any interest in the spectacular scenery of the North-

west and professed an aversion for the climate, it was evident
that he liked Seattle and the bustling activity connected with
it. Years later, in a slightly mellow mood, Vanderveer conceded to Campbell that there was at least one thing he liked
about Seattle: "I like the way people walk—as if they were in
a hurry to get some place, instead of just dawdling along the
way they do in so many cities." For George Vanderveer that
was a major tribute to his adopted city, for otherwise he
avoided anything resembling the Chamber of Commerce approach.

To David Vanderveer, his son's sudden departure from
New York remained more of a mystery, but he consoled himself with the reassurance that the boy was old enough to
know his own mind. That reassurance was shattered in 1904,
however, when he received a letter from George which mentioned—almost too casually—that he had turned down a position as head of the legal department for the Great Northern
Railroad Company which was just opening offices in Seattle.

For several days the old man wondered about that, and
finally he boarded a train and headed for Seattle. For two
weeks he stayed with George at his boardinghouse and at first
he avoided any reference to the position his son had declined.
He relished the little attentions of the other guests, and he
enjoyed meeting George's friends, almost all of whom were
young attorneys. Each in turn assured David Vanderveer
that his son was generally considered about as shrewd and
about as capable as any young lawyer in the state.

George, in turn, had words of praise for each of his friends,
but his most enthusiastic comments were in tribute of Bruce
Shorts, a pleasantly smiling young giant who had played
tackle on Michigan's point-a-minute wonder team.

Then, as throughout his entire life, George Vanderveer
made no attempt to disguise his admiration for men of ath-
letic aptitude; and he contended that he could better appraise
a man by watching him on the football field or in the prize
ring than by observing him in an office.

He belligerently defended his habit of selecting his friends from among young men of his own profession, and he expressed contempt for those who cultivated friendships for business reasons—classifying the latter practice as a cheap form of prostitution. He insisted that he would get his clients from his ability in the practice of law, and not from licking their boots on social occasions.

He explained to his father that he had received Judge Burke's endorsement to serve as one of the attorneys and handle some of the legal work involved in buying up the city's many independent street railway companies in order to consolidate them into one big system. However, because Judge Burke was the owner of one of the street railway companies involved and it would not be proper for him to be negotiating in the transaction with a member of his own staff, it had become necessary for George to move down the street and become employed by the firm of Pyles, Donworth and Howe. He indicated it was little more than a technicality on the fine points of legal ethics, and he did not mention the job offer from the Great Northern.

At the boardinghouse, David learned that his family name had become established as a common noun in Seattle, particularly among the streetcar operators. George shied away from the subject, and David had to piece together what information he could get from his son's friends; usually when George was not present. Down around the carbarns, he learned, it was common practice to refer to a black eye as a "vanderveer."

The system of transfers used on Seattle streetcars had been complex, he learned, and during the months of consolidation the city's public transportation had inspired widespread criticism and ridicule and public opposition. It had become quite common for passengers boarding a streetcar to request a transfer even if it was not needed, and generously to hand the transfer to some stranger waiting at the curb when the passenger disembarked. The operators of streetcars had come to

gaze upon all transfers with suspicion, and to offer a pre-
emptive challenge almost as a matter of course. If a man
could be bluffed out of using a transfer, it was a pretty fair
guess that he had not come by it honestly.

As nearly as David could learn, his son had not taken these
challenges gracefully. Apparently he had considered them as
personal affronts, and the weary and beleaguered operators
were never very quick to offer their apologies. Generally,
too, they were less familiar with the legal responsibilities of a
public carrier than was their belligerent passenger who stood
on his rights as a matter of principle.

On one occasion, David learned, his son had held the motor-
man at bay by threatening to drop the conductor overboard
so that his head would strike the pavement. On another occasion he had expelled the operators of a cable car after a heated
argument, and had proceeded to operate the car himself
while passengers huddled in their seats and made a stampede
for the exit when he finally brought the car to a halt.

It wasn't George's fault, his friends insisted. At least, it
wasn't all his fault. Probably the streetcar men had compared
notes and determined to make it so rough for George Vanderveer that he would quit riding streetcars altogether. Beyond a doubt there was a coordinated plot to pick fights with
him on every possible occasion. But on these points David
was never completely convinced. However, with a wry
smile, he noticed that George was still riding the streetcars
and apparently enjoying it.

Bill Campbell arrived from Grays Harbor a few days after
receiving a letter from David and while George was working
he took the old man for several trips on the small steamers
that plied the waters of the Sound. They sat for long hours
gazing at the rugged and spectacular scenery, and they talked
of many things.

One bit of information picked up at the boardinghouse
during his first week interested David particularly, and offered the first possible clue to his son's reason for turning

down the position with the Great Northern. George's friend and former classmate, Kenneth Mackintosh, was running for Prosecuting Attorney on the Republican ticket and George anticipated a place on his staff if he was elected.

By random and discreet questioning of Bill Campbell, David learned that a position in the Prosecuting Attorney's office was not a prized political plum. The salary could hardly compare with the amount George must surely be earning with Pyles, Donworth and Howe, and certainly it could not compare with the amount that would be paid to the head of the Great Northern's legal staff in Seattle. It became apparent to David that his son had made a very foolish mistake in turning down the proffered job, and he decided to discuss it frankly with Bill Campbell.

"All of his life, I tried to give the boy every possible advantage," the old man explained. "He's never known what it's like not to have almost anything he's wanted. For his mother's sake, particularly, I wanted him to have everything I could possibly give him." He paused and gazed thoughtfully at the horizon. "I'm afraid now that maybe I've given him the biggest handicap of all. I've never let him learn the value of money. I've never let him learn what it's like to be broke, and really up against it. I don't think you ever learn to appreciate money or financial security, if you haven't ever been without them."

Not until the final night before his scheduled departure did David broach the subject to his son, and it is probable that he completed the discussion more confused than at the outset.

"I don't think Dad ever really understood why I turned down that job, and I don't think he ever completely forgave me," George Vanderveer told his law partner, Sam Bassett, a great many years later. "You can understand, Sam, because you're a crazy bastard like I am, and you don't know the value of money, either.

"I just couldn't see myself stuck off in an office, representing just one corporation. I knew it was a good job, and I was lucky to get the chance—but it came too damned easy! It was like spending six months training for a fight, and then having somebody offer you more money if you'd just stand at the door and take tickets. Hell, it isn't just money! You get keyed up to a fight, and you want to go through with it. Or you spend years studying criminal law, and you think about how you'll act and what you'll do when you get into the courtroom. You don't want somebody to come along then and buy you off, and stick you in an office to draw up contracts. At least you want to get in there long enough to find out what you can do!"

Perhaps George Vanderveer was in error, though, when he speculated that his father had never forgiven him for turning down the Great Northern assignment, for he related that as the two of them shook hands at the time of the old man's departure, David conceded: "I guess every man has to live his own life and make his own decisions, son. After all, if I'd followed the advice of my father, I'd still be a blacksmith."

CHAPTER THREE

The history of the world is the record of a man in quest of his daily bread and butter.—HENDRIK WILLEM VAN LOON

THE HEAVY INFLUX of labor to the Pacific Northwest after the turn of the century brought its problems to the mills and the logging camps where men were engaged in the harvest of a great crop of virgin timber which Nature had taken thousands of years to produce.

The experienced and skilled loggers in the hills clung to their jobs with a new-born desperation, each knowing that a dozen men waited to take his place—and all of them bidding against each other with the promise to work a little harder, and to work for a little less money.

The men in the lumber mills and the shingle mills gradually increased the speed of production. "You can't afford to dog along, Joe, when there are that many men waiting for a crack at your job—not if you got a wife and kids to feed."

The law of supply and demand applied itself to labor as surely as it applied itself to hotel rooms, and steamship tickets to the Yukon; and the tempo was contagious. Crew foremen and straw bosses and superintendents were not immune, and there came an ever-increasing competition in the race against time.

"Those damn Swedes on the other side of the hill aren't any better loggers than we are. Come on! Snap into it, men!

We'll show those snoose-chewing bastards what logging
really is!"

"Highball!"

"Highball!"

The mighty trees crashed to earth in the rhythm of the
frenzy. "Timber!" The fallers on their springboards learned
to save a little time by taking a smaller margin of safety—
agile men suspended six or eight or ten feet above the ground,
sliding and gliding the long falling-saws through the heart of
a forest giant, and shouting their triumph of achievement in
each lusty call: "Timber!"

The axes flew and the cables whined. "Highball!" "Highball!" And the logged-off areas crept higher and higher up
the hills. Faster and faster.

Now and then the whistle punk gave five short blasts, and
all was still. The singing saws broke their melody, half complete. The swinging axes took one last bite into a log and
stayed there. Men came swarming out of the woods and out
of the underbrush to see if there was anything they could do,
for the five short blasts were the call of distress. Usually the
crew gathered around and made hurried plans to take the injured workman out of the woods; and after that, for several
hours, the men were sober and thoughtful.

"What do you think, Joe? Is he goin' to live?"

"I don't know. It's hard to tell."

"Somebody says he's got a wife and couple kids back in
Nebraska. Planned on sendin' for them this summer."

"Yeah? Well, I'll tell you something: there's too God
damn much highball in this outfit, and I don't care who hears
me say it!"

"You're damn right! Kill men off, so they can pile up a
few more filthy dollars!"

And the foreman spat on his hands, and hunched his shoulders, and shook his head. "Jesus Christ! I thought this was
going to be our biggest day, the way it started out—and now

we've lost nearly an hour and we'll have to finish up short-handed!"

In the frame office buildings far from the scene of falling timber, other men were frowning over other problems: freight rates and lumber prices, and the competition of southern pine in the markets of the nation. Almost always there was the fear of calamity close at hand—the fear of fire that could wipe out the profits for the season and send the company into receivership—the fear of a drop in the price of lumber that could spell financial ruin—the fear of a thousand things that could send an operator out of the woods flat broke and heavily in debt, with nothing to show for his years of struggle and his countless sleepless nights.

When lumber prices were down, when freight rates were up, when seasons were short, they drove their foremen with a frenzied desperation: "My God, man! We've got to find some way to cut a little more, just to keep even! Either that, or we might as well walk off and let the bank take over!"

When prices were up and freight rates down and the weather ideal for logging, the operators urged their foremen ahead with an almost equal desperation. "My God, if we can't make 'er now, we never will! It's our one big chance, boy, so let's make the most of it!"

Back up in the logging camps, men sat around in the evening and discussed the problems of American labor, and they discussed their own particular grievances, for their work was hard and their days were long, and the hours were filled with danger. It was a rough and tough life. The logging camps often were crude affairs far back up in the hills, affording a minimum of convenience, with cold water hauled from a spring, cookhouse food that wasn't always the best in the world, no pretense of entertainment and no pretense of sanitation. Encouraged by those workmen who had brought their bedrolls purchased from the Northern outfitters, there was an increasing dependence upon the logger to furnish his own bedding, or bindle, and to see to its sporadic laundering the best way he could. Bunkhouses, when provided, were often miserable affairs constructed from the nearly worthless slabs ripped from the outer portion of the giant logs and hauled back from the mill. With a lack of sanitation and with ever-changing occupancy, they tended to become vermin-infested and to remain that way.

As an added and ingenious innovation, there was the company store which operated without competition in its isolated area, and frequently made the most of its opportunity with minimum quality, maximum price, and reluctant service. The typical company store operated on credit, and balanced its books by collecting its accounts from the paymaster before the logger received his wages. And it offered a stock reply to those who complained: "What in hell are you bellyachin' about? You don't have to buy stuff here if you don't want to, do you? Ain't nobody draggin' you in here and makin' you buy the stuff!"

There were inevitable periods when the mills would close down waiting for logs, or when being overhauled. There were times when the logging crews would be pulled out of the hills because of fire or weather conditions, or when shifting equipment to a new stand of timber. In between these times there was the eternal turnover of labor as individual workmen quit their jobs, or were fired, or failed to show up again after a Saturday night in town.

Like a great magnet, the Skid Road district of Seattle pulled in the men temporarily out of work, for here they could find cheap rooms and cheap meals, and often lurid entertainment. Here they could mingle with other workmen from other camps, and compare notes, and get the latest reports on jobs and working conditions. Here they could study the big blackboards of the employment agencies; and here they could listen to the fiery speeches of men on soapboxes denouncing the atrocities of an unjust world, and demanding that the downtrodden masses rise up in rebellion.

Many a logger carried all of his worldly goods in the pack

upon his back, as he shifted from one camp to the next. His only home was the bunkhouse where he slept. His only clothes were the sweat-soaked, pitch-stained, work-worn clothes of the woods: heavy shirt; calked high-top boots; sturdy, water-repellent "tin" pants ripped off at mid-calf and bulging at the knees, so that the wearer appeared always crouched to spring. Years spent in tinder-dry woods had altered his preference from smoking tobacco to chewing tobacco, and the dark brown stain at the edge of his lips was almost a badge of his occupation.

The ideas that fermented in the Skid Road district found their way back up into the logging camps as men went back to work. They spread slowly, but they spread into every niche of the lumbering industry; and in the long evenings in the crude bunkhouses men sat and discussed the various ideas and philosophies they had absorbed from the soapbox orators in the city.

There were men who pleaded with their fellow workers to join the craft unions of the American Federation of Labor—to unite for strength in a great crusade for better pay, shorter hours, and better working conditions. But because of the many unclassified and overlapping jobs of common labor in the logging camps, the idea of craft unionism had its limitations. "That's a hell of a thing," the loggers complained. "Maybe the sawyers go out on strike for more pay, so we're all out of work until they get it . . . but what in hell do we get out of it? Nothing!"

There were men who brought back from Skid Road the soapbox-spouted ideas of a twelve-hour day, or a ten-hour day, or—among the more radical—the proposal of an eight-hour day. There were syndicalists who insisted that an eight-hour wage slave was little different from a fourteen-hour wage slave. "That ain't no answer!" they shouted. "What we got to do is to get rid of the parasites! Take over the mills and the factories and everything else! I hear a guy in Seattle tell how it would work."

There were men by the thousands who disclaimed such philosophies. "Aw, I don't go for that radical stuff. To hell with it!" They believed in the rights of ownership, and they cited the provisions of the Homestead Act, intended to provide each man with one hundred and sixty acres of land. "The hell of it is," they conceded, "the God damn lumbermen moved in and faked a lot of names and greased a few palms, and took up all the good land that had timber on it . . . and now they're making us work our tails off on land that was supposed to be ours in the first place."

There were abortive strikes in the shingle mills during the early years of the century, and there was an epidemic of small company unions that collapsed and died. Then, starting late in 1905, a new idea began seeping outward from Skid Road— the idea of one big union, to include loggers and millworkers and shingle weavers and teamsters and streetcar conductors. One big union to encompass all—a union so big and so powerful that the owners would be unable to oppose it. One big union to end forever the jurisdictional disputes and the competition of craft against craft. One big union, calling upon all the workers of the world to unite—to make "an injury to one an injury to all"—to abolish the wage system, and to do away with capitalism. It was radical enough to appeal to many of the syndicalists. It was daring enough to excite the dreamers. And with the timely revision of its preamble, it offered a carefully worded assurance to the more conservative with its promise to "form the structure of a new society within the shell of the old."

The fast-talking proponents of the one-big-union idea generally skirted any specific details of how they intended to abolish the wage system and do away with capitalism. They scorned the political programs of the Socialists who talked about reforms to be enacted by the process of the ballot, and they gave new significance to the term "direct action." "How can you expect to win at the game of politics," they challenged, "when the capitalists have the money to buy the votes, and can beat you every time at the polls?"

To the more cautious, who feared revolution and bloodshed from such a program, they offered provocative reassurance: "Did they call President Lincoln a radical and a revolutionist when he freed the slaves in the South? Of course not! And what we propose to do is to carry on the great work that he started, and to free the wage slaves everywhere! What we propose to do is not so radical as what has already been done! All we propose to do is to carry on the work of our beloved Abraham Lincoln to its logical and inevitable conclusion!" And many of the cautious listeners to the soapbox orators nodded their heads in agreement. What was good enough for Abraham Lincoln was good enough for them.

The organization of the Industrial Workers of the World was formed in Chicago in 1905, and it put forth its call for membership throughout the nation. It spread through the mining regions and through the heavy industries; it swept through the sweatshops of the East, and through the agricultural areas of the South and Middle West. But nowhere in America did it find conditions more ideally suited to its basic appeal than in the lumbering industry of the Pacific Northwest.

The lumbermen were generally aware of the ideas and proposals filtering through the ranks of their employees. They met and discussed the situation, and made what plans they could, but in large measure they were powerless to stop it. The short-lived company unions were part of their effort to fight fire with fire, but it was futile. The flames of impending revolution leaped across their puny backfires, and the company unions collapsed.

The right of labor to organize and to strike had not yet become entrenched in the public mind. Employers shared convictions that were fortified by precedent, and built upon basic conceptions of right and wrong: "A man has got no more right to come into my mill and tell me how to run it,

than he's got to come into my home and tell me what I can
eat, and who I can invite to dinner! And as long as this is a
free country, that's the way it's got to be."

The right of labor to establish and maintain a picket line
during a strike was particularly questioned, and employers
generally rejected it as fundamentally wrong. Most of them
honestly and sincerely felt that employment constituted a contract between the employer and the employee—that a work-
ingman was free to accept or reject an offer to perform a
certain job for a certain amount of money, but that he had
no conceivable right to prevent another from accepting the
job and the wages he had rejected. The majority of employers, striving to be reasonable about it, agreed among themselves that dissatisfied workers had an inherent right to quit
their jobs, individually. By stretching a point, they might
even have the right to quit in large numbers at a given signal,
decided among themselves. But by no stretch of the imagination could they possibly have the right to stand out in front
of the mill and interfere with other men who came seeking
the jobs they had quit.

The lumber operators, as surely as the lumber workers,
were busy organizing and exchanging ideas, reëxamining their
philosophies, listening to speeches, and seeking strength
through unity. The less articulate tended to follow the lead
of the more articulate; and the more articulate generally represented the larger corporations. Many of the smaller, independent operators were men of moderate education who had
learned their logging through years of working in the woods,
and while most of them were experts in the actual logging
operations, they frequently lacked the delicate touch of political finesse and the financial backing required to gain access
to the large tracts of government-controlled land, heavily tim-
bered. Hemmed in by economic pressures from all sides, the
smaller operators were totally incapable of meeting the demands of their employees, and they followed the lead of the
larger corporations with a sense of desperation. It is perhaps

significant that of the hundreds of small owners who devoted
their lives to the actual operation of lumber mills and logging
camps, only a bare handful ever pulled through without winding up heavily in debt.

The speaking and the organizing went on, but the workers
were not invited to the closed meetings of the operators; and
few if any of the operators listened to the arguments being
presented along Skid Road. Each lacked an understanding of
the other's viewpoint; and possibly the inevitable prejudice
of each group would have made the other's arguments mean-
ingless, if the actual words had been overheard.

Even before the first I.W.W. cards were issued, the operators knew there was trouble ahead. They could read the
unmistakable signs on the faces of sullen men who infiltrated
the mills and the logging camps—Typhoid Marys of discontent, spreading their epidemic of eternal opposition. It did
little good to weed them out and send them on their way, for
they left the infection behind them. The faces might change
from day to day, but the sullen looks remained.

There was nothing you could really put your finger on.
Just the infinitesimal pause after a worker received an order
and before he put it into execution; and the level, unflinching
look that filled the pause and spoke of the thoughts behind it.
Just the way men spat when they turned away. And the cold,
defiant way in which they paused in their work to take a
pinch of snuff or to carve off a bit of chewing tobacco—head
up, shoulders back, as if offering a challenge to the world:
"I quit my work for a minute. Does anybody want to make
something of it?"

Undoubtedly there is some foundation for the argument
that the I.W.W. did not create the discontent in the lumbering industry nor cause the eventual rebellion; that it merely
gave shape and direction to something that was already there.
Down along Skid Road, at least a year before the I.W.W.
was organized in Chicago, it was common knowledge that
trouble lay ahead, somewhere in the uncertain future. Men

talked of it as they sipped their beer, or as they sat on the
benches of Pioneer Place and read the editorials of the ever-
present labor papers. They talked of it as they lay in their
beds in the flophouses and as they gathered in the barnlike
rooms leased by enterprising labor organizations: "Some day
all hell is going to break loose, and God only knows what will
happen after that."

They listened to the fluent speakers who traced the history
of American labor, discussed the philosophy of Karl Marx,
and quoted passages from the Bible. They listened with equal
impartiality to anarchists, syndicalists and Socialists; and each
man remembered what he wanted to remember, and forgot
what he chose to forget.

In uptown Seattle the good people of the city were deeply
concerned about another problem, and they paid little heed
to the rumblings of Skid Road. Mayor Ballinger was holding
public demonstrations to prove that the city streets could be
efficiently sprinkled and washed, and thus be made much
cleaner than streets that are merely swept. The people
watched and applauded, and the city's press approved. Over
much of Seattle there lay a general feeling of civic pride and
social contentment, and the conviction that God was in His
heaven and all was right with the world. It was very pleasant
to live in a city with nice clean streets.

CHAPTER FOUR

If the great gods be just, they shall assist the deeds of justest men.
—SHAKESPEARE

THE GOOD PEOPLE of Seattle who applauded Mayor Ballinger and his program of clean streets joined with other voters throughout the nation in the fall of 1904 in electing Theodore Roosevelt to his second term as President of the United States, and they joined with voters outside the city in electing Kenneth Mackintosh Prosecuting Attorney of King County.

On the other side of the world, Russia and Japan had drifted into war over the question of access to Chinese ports in Manchuria and Korea, and were busy setting up barbed-wire entanglements of political destiny over which men would trip in a later generation. But the news was not really big news in the United States, for the battleground was far away and the names of the cities and rivers were unfamiliar and hard to pronounce.

Teddy Roosevelt, the beloved Rough Rider, was speaking ambitiously of a second Hague Peace Conference and a permanent Court of Arbitration as a substitute for war in international disputes. This was something that could be discussed in simple terms, with familiar words, and it met with almost universal enthusiasm on the part of the American people. Gradually there arose a prevalent belief that the nasty business going on somewhere in Asia was merely the final skir-

mish of an ancient folly destined soon to become extinct.
Reason and common sense had entered the world, belatedly—
like a teacher entering a disorderly classroom. It could be
little more than a matter of time until the brawling and the
mischief would stop, and order would be maintained forever
more.

Similarly, the good people of Seattle paid little attention to
the goings-on down around Skid Road for, although it was
not so far removed, geographically, still it was another world.
Its words and its terms were not difficult to pronounce, but
they were nevertheless barred from general conversation and
mixed-group discussion. Prostitution was not a subject for
nice people to ponder, and drunkenness had not yet become
fashionable.

Among the more philosophical there existed the belief that
the Skid Road district was a by-product of a city's growing
pains, and a conviction that some day it would be outgrown;
but among the vast majority there lived the belief that nothing was needed except more vigorous law enforcement.
These people had faith in their young, vigorous, dynamic
Prosecuting Attorney. They had faith that the pressure of
law enforcement could rid the city's streets of its human
scum, just as Mayor Ballinger's sprinkling wagons washed
away the debris, and Seattle could turn its clean, bright,
freshly scrubbed face to the future as a decent, wholesome,
happy city of fine homes and beautiful public parks.

Kenneth Mackintosh became Prosecuting Attorney of King
County before he was thirty, and he immediately gathered
around him a staff of young men willing to dedicate themselves to the task which had been such a clear mandate of the
people. Financially, he was not able to offer any great inducement which might lure established lawyers from private practice, but the Prosecuting Attorney's office offered two things
which appealed in varying degrees to young attorneys: a
regular monthly income, and a chance to get trial experience
in the courtroom. A deputy prosecuting attorney could ex-

pect to have more trial experience in one month than he might have in many years as a junior associate in an established private law firm.

Because there was no room for the Prosecutor's office in the overcrowded Courthouse, the County Commissioners rented space in the Colman Building for Mackintosh and his staff, and from here they shuttled back and forth to the Courthouse on the hill.

A dozen years before the arrival of George Vanderveer in Seattle, the Commissioners of King County had faced the problem of erecting a courthouse to accommodate the increasing volume of business passing through Superior Court, and a larger county jail to hold the increasing number of persons being dragged in by the expanding net of law enforcement.

Despite the vigorous protests of the Chamber of Commerce, the King County Bar Association, and other interested groups, the Commissioners had gone ahead with their plans to erect the new Courthouse on a block of county-owned land not far from the business district of Seattle. Its one great drawback was the fact that the block of land was located on the brow of a hill which rose abruptly behind the business district, and streets leading to it rose four hundred feet within a distance of just a few blocks.

An appropriation of two hundred thousand dollars had been rushed through, and construction begun on the rectangular building of brick and stone which lacked any semblance of distinctive design, and which was already outgrown before it was ever occupied. But beyond a doubt it boasted the most commanding view of any courthouse in America. Literally at its elevated doorstep lay the skyline of waterfront Seattle; and beyond that, the blue waters of Puget Sound. Still beyond, to the west, could be seen the rugged and sprawling grandeur of the snow-capped Olympics, fringed by their verdant foothills—a scenic spectacle to leave the viewer breathless. But most of the viewers were already breathless by the

time they climbed the hill, and if the compelling panorama
ever inspired any poetry within the souls of those who viewed
it every day, they left no record of it. Perhaps one of the
women employed in one of the county offices summarized it
best with her remark to a fellow employee: "Oh, it's so beautiful . . . and I'm so sick of looking at it!"

Because of the puffing protests of those who climbed the
long hill leading up to the Courthouse, it soon became known
as Profanity Hill; and by that name it was known through a
quarter of a century.

To Kenneth Mackintosh, the securing of offices in the Colman Building was a shallow victory, at best. Because he was
personally fitted for it, he reserved for himself the vast amount
of civil work entailed in operating a multi-million-dollar
branch of local government during a time of tremendous
building and expansion; and his trips up and down Profanity
Hill were almost endless. In setting up his staff, he planned
carefully to utilize the manpower at his command.

Felony cases were assigned to John Murphy, the oldest and
most experienced man on Mackintosh's staff, for these were
the most important of the criminal cases concerning the more
serious crimes. Other assignments were judiciously considered, and George Vanderveer was given his chance to be the
work horse amid the eternal flood of misdemeanors.

To Vanderveer, that assignment was the realization of a
dream, for courtroom experience was available almost to the
limit of his endurance. From his earliest planning of a legal
career, he had always visualized himself in the courtroom.
To him, that was the main arena. That was where the battle
was fought, and either won or lost. The preparation of a
case, the gathering of data, the searching for precedent, the
preliminary interviewing of witnesses—those things were all
part of a necessary evil, like weeks spent in a training camp
getting ready for the big fight.

His legal career up to this point had been dramatic and successful. He was widely respected in his profession, and his

previous employers had been quick to recognize his ability
and his potential. And yet his actual courtroom experience
had been limited. In the private law firms there had been
older lawyers with more experience, ready to take over the
case that had been prepared for court—ring-wise veterans
who, in private life, could call the judge by his first name, and
who knew his every weakness and his every prejudice.

In the handling of misdemeanor cases in the Prosecuting
Attorney's office, Vanderveer had to yield to no seniority. It
was a wholesale business—an ever-waiting dress rehearsal for
the more important courtroom battles in a young lawyer's
future. And George Vanderveer seldom missed an opportunity to perform.

Because of the vast number of misdemeanor cases and because of the shortage of manpower in the Prosecutor's office,
there was seldom time for the careful planning of a prosecution. There was also a lack of respect for the status of the
court itself, because the presiding magistrate was a mere justice of the peace with limited jurisdiction. And because of
the nature of misdemeanors and the status of the majority of
persons accused of committing them—many of them down-
and-outers from the Skid Road district—the defense offered in
court was not always a brilliant masterpiece of legal planning.
The accused were often petty thieves, vagrants, malicious
mischief-makers, persons accused of assault and battery, public nuisances—a sorry lot parading dejectedly before the
bench; expecting little in the way of judicial mercy, and generally receiving even less. Usually they were represented by
young attorneys willing to take a case mostly for the experience it offered, or they were represented by war-weary old
has-beens who clung to dreary offices in the aging buildings
down around First Avenue South and who, for a modest fee,
would offer a client the best efforts of a rusty and alcohol-
beclouded legal mind. Now and then some rugged individualist would insist upon defending himself, and demand a jury
trial. Court proceedings would be interrupted long enough

for the constable to go out and round up a half-dozen prospective jurors from the nearest saloon or pool hall. Many of the defendants fell back upon the services of an attorney appointed by the court; and on rare occasions some weary old veteran of the process would plead guilty and wait glumly for his sentence.

The prosecution of such cases was mostly extemporaneous, based upon the information provided by the arresting officer; and almost from the start George Vanderveer demonstrated a remarkable ability at ripping the makeshift defense to shreds through his often-savage cross-examination. He had an intuitive grasp of psychology, and a genius for judging character. On one occasion, he needled an accused pickpocket into confessing his crime in open court, despite a lack of any compelling evidence against him; he merely pricked at the man's vanity.

"The truth of the matter is that you're not even a good pickpocket," he charged. "When you get down to following a third-rate carnival and then get caught red-handed by a farm hand, it's time to give yourself up!" The outraged defendant, in turn, called upon the arresting officer to verify the fact that the farm hand hadn't even missed the money from his pocket at the time of the arrest.

"It wasn't no farm hand that caught me! I knew you had this deputy tailing me for more than a week and—well—I could tell you plenty that went on right under his nose!"

It was a catch-as-catch-can type of prosecution, and Vanderveer threw himself into the task with the zeal of a crusader, building up his legal reputation like a big-league ball player fattening his batting average against the dubious pitching of a rookie from the hinterland. His percentage of convictions climbed steadily higher, and there was no slackening in his effort or in his zeal. The course of justice unquestionably must have been influenced by the economic disproportion, for the prosecution had legal talent of a caliber which the defense seldom could afford to hire. It was a poor time in King County's history to be haled into court and charged with a misdemeanor.

Because of his excellent record, Mackintosh soon assigned Vanderveer to the prosecution of felonies, sharing the assignment with the more-experienced John Murphy and John F. Miller. In a sense, it was a promotion for George Vanderveer, and it brought him opposite some of the finest defense attorneys of the Northwest. Trials were fewer, generally longer, and were held in the superior court. The prosecution of each case required more detailed planning, with greater attention to the gathering and presenting of evidence. Juries became the rule rather than the exception. And whereas the misdemeanors had rolled through court with drab monotony, bringing occasional yawns to the bailiff, the felony cases were pregnant with headline possibilities, and reporters could generally be found at the table reserved for the press.

It was a step upward to a newer and faster league, and for the first time in his public career, Vanderveer now faced opposing counsel capable of testing his mettle, and equally astute at cross-examination. There were men undeniably eloquent in summing up before a jury; wise old veterans of many a courtroom battle who were masters of psychology and who knew how to gain the sympathy of jurors, and how to tug gently at their heartstrings.

But George Vanderveer was capable of appraising his own strength and his own weakness, and he had gained knowledge and experience through his wholesale prosecution of misdemeanors. He did not consider himself a particularly eloquent man, and he did not place too much faith in his own ability to sway a jury by the power of his oratory, so he played to the mind and not to the heart of the jury—trying to impress them with simple, inescapable logic. He built his cases methodically through the presentation of evidence, and he made his greatest effort to tear down the case of the defense through his cross-examination. These were his strong points, and he made the most of them.

During the course of a trial he would parade back and forth
before the bench, hammering home his points one by one, and
nodding with satisfaction toward the jury as each point was
irrefutably made. There was subtle flattery in his technique,
for he treated the jury members as intelligent adults. He built
his arguments with the exactness of Euclid proving a geomet-
rical hypothesis, and with those frequent nods to the jury he
subtly intimated that he trusted them to understand.

On cross-examination sometimes he would shout, and sometimes lean toward the witness and hiss his questions in a tense
whisper that became doubly dramatic because of the unexpected change of pace. Or he would move forward with his
shoulders hunched and his fists clenched and his eyes burning
with intensity until even the most rugged witness would
flinch and somehow look like a prevaricator trapped in the
mesh of his own falsehood. He was a master of sarcasm that
could leave its welts upon the very soul, and he was one of
the few attorneys who could administer a reprimand to the
court itself, delivered with such subtlety as to leave the jurist
on the bench embarrassed and red-faced with frustration,
while leaving nothing in the record to substantiate a charge
of contempt.

Annoyed at one time by a judge who interposed questions
of his own from the bench and practically took over the
cross-examination of all witnesses, Vanderveer finally rose to
his feet and addressed the Court:

"Your Honor, if that question is asked in behalf of my opponent, I object to it. And if it is asked in my behalf, I
withdraw it!"

A deep crimson flush spread slowly up the jurist's neck
and outward across his cheeks, and for a moment he just sat
and sputtered. "I was only trying to be helpful," he finally
announced with as much dignity as he could command. But
for the remainder of the trial he sat and stared down at the
papers upon his desk, and he asked no further questions.

Such quick and pointed thrusts were Vanderveer's stock in

trade. His verbal weapon was the rapier, rather than the oratorical bulldozer. And yet there were those, even at the start
of his career, who insisted that George Vanderveer could present a closing argument equal to the best of them, when he
chose to do so. Generally he spoke of those things with contempt: "I'm interested in presenting facts and searching out
the meaning of our laws; I'm not interested in oratory. After
all, I chose to be a lawyer, not an evangelist."

He disdained all emotional oratory wrapped around flag-
waving, or pleading through tear-dimmed eyes for the protection of the American home and the glory of motherhood.
With devastating sarcasm he would ridicule any "sentimental
drivel" presented by opposing counsel. When he felt that
closing arguments were necessary to clinch his case, he presented the arguments as he had presented the case itself: a
straightforward array of irrefutable facts building to one inescapable conclusion. He placed his faith in the inevitable
logical-minded juror who would sit in the jury room and
count off his points, one by one, on his fingers: "I tell you,
when everything is said and done, you can't get around these
facts. . . ." To his associates he insisted that logic was enduring and sentiment highly perishable. "If the jury is out for
any length of time at all, the logic will stand up and the sentiment will evaporate."

Almost from the outset, George Vanderveer proved that
he could be as successful in this league as he had been in the
one before it. He prosecuted a charge of manslaughter, opposing Attorney Will Morris for the defense. Morris, at the
time, held the number one spot as the leading criminal defense
attorney of the Northwest, and his client faced a charge of
manslaughter that stood almost without precedent at the
time.

The information filed by Vanderveer charged that the defendant had run an automobile over, and did then and there
involuntarily kill, a certain victim. It was a forerunner of
similar charges that were destined to crowd the court calen-

dars of the future, qualifying the defendant as a hot-rod driver
of his generation—for the information solemnly charged him
with operating said automobile at a speed "exceeding one mile
in five minutes."

The ability of spectators to estimate the speed of a moving
vehicle was savagely challenged by Morris, and not entirely
without reason. Automobiles still ranked as somewhat of a
novelty upon the city streets. Several prosecution witnesses
conceded that they had never ridden in an automobile—and
added that they had no plans of doing so within the foresee-
able future.

With masterful and sometimes emotional oratory, Will
Morris insisted that a grave injustice had been done his client
in the filing of criminal charges as the result of an unfortunate
accident. And it *was* an accident—even the State would have
to admit that! Accidents happen every day—big accidents—
little accidents—and there is no criminal charge involved. Is
a man a criminal because he upsets a glass of water? Is a
housewife a criminal because she breaks a dish? Then how
can it be charged that a big accident constitutes a crime, when
a small accident does not? How can accidents or crimes be
measured in degrees?

The defendant was pictured to the jury as a fine, upstanding citizen—a man who would not knowingly or willingly in-
flict the slightest harm upon a fellow human being—a victim
of the accident as surely as was the girl who was killed, and
a victim of vicious circumstance, haunted by nightmarish
memories of that horrible scene, and dragged into court like
a common criminal.

It was a notable defense, and it did full credit to the ability
of Will Morris; but it was not enough to overcome the me-
thodical and irrefutable arguments of George Vanderveer,
who established the automobile as a lethal weapon, and pointed
to the death of the victim to prove his point. He challenged
the jurors to ponder the future in a country where mechanical vehicles could travel at the rate of a mile in five minutes

... or four minutes ... or three minutes. He took full advantage of the still-existing prejudice, and he demanded for the sake of society that men be held responsible for endangering their own lives and the lives of others when they go careening down the road at fantastic speeds, offering an unspoken challenge to the world: "Get out my way, or I'll kill you!" The jury found the defendant guilty as charged.

The victories of George Vanderveer were not entirely due to his command of the courtroom. His genius was well fortified with unstinting effort, and his preparation of a case was backed by tedious hours of planning and research. There was in his nature no indication of moderation or compromise, and he drove himself relentlessly in this, as in everything else.

The intensity of his preparation for even a supposedly routine case is evident in his prosecution of Laura Haines on a charge of obtaining money under false pretenses. There was no indication at the outset that it would be more than a run-of-the-mill prosecution sandwiched in between more important cases, but by the time Vanderveer had completed his investigation, he had compiled a series of startling disclosures sufficient to curdle the cream of Seattle's society.

According to the preliminary information, Laura Haines was a woman of considerable wealth, recently arrived in Seattle from Kansas City, and the cousin of a prominent Seattle banker. She had sold her home in Kansas City for eighteen thousand dollars and invested much of the money in Seattle real estate. She was a woman of grace and charm and undeniable culture and she had been welcomed with open arms into the top stratum of Seattle society. For some reason, she had refused to pay an amount of $265 due to the Simmons Fur Co., and when the irate Mr. Simmons refused to accept the suggestion that he should institute civil suit for the recovery of the funds, Vanderveer began preparing the case for trial.

Under his savage examination in court, Laura Haines soon went to pieces and admitted that there had been no eighteen-

thousand-dollar home in Kansas City, and there were no investments in Seattle real estate; she was not related to the banker
whom she claimed as a cousin, and never had met the man.
The whole thing was a hoax from start to finish, but it had
been fantastically easy and the social leaders of the city had
competed openly for her friendship. She had been royally
entertained in homes that otherwise would have consigned
her call to the servants' entrance; and there were many red
faces in Seattle by the time Laura Haines stepped down from
the witness stand.

To many observers it appeared as a great triumph for the
clever young Deputy Prosecutor whose brilliant questioning
had trapped the woman in the mesh of her own falsehoods
and brought forth revelations that must have been a surprise
even to him. Few outside of the Prosecutor's office realized
that Vanderveer's intensive preparation for a routine case had
sent him into court fully prepared, and that he had known
all of the answers before asking any of the questions. He had
never forgotten Judge Burke's admonition that the successful
practice of law required using the feet as surely as it required
using the head, and he had interviewed the banker whom the
woman claimed for a cousin. He has investigated real estate
transactions in Seattle and in Kansas City. Much that appeared as extemporaneous courtroom genius had its foundation in plain hard work.

He lost cases, also, and he took his losses to heart. In one
of the first major cases assigned to him by Mackintosh after
he had been moved up from the prosecution of misdemeanors,
he was chagrined and unconsolable as the jury returned its
verdict of not guilty, and he shrugged aside the assurance of
his friends that nobody can win them all. He had been batted
out of the box in his first appearance in the newer and faster
league, and perhaps that original loss inspired the vast amount
of preparation that he put into his later assignments. For days
he brooded over the loss of this case, and he began building
toward that time when he would demonstrate to his friends

that he could come close to winning them all. During Mackintosh's second term in office, he was destined to lose not a single important case in two successive years.

Because the Skid Road district was the spawning place of many crimes that reached the Prosecuting Attorney's office, he spent hours studying it. He studied its people and tried to understand them: how they lived and how they operated and how they looked upon life; how they planned and executed crimes. He learned their language, and he learned about their weapons and their tools.

The Skid Road also had its grapevine and its informers. Many of the habitués of Pioneer Place were well read and well informed, and remarkably proud of their knowledge. They sat for hours on the wooden benches reading the labor papers and the discarded daily newspapers that invariably littered the place. They sauntered at leisure along the street and listened to the various soapbox orators, and they meandered in and out of the union halls, reading the literature and studying the posters. They were an important part of the grapevine, for everybody's business was their business. Their idle hours were filled with the insatiable desire to know everything that was going on, and to pass along some bit of news or gossip that might be unknown to the man on the next bench.

In his explorations of Skid Road, Vanderveer visited the saloons and the union halls, and he joined the crowds listening to the soapbox orators. He read the labor papers, and he listened to the idlers in Pioneer Place. He talked with police officers on duty, and with men out on parole. He joined the throngs that greeted incoming ships, and he gained the confidence of pawnbrokers, theatre operators, parlor-house madams, and an odd assortment of lonely and unwashed characters who were flattered by his interest. He had his informers, and before long George Vanderveer had become one of the reasonably familiar figures of the district. He was recognized and accepted, and he was no longer treated with the aloof resentment that Skid Road held for "slumming parties" from uptown.

Also, he learned other things that he hadn't set out to learn. He listened to confidential reports about pay-offs, police graft, protection policies, and sell-outs in higher places. He discovered that the sundry characters of Skid Road were amazingly well informed about vice and graft and gambling in some of the more respectable districts of the city although, obviously, they had never visited the exclusive private clubs in question. Scandals in connection with city and county and state contracts which exploded unexpectedly over the city of Seattle and left the good people uptown in a state of shock, often revealed facts that had been common knowledge along Skid Road for many months.

To George Vanderveer there was something fascinating and exciting about the Skid Road district, and perhaps even he never could have told just how much of his interest was inspired by his desire to gather knowledge for the better execution of his job, and how much of it was inspired by personal fascination and morbid curiosity.

Frequently his good friend, Bruce Shorts, would accompany him on his forays and stand ready to lend a helping hand when Vanderveer's tempestuous nature got him into difficulty, as it frequently did; for George Vanderveer was blunt and outspoken, and he paraded through the saloons with a chip on his shoulder and with a smile of anticipation on his face. Seldom could he listen to the soapbox orators without offering fiery and antagonistic rebuttal from the sidewalk, and these things were not always accepted with good grace. The debate would shift quickly into name-calling, and this would lead, inevitably, to flying fists. From there it would spread into a miniature riot, with dozens of men elbowing and shoving and trading punches until the police moved in to restore order. Such things were routine incidents along Skid Road.

Vanderveer would not budge an inch to avoid a fight with a logger or a sailor nearly twice his size, and he seemed to delight in trading blows with them. He could turn in a good account of himself on most occasions, for many of the rough-and-ready men from the logging camps and from the ships were powerful and willing, but woefully awkward against the lightning-fast fists of a highly trained fighter.

However, the Marquis of Queensbury rules were not always recognized. Most of the loggers, wearing hobnail boots, found their feet to be far better weapons than their fists. They would kick and stomp a fallen man, and it was all part of fighting as they had learned it. On those occasions when Vanderveer was knocked down and appeared on the verge of possibly fatal injury under the stomping feet of an opponent, Bruce Shorts would move in and rescue his friend; for the big and powerful ex-tackle from Michigan invariably was capable of keeping the balance of power in Vanderveer's favor.

Vanderveer, however, was subject to an occasional error in judgment; and he was not invincible. On one occasion he and Bruce Shorts were walking along First Avenue South when Vanderveer motioned to his companion to stop. They stood for a moment watching a teamster unload beer kegs from one of the top tiers of a low-bed brewery wagon.

"Look at that silly bastard," Vanderveer chuckled a bit too loudly. "If he'd use his head a little more, he could use his back a little less."

The man whirled and grabbed Vanderveer by the shoulder. "If you know so damn much about unloading a beer wagon, let's see you do it!"

Vanderveer spun away and in the next instant fists were flying. The two men were about the same height and the same weight, and for a while they battled on even terms. Spectators closed in to form a large semi-circle on the sidewalk while the thud of bare fists could be heard a block away. Then Vanderveer went down from a smashing right to the jaw. He jumped up almost instantly and moved forward, still a little groggy on his feet. The teamster unleashed a sizzling uppercut and then stood calmly wiping his hands on his thighs as Vanderveer lay flat on his back on the sidewalk, the force of his fall broken somewhat as he had been spun back against the gaping spectators.

For the second time Vanderveer struggled to his feet and staggered forward, while Bruce Shorts grabbed him and tried to hold him back. The teamster stood waiting calmly, with both fists clenched. "What's the matter? You want some more?"

Vanderveer grinned through a split lip and spat blood upon the sidewalk. "Hell no! I just want to shake your hand." And the crowd watched in amazement as the two men soberly shook hands.

"My God!" Vanderveer gasped. "Any man who can fight like that shouldn't be driving a brewery wagon!"

"You're not bad yourself," the teamster admitted grudgingly, "only you sure as hell carry your guard awful low, for a man who fights from a crouch."

Bruce Shorts and George Vanderveer turned and started up the hill, while Vanderveer held a handkerchief over his mouth.

"I've got to get back in shape, get a little more practice," Vanderveer sputtered. "My timing was way off. You could see that, couldn't you?"

Bruce Shorts attempted to reassure and console his friend, but he would not be consoled.

"I'll get in practice and I'll catch that guy and beat hell out him some day," Vanderveer promised. "He's pretty good, but he's not good enough to start giving me lessons on how to hold my guard!"

Vanderveer spent the next two days in the hospital with a broken nose, a bruised jaw, and a pair of painfully swollen hands. Never after his release did he refer again to that fight or mention to Bruce Shorts any ambition to seek out the driver of the brewery wagon. In later years, a slightly crooked nose was to be one of the distinctive features of his rugged countenance. And while Vanderveer denied it, and scoffed at the idea, Bruce Shorts was never shaken in his conviction that the slight irregularity was the result of that encounter with a teamster on First Avenue South.

There were other occasions, too, when Vanderveer left Skid Road to seek medical attention; but those incidents never diminished his interest or his fascination, nor did they tarnish his belligerence. He continued to heckle the soapbox orators, to prowl the seamy side streets, and to savor the peculiar excitement which the district never failed to provide.

It was an era of intense competition throughout America, as growing industries were struggling to capture the markets and as budding labor unions were striving to capture the jobs and the workmen. It was an era when advertising was just coming into its own, when property rights were being widely recognized in such things as good will, brand names, and corporate reputations. It was the era when America was beginning the great shift from its traditional bucket-of-beer-from-the-brewery toward the eventual highly advertised brands in bottles and cans which were to become commonplace later in the twentieth century.

The early years of the century saw the extension of a trend that had started after the Civil War, with the concentration of greater and greater production within fewer and fewer independent factories. Like fish within a tank, the larger mills and the larger factories gobbled up the smaller ones. It was the era of big business, and the trend extended through the lumber mills and the logging camps of the Pacific Northwest where the large mills were becoming larger and their operators more powerful; while the small independent operators were losing their desperate battle to survive.

Nowhere was the era of bitter competition more acutely felt than along the Skid Road in Seattle. Nowhere was the battle for dollars more intense than in the district where dollars were scarcest.

The houses of prostitution found that they could increase their income beyond the two dollar or three dollar limit by selling drinks in the waiting room. The saloons, in retaliation, branched out into services far beyond the pouring of liquor and the setting up of a free lunch. The pimps, the pickpockets, and the prostitutes moved down to the docks to meet the incoming ships, and they joined the hucksters with the hotel hacks in making their initial bid for business. The unwary sourdough returning from the North could be caught in the web of his dismal destiny by the time he was halfway down the gangplank.

The burlesque houses of the district were engaged in a ribald rivalry of lewd entertainment, eager to put up the glaring posters that would lure the remaining dollars from the pockets of loggers and sailors and itinerant workers, and yet fearful of pressing their luck too far and inviting a raid by the city's police. And from the competition there emerged the enigma of the box house.

Box seats in these specially designed theatres offered their peculiar advantages of privacy, comfort, and a certain undeniable luxury. They were completely enclosed except for the strategically-placed aperture which afforded a view of the stage; and a door from the box opened on to an inside hallway. The patron of a box, if he wished to do so, had merely to open the door and take his choice of feminine companions who were strolling eternally up and down the hallway and keeping eager, anxious eyes upon the doors. By happy coincidence, each box was furnished with a broad cushioned bench, almost as large as a single bed, and so situated that the stage remained within view from a reclining position.

From a legal standpoint, it would be difficult to prove that the proprietor of the box house had any connection with the streetwalkers who had changed their beat to an inside hallway, or that he was any more than a victim of circumstance. As an added precaution, the girls usually carried a torn half of a ticket stub to prove that they were merely paying customers of the theatre—customers who had grown a little restless and who had decided to take a short walk. The proprietors of the box houses had their story down pat: "Good lord, you can't hold me responsible! A girl goes up to the box office and buys a ticket, and you can't expect me to go and sit with her and be a chaperone! I'm running a legitimate theatre, see. It isn't my fault if folks get cozy in the box seats, or hold hands in the balcony!"

In effect, however, the box house was little more than a giant brothel with de luxe accommodations and varied entertainment—like the forerunner of a later house of prostitution proudly advertising television in every room. For several years this type of competition threatened to eliminate the old-fashioned and less-imaginative houses which had constituted one of the district's major industries of the past.

Another unique product of the intense competition was the Skid Road's daily "hearse-race"—a macabre type of sporting event which somehow appealed to the morbid and cynical humor of the district. The King County Commissioners had established a flat fee to be paid from public funds for the burial of the pauper dead, and an intense rivalry had developed among certain of the city's undertakers to pick off these modest but ever-dependable windfalls. On an average morning the Skid Road district could be depended upon to provide several penniless corpses fished from the waters of the Sound, or discovered in the back alleys with the coming of dawn. After a cursory examination by a police officer, the bodies were turned over to the representatives of the various undertaking parlors on a basis of first-come-first-served; and thus in the early hours of dawn the horse-drawn hearses of the various funeral homes could be seen racing up one street and down the other with their drivers standing up in the seats and attempting to peer in all directions for any indication of potential business.

It was like a giant Easter-egg hunt, for the drivers would be out combing the district before any reports had been called in; and they would depend upon their moods and hunches as they circled through the area searching out the likely spots where a dead body might be found. Often the drivers would locate a body before anyone else had discovered it, and they would establish their priority through squatter's rights, standing astride the corpse while an assistant dashed off to locate a police officer to come and write out a ticket. At other times, hearses might race two abreast through the otherwise deserted streets, with each driver standing up and whipping his horses and urging them onward in the grim race to be first on the scene after an official report had been turned in.

In at least one saloon, official scores were kept showing the daily "take" of the various undertakers, and men placed their bets on the score for the month, like betting on an elaborate baseball pool. It was a grim and grizzly type of gambling, but it appealed to the odd humor of those who indulged in it; and the winner of a monthly sweepstakes was invariably accused of "stacking the deck" by personally providing a few corpses to make sure his chosen number was reached.

All of these things George Vanderveer observed during his visits to Skid Road, and many of them disturbed him. On one occasion he undertook to trace the background of a man whose body had been fished from the waters of the Sound. He learned, among other things, that the old man had arrived in Seattle from Nome just a few days earlier, and that he had brought with him a small fortune in gold. On his first night in Seattle he had hired a band to march with him from saloon to saloon where he had each time bought drinks for the house. Within a few hours he was surrounded by an entourage of back-slapping men and fawning women, and he had squandered his wealth lavishly. Informers all up and down Skid Road had their stories to tell about that first dramatic evening which had developed into an orgy to attract attention. But after that, no one had seen the old man. Somewhere in the small hours of the morning he had disappeared from sight, and his body had been dragged from the Sound some forty-eight hours later. There was no way to judge, accurately, how much gold he had brought from the North and how much he had spent that night, but it seemed hardly plausible to Vanderveer that a man would thus squander his entire fortune.

Aside from his own unofficial investigation into the background of the case, there had been no particular inquiry . . . merely one more candidate for a pauper's grave. From the Sheriff's office and from the office of the city's Chief of Police he received substantially the same answer when he asked why no investigation had been made: "Obviously, the old boy got drunk and spent his wad, and then when he sobered up and realized what he'd done, he jumped in the Sound. That's as good an explanation as any. We could tie up our whole force trying to run down things like that. We'd have men going in circles and getting nowhere. Even if you found it was murder and you brought the guilty party to trial and convicted him, it would be about as futile as spitting in the ocean. You can't change Skid Road."

There was the contention that any man who made his way about Skid Road with money in his pocket and with the desire to advertise that fact, was deliberately asking for trouble; and there was the concession that such requests for trouble seldom went unanswered. "That's the way it is, and that's the way it's going to be. Why not accept it?"

Meanwhile Vanderveer was steadily building up his reputation at the Prosecutor's office—building it so well, in fact, that the seeds of jealousy were beginning to sprout within the staff, and some of Vanderveer's own friends felt that he was being a little too ruthless, and becoming a bit too ambitious.

"There's one thing that's always struck me as tops in irony," Bruce Shorts told him one evening. "Here you're in the Prosecutor's office, and you haven't any qualms about prosecuting some poor devil who gets picked up for assault and battery; maybe starting a fight on Skid Road. And yet, by God, I've seen you start more fights down there than they ever thought of starting."

"Where's your precedent?" Vanderveer inquired, grinning. "I don't recall any statute to the effect that a man shall not be held to answer for his crime if his prosecutor is guilty of the same crime."

"Oh come off it," Shorts protested. "You know what I'm talking about. A man has to be human, even if he's a deputy prosecutor. I think it's wonderful for a man to take his job seriously, and to put his heart and soul into it, but good lord, there's a limit to everything."

Vanderveer shook his head. "There's one thing I've never learned to do, Bruce, and that's to pull my punches. I just don't operate that way. I couldn't if I wanted to."

"And the hell of it is, you don't want to," Shorts added ruefully, while George Vanderveer nodded his head and grinned.

"Yeah, that's the hell of it."

Judge Campbell recalled a visit with Vanderveer during Mackintosh's first term in the Prosecutor's office. It was during one of Campbell's not-infrequent trips to Seattle from Grays Harbor County, and the two old friends met for lunch.

"I understand you've been building a mighty fine reputation up here," Campbell led off.

Vanderveer shrugged and grinned. "I guess some of the boys think I've been a little too ambitious, trying to ride to glory by tramping hell out of the poor devils who get dragged into court."

Campbell studied his friend intently. "How do you feel about it, Van?"

Once again Vanderveer shrugged. "It's a job. I do the best I can."

"It just shows how wrong you can be," Campbell announced, shaking his head. "I thought it was a big mistake when I first learned that you planned to go in with Mac. When your father was out here, we talked about it—and I told him that I just couldn't picture you as a prosecutor."

"Why not?"

"I don't know. Somehow I just couldn't see you going into court and trying to send somebody off to jail. You've always been pretty much for the underdog, all the years I've known you." Bill Campbell chuckled. "I could picture you taking one look at some poor defendant about halfway through the trial and suddenly deciding to hell with it—and maybe you'd wind up defending him."

Vanderveer turned halfway in his chair and sat for a long time staring off into space. "I'll tell you how I feel about it," he said at last. "I could have become a doctor instead of a lawyer, let's say, and I could be called out to examine some young man and discover that he has consumption. Then I'd have to send him off to some hospital for five years, or ten years, or maybe all the rest of his life. I might feel sorry for him, and I probably would—but that wouldn't make any difference, would it? For his own good, and for the good of everybody around him, I'd just have to do it. Well, it's the same thing here."

Campbell nodded his head soberly. "That's a good way to look at it."

"It's the only way to look at it! You've got to keep in mind that crime is a disease, and these poor devils have been exposed to it—often through no fault of their own. Hell! Some of 'em never had a chance! I'm telling you, Bill—you or I would be just as bad as they are, if we'd been exposed to the things they've been exposed to."

"Not necessarily," Campbell protested. "After all, there is such a thing as strength of character. There've been plenty of fine men grow up in the worst possible environment."

"Oh horse manure!" Vanderveer exploded. "There are

men who can live around crime and not become criminals, just as there are kids who can be exposed to measles and not come down with 'em. They're just not susceptible, that's all! But that's mostly a lot of crap, talking about strength of character. A man can't help being what he is!"

CHAPTER FIVE

Man's love is of man's life, a thing apart: it's woman's whole existence.—BYRON

IN 1896, a year before the steamer *Portland* brought its first cargo of gold from the Klondike, the Samuel D. Hausman family moved from Brooklyn to Seattle. Sam Hausman, a dapper and handsome man and the father of five children, had spent much of his life engaged in the wholesale clothing business in New York and he welcomed the opportunity to find a more leisurely type of life in a smaller community as assistant manager of MacDougall and Southwick, one of Seattle's leading department stores.

The turbulent years which followed in the Pacific Northwest, however, reflected themselves with equal turbulence in the Hausman family relationship. With increasing frequency, Sam Hausman stormed out of the large family home which seemed to be eternally overrun with children of all ages, laughing and screaming and playing their weird games as part of the heinous plot to drive him out of his mind. In addition, there were his wife's guests who paraded through the house in seemingly endless numbers, for Emma Hausman had spent her early years in a fine old family home in Mississippi; and to her, hospitality was a way of life. Within her home she entertained many of the leading social figures of her day; but to her husband the process was somewhat less than entertaining.

A comparatively quiet man seeking serenity in a well-

ordered life, and victim of occasional moods of jealousy
which drove him to petty acts of indiscretion, Samuel Hausman drifted slowly and inevitably away from his family and
away from his home. With the passing years he left home
more often, and he remained away for longer periods, until
finally he failed to return at all.

John Hausman, the oldest of the five children, had married
and no longer lived at home; but Emma Hausman was left
with the other four children, with inadequate and uncertain
income, and without business training of any kind. She was
shrewd enough, however, to capitalize upon her talents in the
one field she had completely mastered. She opened the Hawthorne Family Hotel on Madison Street, between Sixth and
Seventh Avenues, and she became the full-time hostess and
capable manager of a highly successful commercial institution.

The Hawthorne was noted for its excellent meals, its outstanding service, its informal family atmosphere, and for the
convenience and comfort of its rooms. But particularly, it
became noted for something that had not been mentioned in
the formal announcement of its opening. Among its guests
were many of the most eligible young bachelors of the city's
professional life, and some of the most attractive young ladies of
family wealth and social prominence. Each attracted the
other, and Emma Hausman was wise enough to recognize a
successful formula when it appeared. Guests frequently departed amid a shower of rice, and there were always others
waiting for the vacated rooms.

Among the guests who moved into the Hawthorne at the
time of its opening in 1905 were four young attorneys; Bruce
Shorts, Ira Campbell, George Vanderveer, and Bud Cummings. Cummings moved into a room by himself, while the
other three shared a suite on the second floor. They were
four very eligible young men, and they formed part of the
original nucleus which made residence at the Hawthorne more
promising than an ocean voyage for those seeking romance
and potential matrimony.

The four younger Hausmans, Jeanne, Ellinor, Renné and Billy, shared the same privileges and the same restrictions as the guests. Jeanne, at nineteen, was beautiful, and she had acquired many of her mother's social graces. She had a talent for mixing with guests and making them feel at ease. Ellinor, at seventeen, was tall, slender, and attractive; but a little more shy—possibly because she had been all her life slightly over-shadowed by an older sister. Renné and Billy were still young enough to be treated as children by the guests.

Through purposeful planning, Jeanne and Ellinor sat at a table near enough to the four young attorneys to overhear their dinner conversation, for the discussions were usually spirited and varied, and always entertaining. After dinner, one or two of the young men would often join them in the walk out to the lobby, and there would be light and bantering conversation in which Jeanne excelled, and in which Ellinor was just learning to hold her own.

Bud Cummings was the most faithful of the group, and he seldom missed an opportunity to join the girls. He asked them for dates, each in front of the other, and occasionally he took them to shows, or he took them skating at the Hippodrome. If there was anything serious in his intentions, he disguised it behind his eternal wit and good-natured teasing.

Sometimes in the informal after-dinner bantering, Cummings would be joined by Bruce Shorts or by Ira Campbell, but never by George Vanderveer. Seldom did Vanderveer enter the dining room in company with anyone else; and invariably he left alone; stalking grim and preoccupied across the room.

As the weeks passed, Jeanne and Ellinor found themselves watching for his entrance into the dining hall, and they referred to him always as Gloomy Gus—a name borrowed from a comic-strip character of the times. Almost always, Vanderveer would enter the dining room after his companions were seated, and he would slip into his chair without offering a greeting of any kind. In moody silence he would dissolve a single lump of sugar in a glass of water, poking at the sugar with his spoon and studying it intently. After that, he would sip the water slowly and often join the shifting table conversation, expressing his own comments with conviction and clarity. Frequently he contributed the most interesting parts of the discussion which held both girls attentive; but when the meal was ended, he headed resolutely for his room.

It was Ellinor who first asked Bud Cummings about the moody behavior of his table companion, but Bud Cummings dismissed the question with a shrug: "He doesn't mean anything by it; that's just his way."

From informal discussions in the lobby, it became apparent to the two girls that they were not alone in sharing a great curiosity about the aloof young man. Eyelids fluttered, and the gamut of feminine wiles was spent futilely by girls intent upon cracking that aloof shell, but George Vanderveer displayed no interest in any of them.

Christmas Eve, 1906, was an occasion Ellinor was destined never to forget. Bud Cummings came to the Hausman suite on the first floor to extend his greetings to Mrs. Hausman and her family and, well fortified with Yuletide drinks, he soon became intent upon catching Ellinor under the mistletoe. So exciting was the game and so pleasant were his surroundings that he announced a sudden change in plans:

"Look, Mrs. Hausman, I promised to go out and play cards with the boys, but that isn't any proper way to spend Christmas Eve, now is it? So if they call up here and ask for me, just tell 'em that I'm not here and you haven't seen me."

While Mrs. Hausman repeated her succession of evasions on the telephone all through the evening Bud Cummings made himself very much at home and the Hausman family enjoyed an informal but not-too-quiet Christmas Eve.

At a little past midnight there came a knock on the door and Bud made a frantic plea to Mrs. Hausman: "It's maybe one of the boys, and I don't want to be found here! Let me hide in your bedroom!"

While Bud made a dash to the bedroom and Mrs. Hausman stowed his hat and coat in a closet, Ellinor went to answer the door. Bud Cummings' frantic efforts to drag her under the mistletoe had disarranged her hair-do and she had removed the pins and let it down, so that it now hung to her waist. She pushed the hair back over her shoulder and opened the door to face George Vanderveer.

"Is Bud . . ." He left the question unfinished and backed away from the door as he saw her, his face flushed with embarrassment. He apologized for the intrusion and then was gone before she had an opportunity to reply.

The next day was Christmas, and Mrs. Hausman had planned a big Christmas dinner to be served early in the afternoon. A number of the guests had left for the holiday, so that a smaller number of tables than usual had been prepared in the dining room and it was necessary to assign guests to new seats for the occasion. Consequently, nearly everyone remained in the lobby instead of wandering into the dining room as had been their custom.

Ellinor was standing near the foot of the stairs when George Vanderveer came down, and he walked directly to her and again apologized for his intrusion on the night before. In the presence of numerous guests he asked her to go with him that evening to the theatre; and after one triumphant glance around the room she accepted. Ellinor Hausman, just turned eighteen, had won the unofficial but highly competitive sweepstakes by getting the first date with Gloomy Gus.

After dinner Bud Cummings slipped into the Hausman suite to talk to Ellinor. He told her that George Vanderveer had spent most of the morning raving about her long hair, like a man entranced. He stood for a time with his hands in his pockets, staring glumly out the window.

"It's a funny thing," he conceded at last. "Chances are if he hadn't seen you with your hair down he never would have asked you for a date. It just goes to prove something or other, and God only knows what!"

The days between Christmas and New Year's were filled with dates for Ellinor as George took her walking, sailing, skating and dancing. In partnership with Miller Freeman, an up-and-coming young businessman and civic leader, he owned a forty-two-foot schooner which he kept anchored at West Seattle, and which he could skim across the waters of the Sound with expert seamanship. He was an excellent skater and a very good dancer; and contrary to her earlier impressions, he was capable of all the little attentions which can mean so much to a girl in love. In restaurants, at the theatre, and at a dance he was a perfect gentleman; immaculately groomed and always in command of the situation at hand. But to Ellinor Hausman, George Vanderveer was at his best when he was away from the crowds and the social responsibilities; when they were hiking through the woods out beyond the end of the streetcar line, or gliding swiftly and silently across the waters of the Sound.

On New Year's night they sat at a small candle-lit table at the Savoy Hotel and without word or question he reached across the table and fastened his fraternity pin on to the front of her dress, and then he took her hand in his. They sat for a long time in silence. Never then or later did George Vanderveer ask her to marry him, and apparently he took her consent for granted. From Ellinor's standpoint it was just as well. Words would have been superfluous.

Two days later he informed her that he had secured a leave of absence from his job and that he and nine other men were taking his boat, the *Imp*, up the Inland Passage to Alaska. He explained that arrangements had been made far in advance. He didn't offer to change his plans, and she didn't suggest it.

"It will do you both good to be separated for a while," Mrs. Hausman suggested; and Ellinor stood with a dozen others at the end of a small dock not far from Alki Point, waving frantically as the *Imp* scooted past under full sail at the start of her northbound journey.

It was late in February when the *Imp* returned to Seattle, and immediately upon his arrival at the Hawthorne Hotel, George Vanderveer slipped a diamond engagement ring upon her finger. There were no words spoken; no questions asked. Obviously he was a young man who knew what he wanted, and he was inviting no obstacles or opposition.

The next ten weeks were filled with beautiful days and unforgettable evenings for a young couple in love. Mostly they were days devoted to hiking and sailing and swimming and horseback riding; week-ends on Lake Washington; evenings spent under the stars with beach fires, or walking hand in hand in the moonlight. He gave her a .22 target pistol, and spent hours teaching her to shoot.

She told him how she and Jeanne had always referred to him as Gloomy Gus; and from that day forward he called her Gus. It was their own private little joke to begin with, and his way of teasing her; but it was the start of a nickname she was destined to carry for many years.

Bud Cummings, meanwhile, had instituted divorce proceedings in Mrs. Hausman's behalf, and Ellinor explained that her mother was perplexed by a problem of professional ethics: "If she's going to have a lawyer for a son-in-law, it seems a little odd to have somebody else represent her in court; and yet she doesn't want to hurt Bud's feelings by asking him to turn it over to you. What should she do?"

George Vanderveer laughed at her. "It's Bud's case, so let him handle it. I don't see where there's any problem involved."

However, when a separate problem appeared as a by-product of the divorce action, Ellinor insisted that George should handle it, and her mother consented. Sam Hausman was holding a brooch that had belonged to his wife before her marriage, and although it had little value except for Emma Hausman's sentimental attachment, he had refused to give it to her.

George Vanderveer grinned when Ellinor told him about

the brooch and asked him to institute proceedings to make him surrender it. "That's one of the things wrong with this country, Gus. Our courts get all cluttered up with things that ought to be settled out of court—little piddlin' things that shouldn't take up time on the calendar." He assured her that he would call on Mr. Hausman and secure the brooch without any legal involvement or delay.

The next evening he presented the brooch to Mrs. Hausman. He explained to Ellinor that her father had sat at his desk acting smug and supercilious at first, but that he had grabbed the older man by the collar and yanked him to his feet, and immediately Sam Hausman had undergone a change of heart. "He couldn't give the thing to me fast enough," Vanderveer grinned, "and then after that we shook hands and he apologized for being petty about it. He even sent his love, and wished us all kinds of happiness."

George Vanderveer and Ellinor Hausman were married on May 22, 1907, at St. Mark's Church in Seattle, and they left immediately for a two months' honeymoon in California. They spent their wedding night at the Oak Bay Hotel in Victoria, British Columbia, with reservations for the California-bound ship to be boarded the next day.

They walked for a while in the cool of the evening, and then sat on a wooden bench holding hands and looking out over the twinkling lights of the harbor, and sharing their dreams of the life ahead.

Suddenly he got to his feet and began pacing back and forth before the bench, pounding his fist into the palm of his hand. "There's one thing I've got to ask of you, Gus," he announced grimly. "There's one thing you mustn't ever ask me to do!"

She was taken aback by the sudden tenseness of his voice, and just a little alarmed. "What is it, George? Just tell me."

He stopped pacing and stood in front of her, bending forward until his face was near hers and his eyes burning with intensity: "Don't ever ask me to get into politics! Don't hint it! Don't urge it! Don't suggest it! Don't try to influence me in any way! You mustn't ever encourage me to go into politics!"

She smiled up at him. "Don't you know I wouldn't ever do that, George? Those things you'll work out for yourself, and I won't try to influence you."

A fleeting smile crossed his face and he shook his head. "I know you wouldn't, Gus; not purposely. But I'd do almost anything in the world for you, if I thought it would make you happy—anything but getting mixed up in politics. It's a mean, rotten, dirty business and I don't want to get sucked into it! I just thought we better both understand that, right from the start. Sometimes it doesn't take much to influence a man, either way."

He didn't mention the subject again, and the weeks that followed were unmarred by sober thoughts or reference to his professional career. They spent two weeks at Santa Barbara. Together, on horseback, they explored the more remote trails, far back up in the hills; and they shared dreams of some day owning a sprawling mountain ranch, raising thoroughbreds, and living the good life of the out-of-doors amid the peaceful solitude of pine-covered hills. They spent considerable time in Los Angeles, and enjoyed carefree days on the sandy and sunswept beaches of southern California. Together they swam far out into the seemingly tepid surf, for both were excellent swimmers. They spent many days fishing the waters off Catalina in June, and they prowled the steep trails of the island.

It was toward the end of June when George Vanderveer announced that it was almost time to end the honeymoon. They were drifting idly in a small boat in the sheltered waters of the bay, soaking up sunshine and listening to the peaceful ripple of the small waves against the side of the hull.

"Will you be glad to get back to Seattle?" he asked quietly. "Have you missed it much?"

She shook her head. "I've missed Mother, of course; and

the family. I'll be glad to see them when we get back, but I haven't ever wished it would end. Have you?"

He sat for a long time staring idly out over the water. "No, I haven't ever wished it would end," he said at last. "And I'll tell you something, Gus: I've been happier these past five or six weeks than I've ever been in my life—happier than I ever knew I could be."

She reached over and patted his hand. "I'm glad."

She felt his hand tighten, but his gaze remained on the far horizon. "Damn it all," he said slowly, "this is the way Nature intended for a man to live—with the sun on his back and the wind in his face and a kind of strange contentment in his heart. My God, Gus! I don't think I've ever let myself completely unwind this way before, ever in my life! I can't tell you how I hate to see it end!"

She tried to assure him that it wouldn't need to end, and they could take their week-ends in Seattle and explore the San Juan Islands; go swimming and hunting and fishing together; that the years ahead could be much like the weeks just past.

He shook his head, turned his hand over to encompass hers, and looked directly into her eyes. "You just don't understand. That's a different world, and it's a different life. A man can't be half this and half that."

Little more was said at the time, but one evening on the ship headed north, Ellinor Vanderveer tugged at her husband's sleeve as they stood together at the railing staring down at the dark water slipping past. "I've got a wonderful idea, George! Let's jump ship when we get to Victoria! We can have one last week-end together at the Oak Bay Hotel, where we spent our first night together."

He shook his head. "We've got too many things to do. We've got to unpack, look around for a place to live, and all that sort of thing. I'm kind of anxious to get everything ship-shape so I can start in at the office on Monday morning."

And even before the ship docked at Seattle, Ellinor knew what he had been trying to tell her that day in the shelter of Catalina Island: George Vanderveer, attorney, would always be dominant over George Vanderveer, husband and week-end companion. All the springs of inner tension were being wound once again as the fighter headed toward the arena.

George Vanderveer went back to his job in the Prosecuting Attorney's office on Monday morning, and he left to his wife the task of selecting their future home. She studied the classi-fied advertising columns of the daily newspapers, and she combed the city until she found exactly what she wanted—a tiny house set in the midst of a wooded plot, not far from the shores of Lake Washington.

"You'll love it," she told George that evening. "We can swim in the lake, hike in the woods, and even sit on our front steps and practise shooting!" But he laughed at her and he teased her, and he refused to go to see it.

"You've got to be practical about it, Gus. I'm a deputy prosecuting attorney, and I've got to be able to get down to the office on short notice at almost any time of the day or night. Let's try to remember that the honeymoon is over."

"But it's to be our home," she protested. "Our first real home together. Don't you think it's important to find exactly the right kind of place?"

He shrugged his heavy shoulders. "Actually, I don't see that it makes too much difference. After all, there are just two of us and we'll probably spend a lot of time on the boat. All we really need is some place where we can eat and sleep and have a little privacy."

He scanned the newspaper momentarily, made a telephone call, asked several questions, and then hung up. "You see, Gus, it's not really much of a problem if you don't try to make a problem of it. We'll run over and look at this place after dinner, and if it's all right, you can start moving our stuff in tomorrow."

The following day George and Ellinor Vanderveer moved into the Eulalie Apartments at Boren and Cherry Streets, not far from downtown Seattle. It was almost exactly the opposite of everything Ellinor had dreamed of when she had tried to visualize their first home. But it was handy to George's work.

CHAPTER SIX

For slander lives upon succession, forever housed where it gets possession.—SHAKESPEARE

CHARLES W. "WAPPY" WAPPENSTEIN had become Seattle's Chief of Police following the election of Mayor William Hickman Moore in 1906; and while the Prosecuting Attorney's office, as a part of the county government, had little direct responsibility to the city's police force, still there were many occasions when cooperation between the two was considered mutually beneficial. There had been a measure of such cooperation before the appointment of Wappenstein, but the new chief would have none of it. He preferred to run his department as he saw fit, and to recognize his responsibility only to the man who had appointed him.

There is little doubt that Wappy's resentment toward the Prosecutor's office was a by-product of his personal antagonism toward Deputy Prosecutor George F. Vanderveer, for the two men had met several times previously, and never under particularly happy circumstances.

At the time of Vanderveer's arrival in Seattle in 1901, Wappenstein had been a detective in the Seattle Police Department, and Wappy had made the headlines temporarily when a committee composed of members of the City Council had offered to produce evidence that he and his chief, W. L. Meredith, had accepted protection money from the operators of bunco games within the city. Chief of Police Meredith had promptly written out his resignation and then had gone out and got himself killed in a gun battle before the resignation had time to become effective.

Crowded off the front page by the more dramatic details of the fatal shooting, Wappenstein had quietly left the police force to work as a special investigator for the Great Northern Railway Company, at about the time when Vanderveer was handling some of the company's legal work and was being considered to head its legal staff in Seattle. Despite the fact that Wappy's investigations served as legal ammunition, George Vanderveer looked upon the older man as an opportunist—a man who would sell his honor to the highest bidder, and whose sworn testimony ran a fifty-fifty chance of being perjury.

Wappy was short of stature and, in Vanderveer's opinion, equally short of character. He wore a walrus-type moustache, and his unflinching gaze seemed always coolly calculating. His attire inclined toward the flamboyant, but in his own way he could be as hard and as uncompromising as Vanderveer. The City Council had produced evidence that he could be bought, but no one had produced evidence that he could be bluffed or intimidated.

Undeniably, Wappenstein had an ability to make friends and to hold them, and he had his own peculiar sense of loyalty upon which he had never set a price. There was about him a certain personal charm, and he prided himself in delivering what he was paid to deliver. During his years on the force he had rendered a number of favors to Colonel Alden J. Blethen, owner and publisher of the *Seattle Times*, and he had won the Colonel's friendship and unfailing support. Even at the time when Wappy was being accused of accepting protection money from the city's gamblers, the *Times* had filled its front page with journalistic blasts—not against the accused officers, but against the members of the City Council for their high-handed action and their star-chamber sessions, which had produced the unsavory charges.

With Wappenstein's appointment as Chief of Police in 1906 there came a flood of praise in his behalf printed in the *Times*, and intended to quiet the rising protests from the many thousands who had supported Mayor Moore in his campaign as a reform candidate and who stood aghast at his choice of a police chief. To his close associates, Mayor Moore explained that Wappenstein had been appointed as the result of a pre-election side-deal for support; that he had been part of the price of victory—and that the reformists should be willing to accept a little bit of bad, in order to accomplish a great deal of good. Within a few weeks all was quiet, and the *Times* was able to override the wave of disorganized protests.

Wappenstein's first few months in office brought reassurance even to his critics. He was a capable man and, according to reports, he was making the most of his opportunity to vindicate himself and to prove that he was able to give the city the best police administration in its history. The police cracked down on crime wherever it was found, apparently without fear or favor. The only exception was the Skid Road district, where Wappy maintained a hands-off policy. "You can't solve the problem," he insisted, "so you might as well learn to live with it."

The first few months saw no particular conflict with the Prosecuting Attorney's staff. At the time the deal was being consummated for Wappenstein's appointment, Vanderveer was on his trip to Alaska; and not long after his return he had departed again—this time on his honeymoon.

Shortly after Vanderveer and his bride moved into the Eulalie Apartments, however, the animosity between the two men once again began to smolder. Reassured by the laudatory comments in the *Times* paying tribute to Seattle's outstanding Chief of Police, the great majority of the city's people had come to accept Wappenstein as a righteous and upstanding man who had made amends for his earlier transgression. But through his contacts and informers along Skid Road, Vanderveer heard new rumors of police pay-offs and the

skyrocketing price of protection. Rightly or wrongly, he
was convinced that the hands-off policy toward Skid Road
vice was being bought and paid for, and that Wappenstein
was sharing in the profits.

The mounting bitterness between the two men branched
out into a spreading political rift. Colonel Blethen of the
Times fitted automatically on the side of the Police Chief
and he began his journalistic left-hand jabbing at the Deputy
Prosecutor. The *Seattle Post-Intelligencer*, the city's other
leading daily newspaper and familiarly referred to as the *P.I.*
by almost everyone, found itself lined up just as automatically
on the side of George Vanderveer. The independent and
often-erratic *Times* and the staunchly Republican *P.I.* opposed and contradicted each other on nearly everything from
political questions to weather forecasts; and the *P.I.*'s mounting admiration for Deputy Prosecutor Vanderveer grew in
direct ratio to Colonel Blethen's criticisms in the columns of
the *Times*. The name of George Vanderveer had become a
political football on the journalistic gridiron, and Seattle was
keeping its eye on the ball. The *Seattle Star* and other smaller
papers divided along partisan lines.

Within a few weeks of the time when they returned from
their California honeymoon, George Vanderveer arrived
home at the Eulalie Apartments one evening with information that came as a complete surprise to his young bride. He
explained that prolonged discussions had been going on at the
office, and that the consensus seemed to be that he should
seek the Republican nomination for Prosecuting Attorney the
following year. Some of the party leaders felt that because
of the great amount of publicity he had received in the newspapers, he might be the most likely candidate with the greatest
chance of success. He told her that he had decided to accept
the responsibility.

Ellinor Vanderveer made no attempt to disguise her amazement, and she reminded him of his sober words on their wed-

ding night in Victoria when he had insisted that he would
not enter politics.

He smiled at her, and winked. "Of course I didn't know
then that they'd ask me."

Already, in her married life, Ellinor Vanderveer had learned
to expect the unexpected, and she had learned the futility of
probing for information. She knew that he would explain the
reasons for his abrupt change of plans when he felt in the
mood to do so, and she was willing to wait.

It was nearly a week later when he explained to her that
under the terms of the state constitution, Kenneth Mackintosh would be ineligible to seek reëlection after the comple-
tion of his second two-year term, and that ordinarily the office
and the party leaders gave their support to the Chief Deputy.
He had assumed that John Murphy would receive the endorsement almost automatically; but party leaders, facing the
future with a sense of apprehension, determined to put their
strongest candidates on the ticket to combat a rising surge of
independent progressive voters.

"But you don't have to agree to run just because they've
asked you," she pointed out. "You could tell them that you
don't want it."

He shook his head. "That's where you're wrong, Gus. A
man can't very well turn his back and run away from a fight
after somebody has started swinging at him, and just say that
he's not interested."

From Vanderveer's standpoint, probably there was no al-
ternative. Colonel Blethen was snorting fire and alternately
threatening to have Vanderveer disbarred or to run him out
of town if he had the temerity to seek election, and it was
contrary to everything in Vanderveer's nature to back down
in the face of such threats.

"Besides that, I don't want to try to start in private practice
right now," he told Ellinor impatiently. "I've spent a lot of
money in the past year, what with that trip to Alaska and the
one to California, and I'd like to have a little more cash in the

bank before I try to start out of my own. It's a sort of a responsibility for a man when he has a wife and a home."

She didn't say any more then, but a few days later when they were dressed in old clothes and were working side by side scraping the decks of the *Imp*, she tried to tell him how she felt: "George, if you really don't want to enter politics, I hope you won't do it just because you have a wife to support. We can get along, just the two of us—no matter what. I don't want you to do anything like that on my account."

He insisted that his interest in a monthly paycheck was purely incidental; that Colonel Blethen had delivered a few low blows, and that now he was determined to stay in the battle to the finish. "And it isn't just getting elected that I'm interested in," he told her earnestly. "I'm going to be the best Prosecuting Attorney King County ever had. I can do it, and I'm going to do it, just to make that old frizzle-headed bastard eat his words!"

There were a few cautious leaders in the Republican camp who felt that George Vanderveer might not be the most likely candidate to represent the party because of the inevitable opposition of Colonel Blethen. "The poor boy will be crucified," they pointed out. "It seems just a little like deliberately asking for trouble." They suggested that a new candidate should be selected who would incur the wrath of neither newspaper, and thus stand a better chance of being elected.

There were others who argued that the Republican party would be practically dead in Seattle when it began selecting its candidates on the basis of Colonel Blethen's approval. And their enthusiasm for Vanderveer gained momentum in the face of new developments at the Prosecutor's office.

On September 20, 1907, Seattle residents received with their morning milk delivery a small card announcing a new price schedule for milk sold within the city and to become effective October first. Under the price structure set up by members of the Seattle Milk Exchange, whole milk would not be sold for less than ten cents a quart or six cents a pint, whether bottled or in bulk. Special prices were posted for deliveries to boardinghouses and grocery stores, but all along the line Seattle faced the grim prospect of a rise in the price of milk. The Seattle Milk Exchange represented the great majority but not all of the persons and organizations selling milk within the city, but it was announced that all members would observe the uniform price schedule.

There was no effective anti-trust statute in the State of Washington, but Vanderveer promptly received permission to swing into action and to prosecute the members of the Seattle Milk Exchange under a common law charge of illegal conspiracy.

His first open threat to secure a restraining order was met with jubilation on the part of the milk-buying public, but the members of the Seattle Milk Exchange remained adamant for they had secured competent legal advice in advance, and their attorneys assured them that Vanderveer must be bluffing. Surely he was smart enough to realize that he couldn't make it stand up.

The various milk dealers within the Exchange had agreed among themselves each to raise the price of milk sold, and each to refrain from selling milk to other than his own customers. Attorneys assured the dealers that they had a lawful right to establish any reasonable price upon their own milk, to refuse to sell it for a lower price, and to sell it to such patrons or persons as they desired. On October first, the new higher prices went into effect and they remained in effect throughout the month. Customers paid the new higher prices and resigned themselves to the inevitable. Like the milk dealers, many of them concluded that Vanderveer had been bluffing in his original threat of action.

However, as the month of October began drawing to a close, the members of the Seattle Milk Exchange started a series of emergency meetings to review their legal situation. Word was out that Vanderveer, somehow, had gained possession of some damning evidence in the form of ill-advised correspondence written by one of the milk dealers—letters indicating that the milk dealers intended to control the price of milk throughout the city and to prevent open competition. How Vanderveer had secured the correspondence was a mystery, but the fact that he had the letters seemed beyond question.

Information seeped out concerning other activities of Vanderveer in gathering evidence for the prosecution, and by the end of the month members of the Seattle Milk Exchange were no longer adamant. If found guilty on the criminal charge of conspiracy, they might face jail sentences in addition to substantial fines; and their legal advisers no longer spoke with such assurance. In an attempt to evade such grim possibilities, they called off the entire campaign. Prices dropped two cents a quart, and milk dealers let it be known that they would sell to anybody and to everybody who wanted to buy.

As the price of milk tumbled and as customers rejoiced, the *Seattle P.I.* paid tribute to the dynamic young Deputy Prosecutor who had won the battle in behalf of Seattle's mothers and children, and Republican party leaders wiped away their last doubts as to whether Vanderveer should be their candidate. He was the man of the hour.

At the Prosecutor's office, however, Vanderveer took little cognizance of the altered situation. He went doggedly ahead preparing for the prosecution. He filed an information against A. Z. Erickson, one of the milk dealers, who later was found guilty, sentenced to ten days in the county jail, and fined five hundred dollars. He also fought Erickson's appeal in the State Supreme Court where the judgment was affirmed (54 Wash. 473). Among lawyers of a later day, his successful prosecution of the case without the benefit of pleading any state statutes was destined to rank as a major legal achievement.

The *Seattle Times* scrupulously avoided giving Vanderveer any credit for restoring the lower price of milk, but it also refrained from sniping at him during the course of the primary campaign. The *Times* concerned itself largely with national issues and with the timely arrival in Puget Sound of all the great battleships of the United States Navy in the course of an around-the-world cruise. Apparently there was little room in the crowded columns for the mention of such things as local politics, and the selection of a Republican candidate for the office of Prosecuting Attorney.

Vanderveer won the nomination without serious competition and he turned his attention to the forthcoming general election, with the *Times* still giving his campaign a journalistic cold shoulder. Blethen was all out for Bryan and his free-silver campaign, and his local interest had shifted from the field of politics to the field of public service.

The Arctic Club, some time earlier, had approached the *Times* with a request for publicity to aid in its plan to establish in Seattle a permanent Alaska exhibit in order to encourage more travel to the far North; and Colonel Blethen's city editor, James A. Wood, had suggested enlarging the plans to encompass something in the nature of a World's Fair. Nearly a decade had passed since the city's businessmen had first sent out their nation-wide blast of publicity to promote Seattle as the gateway to Alaska. The great Northwest boom was tapering off, and other cities were beginning to press their claims for the title of the fastest-growing city in the United States. Something was needed to stir up the dying embers; and it would take something more than a few stuffed polar bears and glass-encased samples of ore in a special exhibit in downtown Seattle.

A committee was formed to promote the Alaska-Yukon Exposition in Seattle, and it went about its task with businesslike efficiency. The original committee had its shortcomings, however, as the publisher of the *Times* proceeded to point out —not the least of which was its failure to include Colonel A. J. Blethen on its board of trustees. This oversight was promptly remedied, and one more word was added to the title: it now was designated as the Alaska-Yukon-*Pacific* Exposition. After numerous discussions, with the plans growing larger at each session, it was decided that the word *Pacific* should be given the broadest possible interpretation, and that invitations should go out to all countries bordering upon the Pacific Ocean.

Several of the more active members of the Arctic Club felt that their original idea had been lost somewhere amid the mounting enthusiasm, and they protested that too much attention was being shifted away from Yukon gold toward Japanese lanterns, Chinese dragons, and boxing kangaroos from Australia. Colonel Blethen, however, displayed little patience for those who failed to believe as he believed, and who lacked his almost-boundless enthusiasm for this classic event of Northwest history.

He was short-tempered with all who failed to offer financial help to get the exposition launched, and he was not subtle in his threats against them. On the front page of the *Times* he ran a glaring box with the threat to publish the names of men who had been made wealthy by Seattle's growth, and who had declined to aid the Exposition project. The caption put it squarely up to them: "RICH MAN! Do You Want Your Name On This List?" Less than a dozen names were actually published, and to each the Colonel openly suggested the purchase of a five-thousand-dollar bond. And later, amid the list of donors, there appeared the name of the *Seattle Times* as the purchaser of a five-hundred-dollar bond. The threat to publish more names of financial slackers turned the trick, and before the announced deadline Seattle had subscribed its requested quota, thus proving to the Colonel's printed satisfaction that the city was enthusiastically behind the great project.

Vanderveer, meanwhile, was going quietly ahead with his campaign. At the request of party leaders he had made a personal call upon Colonel Blethen to assure him that there was nothing nefarious behind his desire to become Prosecuting Attorney. The Colonel heard him out without commitment, and the *Times* continued to refrain from any attack.

On October 26 it printed its sample ballot listing the two

candidates for Prosecuting Attorney: George F. Vanderveer, Republican; and C. R. Hawkins, Democrat. It suggested no preference to its readers, and for two days following, the sample ballot appeared as first printed.

In the spring election, Seattle voters had rejected Mayor Moore in his bid to win reëlection, and Charles Wappenstein was out of a job once again. Now, amid the rumors floating through Skid Road, Vanderveer heard the report that Wappy was to serve as head of the special police appointed to guard the Exposition grounds. He called upon a member of the committee and learned that the rumor had ample foundation; that Colonel Blethen was beating the drums in Wappenstein's behalf, and that other committee members felt that they owed the Colonel consideration because of the great amount of good work he had done. He learned also that Colonel Blethen was intent upon pushing through the Wappenstein appointment some time before the general election.

That night George Vanderveer relayed the information to his wife. "Right there is the reason old Blethen has been letting me ride along without sniping at me," he told her. "He thinks I wouldn't dare object to the appointment so close to the election, for fear of upsetting things! If he'd been pounding away at me, he knows I'd protest the appointment, but he's been letting me alone and he thinks I wouldn't dare protest now!"

He assured his wife that he intended to protest, regardless; and that his failure to do so would be tantamount to accepting a bribe. "People are going to be watching to see if I've got the guts to stand up and protest," he told her earnestly. "They'll find out!"

"Who's going to be watching?" she asked quietly. "I'll bet not one person in a thousand will interpret it the way you do."

He whirled and faced her. "That doesn't matter! Blethen will be watching. So will Wappenstein! They'll figure they've bought me off, if I just let it ride and don't put up

any protest. They'll probably laugh, and figure they've handled me the right way."

Ellinor's eyes were puzzled as she studied her husband.
"Do you really care what they think? Is that important?"

He shrugged his shoulders. "I don't know whether it's important or not, but I know I couldn't do it. I'd never feel
right about it, Gus—never for the rest of my life! A man
can't compromise himself on a thing like that, and have any
self-respect."

He attempted to still his wife's fears when she asked how
Blethen would respond. "Actually, he can't do very much,"
he assured her. "The *Times* will probably come out strong
for Hawkins, but he can't very well hit at me. There isn't
any scandal in my life. I've done my job the best way I know
how, and I've got a pretty good record. The people all know
that. I've never taken a nickel of hush money or been mixed
up in any kind of graft that they can spring at the last minute. Even Blethen's got to have *some* foundation for his
tirades and I don't see that there's much he can do, when you
come right down to it."

The following morning he submitted his protest against the
Wappenstein appointment. He warned influential members
of the committee that Seattle might derive more harm than
benefit from the Exposition if concessions were sold to pickpockets, gamblers and confidence men by an unethical chief
of the special police force, just as the legitimate concessions
had been sold by the committee. And he emphasized that
Wappenstein was not the man for such a job. On the record
and off the record, he insisted, Wappenstein had demonstrated an unvarying contempt for ethical behavior.

Committee members listened but each, in turn, assured
Vanderveer that the matter was out of his hands. Reports fil-
tered back that Colonel Blethen was furious, but there was no
ripple in the serenity of the *Times*. It continued its policy of
praising Bryan and lambasting Taft, and stirring up interest
in the forthcoming Exposition, while shunting mention of

local politics to the inside pages. It refrained from any mention of the Republican candidate for Prosecuting Attorney.

On Thursday, October 29, 1908, at the beginning of the final week before the general election, the *Times* once again waded into local politics. With banner headlines across the front page it charged that Vanderveer was up to his old tricks, employing methods of "darkest Russia." With crocodile tears, it told of the heart-rending case of an elderly doctor, dragged from his office, brutally deprived of his liberty by police, aided and abetted by Deputy Prosecutor Vanderveer. It described how the poor old doctor had been forcibly taken from his office at four o'clock in the afternoon, locked up in the King County jail and refused permission to communicate with attorney or friends. It mentioned—almost as an irrelevant detail—that the doctor had been charged with practising medicine without a license; and it did not mention that it was almost universal practice to hold all prisoners incommunicado during the booking process—a police procedure having no possible connection with the office of Prosecuting Attorney.

Friday's paper picked up where the Thursday edition had left off. The three center columns of the first page were devoted to an unflattering picture of Vanderveer, under the heading: "He Abused Old Man." It repeated the story of the poor old doctor being brutally bulldozed until he was forced to sign an affidavit, and it branched out into additional charges of Vanderveer's brutality. And buried deep on the inside pages of the same edition was a small announcement that Charles W. Wappenstein had been designated to head the special police force on the Exposition grounds.

The climax of the campaign was reserved for the Sunday edition, with its wide circulation throughout the county. The *Seattle Sunday Times*, on November first, devoted all of page three to Vanderveer, with a sensational account of George Vanderveer assaulting his prospective father-in-law, S. D. Hausman. Somehow, the *Times* had uncovered the story of Vanderveer's call upon Ellinor's father the year before, when he had demanded the return of the brooch belonging to Ellinor's mother. However, the story in the *Times* bore little resemblance to the story Vanderveer had related to his fiancée. The newspaper story deleted mention of the brooch. It described the incident as an "unprovoked and ferocious assault," and it quoted Vanderveer as threatening Mr. Hausman's life: "I've got a d——d good mind to kill you now! If you repeat this conversation I will kill you." And it carried an affidavit, sworn to by S. D. Hausman, stating among other things: "I am a Republican and want to vote the Republican ticket but nothing on earth could induce me to vote for such a man as Prosecuting Attorney. He is no man for such a position."

Vanderveer responded with a threat to sue Blethen for libel, and the Colonel was almost beside himself. Monday's edition of the *Times* broke with a pen-and-ink sketch which occupied more than half of page one. It portrayed a dignified old gentleman seated in a chair, and cowering under the threatening gestures of a viciously caricatured George Vanderveer towering above him with upraised fist. Taft, Bryan, free-silver, and the Alaska-Yukon-Pacific Exposition by now had been banished from the front page of the *Times*, which was devoted exclusively to the broadside against Vanderveer, under the banner heading: "Threats And Lies From Vanderveer."

Warming rapidly to its subject, the front page story led off with a description of Vanderveer as a "brutal, domineering, bigoted and unforgiving character in whom it is unsafe to entrust authority." It mentioned his relentless pursuit of C. W. Wappenstein, and it bristled under Vanderveer's threat to sue for libel:

"The *Times* is not an old, feeble man or a defenseless woman. Nor is it an immature youth held helpless by you in the county jail and denied the right to communicate with friends or lawyers.

"If you should be elected to the office to which you aspire, the *Times* will still be in the same old place, with the same old proprietors. Fulfill your threats if you dare. But remember— you must stay within the limits of the law! . . .

"It won't be the same thing as frightening the wits out of an aged doctor! It won't be the same thing as striking a 60-year-old, be-spectacled father-in-law!

"The *Times* has been threatened many times. It rather enjoys being threatened by such as you.

"Never before in the history of King County at least, has any man running for office dared to threaten a publisher with persecution and criminal arrest for defending the downtrodden, the poor and the worthy—and no one would believe that such a thing could occur at the present time, under normal conditions.

"In spite of your threats, rascals will be exposed, criminals will be attacked, whether they be in office or out, just the same when this community may be unfortunate enough to be burdened with you as a public official, as they have been in the past!

"Whom the Gods would destroy they first make mad!"

On election day the *Times* apparently heard the call to a higher duty, for it devoted its first page to a calm appraisal of the platforms and the policies of the major political parties, and it refrained from taking any closing shots in the local campaign.

On November fourth, the day after election, it conceded election to Taft and ran a front-page picture of the President-elect and his daughter; but it reserved the two left columns for a triumphant heading: "VANDERVEER REBUKED!"

The story about Vanderveer told how the people of Seattle had streamed to the polls to reject the Republican candidate for Prosecuting Attorney; but like the earlier story concerning the arrest, it included a pertinent fact which had been disregarded by the writer of the bold heading: Vanderveer's heavy majority in the county precincts had more than offset his adverse vote in certain urban wards, and the over-all totals were undeniably in his favor.

Despite its triumphant heading which claimed that Vanderveer had been rebuked and rejected, even the *Times* conceded on the basis of early returns that George F. Vanderveer had been elected Prosecuting Attorney of King County.

CHAPTER SEVEN

As diseases must necessarily be known before their remedies, so passions come into being before the laws which prescribe limits to them.—CATO, THE ELDER

ALFRED LUNDIN, when he arrived in Seattle in the fall of 1906, was a young man with two related problems: he had to establish himself in the practice of law in order to make use of his newly granted degree from the University of Nebraska, and he had to convince his fiancée back in Nebraska that she should board a train and head for the Pacific Northwest to marry him. Inasmuch as the solution of the second problem was contingent upon the solution of the first, he devoted himself to the task of establishing a private practice.

He rented desk space in the offices of Todd, Wilson and Thorgrimson in the Lowman Building at First and Cherry Streets. He hung his framed diploma upon the wall, and he awaited the call of his first client. It proved to be a long and discouraging wait, for the great Northwest boom had attracted many attorneys ahead of him, and most of them were firmly established. He went to church and he joined social and fraternal clubs and he widened his circle of friends and acquaints, but always he was rubbing shoulders with other attorneys who had made their contacts before his arrival. There was no shortage of manpower along the legal front of Seattle's progress, and Al Lundin spent fruitless hours at his rented desk and pondered the possible worthy use of time on his hands.

He recalled the widely shared dreams of the men back in law school who had planned to start their careers as deputies in some legal branch of local government, and he called upon Scott Calhoun, corporation counsel of Seattle. "Most of my problems would be solved if I could just land a regular job with a regular monthly income," he explained earnestly; but he was informed that there were no existing vacancies in the office and none expected.

The United States, in the months that followed, rippled with rumors of impending war with Japan, and nowhere in the nation were the rumors more widely discussed nor more seriously considered than along the Pacific Coast. It was a dominant topic of conversation on the street and in offices, in saloons, and all along the waterfront. Batteries had been completed at Forts Worden, Flagler and Casey, guarding the entrance to Puget Sound, but personnel to man them was wanting. Frenzied recruiting programs were under way to build up the enlistment in the National Guard.

Al Lundin, with time on his hands and with patriotic fervor in his heart, joined Seattle's Company L and left for two weeks' encampment at Fort Worden on the Olympic Peninsula. There were days of intensive drill for the infantrymen, and long hours on the target range as Company L, under Captain Howard Darlington, established the best shooting record of any company in the United States.

There was competition and inter-company rivalry which grew intense when Company K, from Everett, produced a couple of pairs of boxing gloves and a complete boxing team, with a challenge to take on all comers. Its offer was quickly followed by a claim of championship through default, for the other companies failed to produce any competition in several weight divisions.

First Sergeant Charles O. Curtis of Company L pleaded with his men to meet the challenge, for company spirit was running high and he was not a man to shrug off the taunts from across the parade ground. It had all started in the spirit of fun, but the taunts had a way of becoming pointed and personal, and the smiles slowly disappeared.

For two days Al Lundin waited hopefully for someone else in his company to offer to fight in the middleweight division, but when no one stepped forward he finally confronted Sergeant Curtis with his offer to represent Company L: "I've boxed a little in my life but I'll probably get hell beaten out of me," he explained with a grin. "I'm willing to try it if you can't get anybody else."

The reluctance of others within the company to face Company K's middleweight contender was fortified, no doubt, by the fact that Everett boasted a particularly well-qualified candidate—a powerful man of considerable experience, who was reputed to be the outstanding boxer and the heaviest hitter of the K Company team.

Al Lundin, at one hundred and sixty-three pounds, was tall and rangy and well-muscled, but he was comparatively inexperienced. He depended greatly upon the advice of Sergeant Curtis and others within his company to show him how to hold his guard and how to cover up under a barrage of sudden blows such as his opponent was expected to deliver.

"I'll be right there in your corner," Sergeant Curtis promised. "No matter what happens, you listen to me! I'll tell you when to cover up, when to back away. You do just what I tell you."

The day of the fight was clear and bright, but with a crisp wind whipping in from the Strait and kicking up whitecaps on the surface of the Sound. Officers and men of both companies gathered around the improvised ring, and for a while they watched Al Lundin take a merciless beating at the hands of his opponent. Somehow, his long arms seemed to be all elbows and he was unbelievably awkward as he tried to manipulate his guard in response to the advice being shouted from the corner by Sergeant Curtis. It was a pitiful thing to watch, but the members of Company L attempted to console themselves with the philosophy that it was a moral victory—merely having a man willing to step into the same ring with the Everett mauler.

Somewhere in the second round, Lundin received a sharp right hook to the ear that sent him sprawling across the ring. He was angered and stung, and perhaps a little humiliated. He forgot all of the well-intended advice of his friends, and he completely disregarded the frantic shouts of Sergeant Curtis in his corner as he waded forward with both fists flying. It was all offense and no defense, and with no slight resemblance to boxing skill. Blows bounced off his head and shoulders and chest with terrific thuds that could be heard clear across the parade ground, but he landed blows of his own also—wild, swinging, vicious blows so completely unorthodox as to be confusing. When the round ended, his opponent was splattered with blood from a hard smash against his nose, and when it was time to start the next round the man was unable to answer the bell. It was nearly an hour later before the bleeding could be stopped, and by that time Company L had proudly claimed the championship of the middleweight division.

It was but one of many fights in the inter-company competition, and but one of the many incidents that filled the two weeks of training encampment, but Al Lundin, in later years, would have reason to believe that those few moments of frantic and unorthodox fighting at Fort Worden helped to shape the course of his life.

He returned to Seattle and to the same discouraging routine he had known before. He was able to pick up enough legal work to remain solvent, and to pay the ten dollars a month for his desk space; but his clients were few and his fees were small—and the letters from Nebraska seemed to hint of a slight impatience.

In the spring of 1908 he heard rumors that George Vanderveer would be the Republican candidate for Prosecuting Attorney, and he determined to make one more try for a regular income, which would enable him to send for his intended bride. He called upon George Vanderveer at the Prosecuting Attorney's office and offered to work untiringly in the forthcoming political campaign in exchange for the promise of a job as a deputy if Vanderveer were elected.

Vanderveer shook his head. "If I'm elected, I'll choose my deputies on merit, alone. There'll be no political considerations involved."

Al Lundin left the office convinced that he had been given the brush-off and that he would have no opportunity at a job in the Prosecutor's office if Vanderveer were elected. He was even more convinced of it when he received a report from his friend, John C. Higgins, who had undertaken to speak to Vanderveer in Lundin's behalf.

"You must have made one hell of a big impression on Vanderveer, with your promise to work in his campaign," Higgins reported. "When I asked him to reconsider, he couldn't even remember who you were."

Lundin followed the course of the campaign without taking any active part in it, and when he read the report of Vanderveer's election he parted with his last hope of entering the Prosecutor's office for at least two more years. He paid out another ten dollars for desk rental, and wrote a long, discouraged letter to his fianceé in Nebraska, explaining that there were nothing but dark clouds on the horizon in all directions.

Two days later he met Vanderveer on the street and was greeted with an impatient reprimand. "Where in hell have you been? I thought you wanted a job as deputy on my staff!"

He accompanied Vanderveer to his office, and joined in the general discussion of staff organization and the distribution of responsibilities. He also learned the reason for his selection.

"Howard Darlington told me about that fight you put up over at Fort Worden," Vanderveer told him. "I liked that,

Al. That's the kind of deputies I want in my office—men who've got the guts to fight, even when things look tough."

During the months that followed, Lundin had reason to believe that Vanderveer had been sincere in his original statement about choosing his deputies on the basis of merit alone. He had his own peculiar yardstick for measuring merit, but it never appeared to be particularly influenced by political considerations. From his staff, Vanderveer demanded unwavering integrity, absolute honesty, and an unflinching devotion to duty. He respected his men for their personal courage, and he disregarded their occasional shortcomings in the knowledge of the law.

In one of his earliest prosecutions, Al Lundin moved for the dismissal of a defendant because of the lack of sufficient evidence and his motion was granted. He was called into Vanderveer's office later in the day and asked to submit his reasons for the motion.

Vanderveer listened, and nodded his head with satisfaction. "That's all right, if that's the way you see it." There was no reprimand spoken or implied, although Lundin discovered that his motion had been based upon a grievous error of judgment and an ignorance of the law.

"We all make mistakes every day," Vanderveer assured him. "As long as you're honest and sincere in your mistakes, I'll back you to the hilt."

The *Seattle Times* and the *Seattle Star* took turns at lambasting the Prosecutor's office from the day Vanderveer took over, and he appeared impervious to their assaults. He ran his office like a quarterback running a football team, and on several occasions he covered up the errors and failings of his deputies by bluntly informing the press that these men were working on direct orders from him. He relished the "team spirit" which he had missed in college. He enjoyed his role as the signal-barking quarterback who called all of the plays, and who constantly slapped his men on the back and urged them to get in there and fight. To him, this was no mere job wherein he exchanged legal services for a monthly paycheck; it was a running battle every inch of the way, with his salary an incidental perquisite to his love for playing the game.

Even though the *Times* and the *Star* did not appear to be impressed, those who worked close with George Vanderveer in the Prosecutor's office became unalterably convinced that he had one unwavering goal—to build his record as the best Prosecuting Attorney in King County's history and to destroy completely the tentacles of crime that had entwined themselves in the political and civic life of the community. He was a man embarked upon a crusade, and he planned his prosecutions without fear or favor. He disdained all mention of political expediency. He prosecuted men for the violation of laws which he personally opposed. He refused to listen to the pleas of party leaders who had helped to put him into office, when they came seeking special consideration for personal friends. He alienated influential men who promised to guarantee his reëlection in exchange for special handling on certain cases. He flatly informed a member of the Republican Central Committee that he owed no party obligation in the conduct of his office, and that his one and only consideration would be to live up to his oath of office in letter and in spirit.

The office of Prosecuting Attorney had been designed to handle the legal end of the county's business, and particularly to prosecute those accused of crimes who had been arrested by the Sheriff or his deputies, or other duly designated officers of the law. It had never been the duty of the Prosecutor's office to attempt to enforce the law, or to make arrests. It had neither the responsibility nor the manpower to enter the enforcement field although, theoretically, the Prosecuting Attorney or his deputies retained the citizen's right to make an arrest or to swear out a warrant.

During his early months in office, Vanderveer seethed occasionally at the limits placed upon his office, and he discussed these things with his deputies. "It's a damn shame," he told Al Lundin one afternoon. "There are things going on in this town that shouldn't be going on. You know it and I know it —but what can we do about it? Until an arrest is made, we can just sit here and twiddle our thumbs! And if they're paying protection money to keep from being arrested, we could twiddle our thumbs to eternity!"

In 1909, a few months after his election, George Vanderveer created an innovation by adding two investigators to his staff, and sending them out to get evidence of law violation. This was a step beyond the usual practice of the Prosecuting Attorney's office, and the *Times* and the *Star* promptly shifted their campaign of criticism into high gear. They protested that Vanderveer was stepping beyond the bounds of his rightful authority; that he was attempting to set himself up as a czar, reproducing the dreaded inquisition of "darkest Russia"; that he was building his own private police force in order to find new outlets for his ruthless brutality. Both newspapers, at the time, were sending their reporters into the field in an identical search for law violation in order to fortify their occasional exposé articles which were intended to reflect discredit upon those charged with maintaining law and order; but apparently the irony of the protests was lost upon publishers and readers alike.

Vanderveer's two investigators, Peyton and Church, drifted quietly through Skid Road. They visited houses of prostitution, and they placed their bets on illegal gambling wheels. They shuffled up to doors where drinks were being sold after closing hours. When the Alaska-Yukon-Pacific Exposition opened, they circulated through the crowds and they talked to the hucksters and the exhibitors and the roustabouts.

They brought back to the Prosecuting Attorney many reports of law violation, and in each case Vanderveer was able to take his information to the Sheriff or the Chief of Police and demand immediate arrests, under the threat of taking matters into his own hands if action was not forthcoming. Skid Road, for one of the few times in its erratic history, be-

COUNSEL FOR THE DAMNED 113

gan to acquire an air of dismal dignity. Houses of prostitution closed their doors after successive raids and prosecutions.
Streetwalkers shunned the area and moved on to less hazard-
ous markets. Saloonkeepers were forced to observe the nearly
forgotten ordinance establishing closing hours, and they lived
in fear of the nearly fatal error of selling alcohol to minors
and accepting marked money. Word spread up and down
the coast that Seattle was a closed town; and seamen generally looked forward to a stopover in Seattle's port with about
as much eagerness as to a duty-visit with a maiden aunt.
Peyton and Church were only two men, but they got around;
and they created as much apprehension as a scale-model
Gestapo. Never, however, did they uncover any evidence
of collusion or conspiracy at the scene of the Exposition,
where Wappenstein was serving as chief of the special police
force and apparently doing a creditable job.

The charges of the *Times* and the *Star* that Vanderveer
was taking a great deal of authority into his own hands were
not entirely without foundation; and beyond question, his
methods were unorthodox. He rebelled against circumscribed
procedure, and he demonstrated no tolerance for tradition.
He was engaged in a free-for-all battle against crime and law-
lessness, and he was not inclined to disregard the occasional
short-cuts toward his goal. Shortly after taking office, he had
moved his staff from the Colman Building to new offices in
the recently completed Alaska Building; and here, behind
closed doors, he planned strategy of his crusade and gave
daily orders to his lieutenants. It was a rough and tough battle toward an unwavering goal, and the winning of that battle
was all important. There were no holds barred.

He listened, one afternoon, to the complaints of a man who
insisted that he wanted to swear out a warrant for Dr. David
Buckley, a Seattle physician. "We got into a little argument,"
the man complained. "One thing led to another, and all of a
sudden he started pounding hell out of me, for just no reason.

I'm not a well men, Mr. Vanderveer, and I want him arrested."

George Vanderveer listened, and then invited the man into
his private office. "I know this Dr. Buckley," he explained.
"Maybe he's inclined to be a little hot-headed, and maybe
you said a few things you shouldn't have said. I don't know
about that. But don't you realize you could ruin a doctor's
reputation by swearing out a warrant and charging him with
assault?"

"He should have thought of that before he hit me," the
man protested. "It was absolutely unprovoked, and I'm not
going to let him get away with it."

"You'd be willing to go into court and insist that he struck
the first blow, that it was absolutely unprovoked, and the
doctor, alone, was responsible? You'd be willing to see his
reputation ruined, his family disgraced, his practice destroyed
—all because in one fleeting fit of temper, during an argument,
he hit you with his fists?"

The man squirmed. "I don't want to be unreasonable, and
I don't want to hurt his family, or anything like that; but I
don't think he ought to have hit me." He stared glumly out
the window. "I just wish I was big enough and strong enough
to have beaten hell out of him, after he hit me. That would
of served him right."

Vanderveer flashed the man a smile. "In other words, you
think the doctor has a whipping coming to him, and you'd
like to see him get it. Is that right?"

The man nodded, and Vanderveer reached for his desk
telephone and called the doctor's office: "Doctor, I've got a
man here who wants to swear out a warrant for you, and I've
tried to tell him that something like that might ruin your
professional reputation. He says he'd be happy if somebody
just beat hell out of you. What do you think?"

That same afternoon, by arrangement, George Vanderveer
and Dr. David Buckley met in the doctor's office, with the
complaining patient as a witness. For nearly a half hour

George Vanderveer and Dr. Buckley engaged in a bruising battle during which medical cabinets were overturned and office furniture broken. It ended with the doctor on the floor, Vanderveer bleeding at the mouth, and the excited patient shouting his regrets that he hadn't just gone home and forgotten the whole thing.

"I hoped to Christ you're satisfied," Vanderveer puffed. "The doctor has had a rough beating, his office is all smashed to hell, but at least we haven't ruined his whole life. And by God, we're both going to hold you to your word to never breathe a word about this to anybody."

"I won't mention it to a soul," the man promised, and apparently he was true to his word. It was such a story as would have made headlines in the *Times* and in the *Star*, but the first report of it did not leak out until shortly before Dr. Buckley's death in 1923.

As Prosecuting Attorney, Vanderveer bore the responsibility of defending the county in civil actions and here, too, upon at least one occasion, he stepped beyond the circumscribed limits of usual legal procedure and risked a judicial reprimand.

The unusual case concerned a plaintiff with remarkable powers of self-control, or a master of the technique of self-hypnosis. She claimed complete paralysis of the lower limbs as the result of an accident, and there was ample proof that the accident had been caused by the negligence of a county employee who had walked off and left a road grader straddle of a dark country road without bothering to put out red lanterns or warning flares of any kind.

The county's physician had examined the woman who lay quiet and unperturbed as he prodded the flesh of her calves and thighs with the point of a pin. Not so much as the flicker of an eyelash indicated any awareness of pain, and yet the physician became convinced that she was not paralyzed. He explained to Vanderveer that he had noted indication of muscle spasm—the involuntary reaction of muscles to the prick of a pin.

The plaintiff's physician, however, differed sharply in his opinion during the course of the trial. He insisted that in his opinion, the woman's lower limbs had become completely paralyzed as a result of the accident, and his testimony did not waver on cross-examination. He had been qualified as an expert, and it was obvious to everyone in the courtroom that he had stated his honest conviction.

When the woman was wheeled into the courtroom on a stretcher, Vanderveer knew that the case was all but lost. She was frail, and wistful in appearance. Tears shimmered in her eyes as she answered the soft-spoken questions of her attorney, and it was apparent that any savage cross-examination from Vanderveer would prejudice the jury even more in her favor. Thus, when Vanderveer began his questioning, he also spoke softly and stood directly beside her.

There were a few routine questions . . . and witnesses could not agree exactly what happened next. A blanket tumbled to the floor, and there was an ear-splitting scream. The woman sat up and grabbed for the calf of her leg, tipping the stretcher as she did so; and there was a wild flailing of the "paralyzed" limbs as she struggled to avoid a fall to the floor. The judge, the jury, the courtroom spectators, the woman's attorney, the bailiff, all stared wide-eyed with astonishment, and then everything collapsed.

The woman was standing on the floor and her attorney was on his feet, literally quivering with indignation and pointing a wavering finger in the direction of Vanderveer. "That's assault! It's contempt of court! It's unethical conduct!"

Every eye in the courtroom was riveted upon George Vanderveer who stood in apparent confusion. The woman's attorney, Thomas J. Casey, hurried to her side and began firing questions at close range, and she gazed up helplessly.

"I don't know what he did. I think he stuck me with a pin. It felt more like a bee sting. . . ."

Casey was still on his feet, angrily demanding that the judge declare a mistrial and find Vanderveer in contempt. Interspersed with his demands were extemporaneous threats to have Vanderveer disbarred. Vanderveer continued to look bewildered.

Judge J. T. Ronald rapped for order and took a few moments to ponder the motion before offering any judicial decision. He stood momentarily upon untrodden ground, without legal precedent to guide him. Never to his knowledge had exactly the same situation appeared in a courtroom and he contemplated the various avenues open to him. Ultimately he denied the request that he declare a mistrial, and he refused to find Vanderveer in contempt of court. A slight smile played at the corners of his mouth as he glanced about the courtroom. "Gentlemen—it seems to me that the only thing we can do, in view of the evidence and what has happened here, is to conclude that we have witnessed a miracle." He did, however, accept Attorney Casey's motion for a voluntary non-suit . . . a legal disclaimer of let's-just-pretend-it-never-happened.

Seldom, however, did Vanderveer tread so close to the threshold of judicial reprimand. He preferred to win his cases through the orderly processes of logical argument and irrefutable precedent, but he was willing to risk a great deal when risk seemed necessary to the winning of a case. It was the winning that was important.

George and Ellinor Vanderveer, in private life, were finding their place in Seattle society. Mostly at Ellinor's instigation, they joined the exclusive Firlock Club (which later became the Seattle Tennis Club) and each summer they rented a house at Eagle Harbor and entertained almost endlessly. There were beach fires and sailing parties, clam-digging excursions, and forays out into the waist-deep water over the tideflats seeking crabs; and for those who didn't care for the more active pastimes, there were the eternal card games in the house which invariably lasted into the small hours of the morning.

Guests arrived and departed at the summer home without formality of any kind, and there were seldom specific invitations. The door was open, and the cupboards well stocked with food. Those who wished to remain overnight were granted access to the available beds, usually on the basis of first-come-first-served. There were Vanderveer's old friends —most of them attorneys—and newer acquaintances from his professional life. There were political leaders and precinct committeemen, former residents of the Hawthorne Hotel; neighbors from Seattle and neighbors from the island. There were brother Elks, fellow members of the Firlock Club, and lifetime friends of the Hausmans.

They came in almost endless numbers, and they shared in the informal hospitality. Ellinor had acquired much of her mother's skill at making guests feel welcome; and while George was far from being the hail-fellow-well-met, he nevertheless enjoyed the informal comradeship and his engaging smile became more frequent and more familiar. He was an avid card player; and once started in a game he would remain until the last guest had departed over his strenuous protests. The usual game was bridge, played for modest stakes; and in this, as in all things, he played to win. He was impatient with those who failed to take the game seriously, and he was intolerant of any by-play which tended to slow up the game. He played an excellent though often-unorthodox game, and he played it as if his entire life depended upon winning.

At the beach parties he was in complete command of the situation. He was the one depended upon to make the fire burn; to judge the height of the incoming tide, to predict the course of a shifting wind.

He excelled in nearly all of the informal sports: rowing, swimming, sailing, pitching horseshoes. But occasionally he would meet his master, and he did not accept defeat with any particular grace. Generally he would practise the sport at which he had been defeated with a grim, unwavering determination; and then demand a rematch.

On one occasion, when they were week-end guests at the Albert J. Tennant home, he challenged Ellinor to join him in an attempt to swim the mile from Mercer Island to the mainland. About halfway across he became exhausted, and had to be pulled into the rowboat which accompanied them, but she continued on and reached the mainland. There were cheers and toasts to Ellinor when the group returned to the house, and much good-natured back-slapping. But as soon as they were alone in their room that night George upbraided her unmercifully for deliberately making her own husband look ridiculous; and for nearly a week he treated her with cool reserve.

There were other times, of course, when the two of them spent evenings and week-ends together without company at their home in the city. They spent much time on the boat, and George had been selected as Commodore of the Seattle Yacht Club. They went for long hikes into the hills; and they continued their target practice until Ellinor, with her .22 pistol which he had given her before their marriage, could almost match him for marksmanship.

"You've got to learn to shoot from the hip," he told her one day. "If somebody came to the door gunning for you, you wouldn't have time to take aim the way you've been doing."

She laughed at him. "I'm your wife, remember? Aren't you getting me confused with Jesse James?"

"I am remembering that you're my wife, and that I'm Prosecuting Attorney," he told her earnestly. "It's a dangerous business, Gus. When you crack down on these thugs the way I'm cracking down on them, there's liable to be somebody to try to strike back—and they might just go gunning for you, to get even with me."

She continued to laugh. "Do you know what you remind

me of, George? You remind me of a little boy playing cops-and-robbers."

His earnest face broke into a slow, wistful smile; but he pinned a paper target to a stump and proceeded to give her instructions on shooting from the hip. And he demonstrated remarkable speed and accuracy in drawing his own revolver from a shoulder holster and firing in one swift motion.

"You can laugh about it if you want to," he told her, "but we're both going to spend a lot of time practising until we can draw faster and shoot straighter than anybody else in the Northwest."

Never a week went past without its practice sessions, and that Christmas Ellinor received from him a heavy wool sweater which exactly matched one he had bought for himself. "We'll wear these when we go out shooting on cold days," he explained. "We mustn't let ourselves get out of practice."

Looking back years later, Ellinor would recall that her heavy wool sweater was the only Christmas present she ever received from him, and there was never a birthday present. George Vanderveer was not a sentimental man.

The changing problems of a changing world had been reflected in the criminal code of the State of Washington. Each new weapon and each new tool, as it appeared, brought with it the possibility of new crimes or new refinements upon the old. State legislators had engaged in a frantic race to add new appendages to the original code as each new problem evolved, until the tail was larger than the dog. George Vanderveer was appointed to head a commission to draft a new criminal code. It was an assignment of staggering proportions, and he gave to it every last ounce of his ability and his undivided enthusiasm so that the code, when it finally emerged, was largely his own personal contribution.

The routine work of his office he left largely to his deputies, and the social life of the Vanderveers became temporarily non-existent. Seven days a week, and far into the night, he toiled over the project; and only by obvious effort could he clear the deep thoughts from his mind and answer the simple questions of his wife or of his associates. The criminal code which evolved from his efforts was to become a model thoughtfully studied by many states, and destined to endure, with certain modifications, up to the present time.

At the conclusion of the final draft he announced that he was leaving for another trip to Alaska, and he invited his father to accompany him and the crew. However, after his arrival in Seattle, David Vanderveer took one short cruise aboard the *Imp* and announced that a sailor's life was not for him. "I don't care how far out to sea I go," he told his son, grinning, "just so long as I can keep one foot on dry land." David Vanderveer remained in Seattle and visited with his daughter-in-law while George and his crew spent several weeks cruising up the Inland Passage. The old man also spent several days visiting with Bill Campbell who came up from Grays Harbor, and once again they cruised the sound on various passenger ships of the mosquito fleet.

"I don't mind riding on boats like these that stay right side up," David confided to Bill Campbell, "but you take that boat of George's—it's altogether too skittish."

The anti-Vanderveer campaign in the *Times* and in the *Star* was building in intensity, and it was beginning to produce its reaction throughout the county. Snide comments of the press began to seep into public conversations: "A guy has got it pretty soft when he can go off cruising around Alaska on the taxpayers' money—and draw his salary all the time he's gone."

Shortly after Vanderveer's return, and after his father had once again departed, party leaders began dropping into the Prosecutor's office to offer their subtle suggestions: "You're doing a swell job, Van, and we're all proud of you—but there is such a thing as being politically smart. If I were you, I'd think it over pretty carefully before taking any more long trips like that. The voters just don't understand."

Vanderveer displayed little sympathy. "Listen," he snorted, "during all of the months when I was working seven days a week and sixteen or seventeen hours a day, there wasn't a damn soul ever raised his voice to suggest, 'Van, you're working too hard; you ought to take a few days off.' And now, by God, you guys are practically wearing out the carpet, parading in here telling me I shouldn't have gone to Alaska!"

He rebelled at every suggestion of political expediency, and to his wife he explained that there was something cheap and shoddy and basically dishonest to the process of playing politics. "When I take time off from my job I do it with a clear conscience, and I don't give a damn who knows it! I'm not going to sneak around like a kid playing hookey!"

David Vanderveer had returned to Nebraska to stay with one of his daughters. At the time when George was just getting back into the swing of his duties at the Prosecutor's office, he received word that the old man was failing rapidly.

Two days later a telegram arrived at the apartment announcing that David Vanderveer had passed away. Ellinor telephoned the information to George at his office, and began packing for the trip back to Nebraska.

"What's all this stuff?" George Vandermeer demanded when he returned home that evening, pointing to the suitcases already packed and standing on the floor in the living room. "What's the idea?"

"We can catch a train out tonight," Ellinor explained. "I've got everything packed and . . ." She paused and stared incredulously at her husband. "What's the matter, George? Didn't you want me to go with you?"

He shook his head. "There's no reason to go back now. He's dead."

"But the funeral!" she protested. "You'll have to go to the funeral. George! You're not afraid you'll be criticized for taking a few more days off? People would expect that, when your father dies. Nobody could criticize you for that."

He sank wearily into a chair. "You can put the suitcases

away, Gus. We had our visit with Dad while he was still alive, and I'm glad of that; and I don't see any damn sense in going clear back to Nebraska just to look at him, now that he's dead."

"But don't you want to pay your respects? At the funeral?"

He sat rubbing his powerful hands together and staring at the floor. "I paid my respects when they counted—while he was still living and could appreciate it. I wish to God I'd done it a lot more often, but now it doesn't mean a damn thing."

Without further word she took the suitcases back into the bedroom and began unpacking them. The next morning at the breakfast table he attempted to explain a little of how he felt:

"You said last night that people wouldn't criticize me if I took time off to go to the funeral, and you're absolutely right. That's the irony of it! They'll criticize you for taking time to visit with your family or your friends while they're living, but they won't criticize you for taking time off to stand beside 'em when they're dead. They'll persecute you if you worship Life and try to make something of it—but they expect you to bow down and pay homage to Death! Well, to hell with 'em! I'll live my life and I'll do my job, and I don't give a damn whether they criticize me or not!"

He returned to his office without taking any time off to attend his father's funeral, and he devoted himself to the duties of his office with an unflinching zeal. His crusade against crime became almost a passion, until party leaders began dropping hints that he should not take his job quite so seriously; and a number of his old friends offered their well-meant advice.

They assured him that the public looked with suspicion upon all great changes and reacted against anything hinting of fanaticism; that he was losing the respect and the confidence of the people by becoming overzealous in his crusade.

He refused to listen to them. He insisted that he had ninety percent of the people of the county squarely behind him— Republicans, Democrats, and Populists alike. He offered to bet his bottom dollar that all of the clean and decent and law-abiding citizens were solidly on his side, and that all of the stench was being raised by the other ten percent who had a direct financial interest in preserving crime.

Despite mounting evidence to the contrary, George Vanderveer clung doggedly to that conviction. The newspaper attacks upon him continued unabated, and they began to give evidence of shaping public opinion. The *Times* was eloquent in its tributes to Wappenstein, and there was no denying that he had done an excellent job as chief of the special police at the Exposition. The public was not allowed to forget that Vanderveer had opposed the appointment, and there arose the inevitable conviction that Wappenstein was a fine, upright, and highly ethical citizen who had been persecuted by Vanderveer for purely personal reasons. Obviously, old Colonel Blethen had been right about that; and maybe he'd been right about a lot of other things in his charges against Vanderveer. Public opinion had started its backswing.

Eventually, under the growing pressure, George Vanderveer irately demanded a grand jury investigation of the conduct of his office.

"I want 'em to dig into every nook and cranny," he told his wife. "I want 'em to investigate everything from all angles, and put my record squarely on the line. I want the public to know that I've done what I started out to do, and that's to clean up a lot of imbedded crime. There's been no favoritism, no partiality, and there've been no pulled punches."

"But what if they should find some little thing that isn't good?" she asked. "Maybe it's something you don't even know about—something one of your deputies has done."

He glared at her. "I know what goes on in my own office, and I know my deputies! I'd trust any one of them with my life. Damn it all, Gus, we've done the best job that's ever been done in that office, and I think people ought to know the truth."

Methodically he began preparing for the investigation, confident that he could depend upon the support of civic leaders, judges, attorneys, businessmen, ministers, social workers, and all who were familiar in any way with the progress that had been made in cleaning up crime in King County. Day after day he met with excuses, apologies, and disclaimers:

"I'll tell you, Van, that's a kind of a political thing, and I don't want to get mixed up in it."

"You understand how it is, Mr. Vanderveer: a man in business can't take chances on offending some of his customers. It just wouldn't be very smart."

"You see, sir, I have a very large congregation made up of people from all the various political parties, and I don't feel that it is my place to take sides in a matter of this nature."

Even before the grand jury convened, George Vanderveer returned to his home one evening, tossed his coat and hat upon a chair, and told his wife that he was a beaten man. "I'm through, Gus. All through. People aren't interested in wiping out crime, or in clean government, or in anything else. All they want to do is sit back and not get mixed up in it, so to hell with it!"

He left after dinner without telling his wife where he was going, and for the first time in his married life he returned home early in the morning smelling of alcohol and staggering slightly as he walked across the room. He flung himself into bed without completely undressing and soon was breathing heavily.

For two days he did not go near the office, and he forbade Ellinor to answer the telephone. He paced endlessly across the bedroom, and he sat for hours on the edge of the bed playing solitaire.

"It's the futility of it that gets me," he almost sobbed. "There's nothing you can do—nothing you can hit at—nothing to fight against. Just a big empty void. Nothing but indifference from people who don't really give a damn!"

However, when Colonel Blethen attempted to ride the crest of a triumphant wave by informing Vanderveer that he would run him out of town, the disillusioned young Prosecuting Attorney struck back with all of the bitterness that was in him.

"You frizzle-headed old bastard," he screamed, "I'll still be here when you're dead and gone—and I'll go out and puke on your grave!" That violent and extemporaneous threat, delivered in a moment of passion, was to become a local classic and one of the most widely quoted statements of his career.

CHAPTER EIGHT

Ne'er look for birds of this year in the nest of the last.—Miguel
de Cervantes

E ARLY IN 1910 George Vanderveer announced he would
not be a candidate for reëlection, and he listened without apparent interest to a committee of Republicans who
urged him to start preparing himself to become a candidate
for Governor. "To hell with it!" he snorted. "The greatest
mistake of my life was getting into politics in the first place."
He extended his personal good wishes to John Murphy, who
had served under him and under Mackintosh, and he recommended him as the logical Republican candidate; but he disdained any active part in the political campaign.

Seattle voters, in the spring of 1910, placed their approval
upon John Murphy as the Republican candidate for Prosecuting Attorney. And upon a separate city ballot they expressed their rebellion against a closed town and an era of vigilant law enforcement. Skid Road had become quiet and docile.
The box houses had torn out their partitions and they operated
now as nearly legitimate theatres with not-too-lurid entertainment. The cherished tradition of the free lunch had disappeared from the saloons. The district below Yesler Way had
lost much of its glamour and excitement, and its dismal streets
were lined with pawnshops and grease-encrusted restaurants,
health-food stores, and offices of advertising dentists, tatoo

artists, and a questionable assortment of medical practitioners. Operators of legitimate businesses and industries uptown had begun moving back into Skid Road to sign up long-term leases on the aging buildings which they used as warehouses; and new coats of black paint appeared on the inside of the tall arched windows which once had looked out upon more dramatic scenes. Foot traffic in the district had dwindled; and the old-time habitués of the district who still remained, rubbed shoulders with stock clerks, warehouse employees, switchboard operators, and many other respectably employed persons who would have been out of place in the district a couple of years earlier. The few soapbox orators who persisted, generally wasted their words on empty air. Skid Road had changed. The colorful and wicked black sheep of the civic family had turned out to be a weary and poverty-stricken relative displaying its shabbiness to all visitors who arrived by ship or by rail, for it had sprawled out to encompass the area between the depots and the docks.

Seattle was in a mood for a change, and it did not indulge in halfway measures. It elected Hiram C. Gill as Mayor, on his outspoken pledge to pull the lid off Skid Road and to maintain it as a restricted district; to recognize the facts of life, and to tolerate that which could not successfully be destroyed. Gill rode into office on a wave of flattering publicity in the columns of the *Times*, and it came as no particular surprise to anyone when he appointed Colonel Blethen's old friend, "Wappy" Wappenstein, as his Chief of Police.

The changes along Skid Road were almost instantaneous. Bigger and better and more elaborate houses of prostitution opened their doors on almost the same day when Hi Gill took office, and later investigations revealed that Wappenstein was in on the renaissance from the start. He helped operators of the houses gain financial backing by giving his personal assurance that these would be profitable ventures, and according to sworn testimony at the subsequent investigation, he personally collected ten dollars a month from the income of every girl in the district. Gambling houses flourished openly; and while Seattle had grudgingly relinquished its title as the fastest-growing city in the United States, it now began to claim a new distinction as the most wide-open city on the North American continent.

Skid Road still had its paupers and its bindlestiffs and its cheap flophouses, but now it also had money. There was new power in the old magnet, and once again it began drawing loggers in from the hills and sailors in from the sea; and it extracted dollars from their pockets. Its dreary streets were throbbing with new life, and the soapbox orators returned like swallows in the spring. The hard, bleak winter of rigid law enforcement had ended and the green buds of dollar-prosperity were appearing everywhere.

National magazines sent their writers to cover the lurid story, and the *Post-Intelligencer* unleashed a barrage of front page criticism against Hi Gill and Wappenstein to rival anything the *Times* and the *Star* had leveled against Vanderveer during his term of office. Alarmed citizens appeared on the streets with petitions to recall Hi Gill. Belatedly, the good people of Seattle began to realize that George Vanderveer had been correct in his appraisal of Wappenstein; but Vanderveer scoffed at the editorials and refused to sign the petitions.

The orgy reached its climax, no doubt, when the City Council voted to vacate a street on the side of Beacon Hill and to grant a fifteen-year lease to a company which was ambitiously and more-or-less openly planning to build the world's largest and most modern brothel. It was all part of Mayor Gill's program for an open city, and his cultural ambitions to remove prostitution from the sordid surroundings of Skid Road. And thus the city that once had refused to vacate public streets for a downtown railway depot, now established the unique precedent of vacating a city street to accommodate the erection of a house of prostitution.

Dr. Mark A. Matthews, whose Sunday sermon had given

Skid Road its name, now headed the fight to recall Mayor Gill. Not only did he lash out with telling effect in his sermons, but he borrowed money against his own life insurance policies in order to hire a Burns detective to gather evidence against Gill and Wappenstein. He also spent his off hours prowling through Skid Road and gathering first-hand reports on vice conditions. The city was split wide apart.

Enough signatures were collected on petitions to force a special recall election, and the people of Seattle went to the polls and turned Hi Gill out of office before he had completed the first year of his term. Construction stopped immediately on the partially completed structure on the side of Beacon Hill, and for six years it stood unattended until a new group of investors took it over during World War I and converted it into a quiet and sedate apartment house for war workers; and it had to wait forty years before again making the headlines by being partially demolished with the loss of several lives when it was struck by an Air Force B-50 bomber from near-by Boeing Field.

Wappenstein was indicted, tried, convicted and sentenced to the state penitentiary (State vs. Wappenstein 67 Wash. 505.) Largely because of his long-standing friendship with Wappenstein and his more recent support of Hi Gill, the activities of Colonel Blethen came in for close scrutiny by the same grand jury which indicted Wappenstein, and the aging Colonel also was indicted. However, the charges against Blethen were dismissed by Judge James T. Ronald following a motion for non-suit by the defendant in the trial of the action. Judge Ronald adjudged the state charges to be flimsy and highly technical in nature. Even the severest critics of the Colonel had to admit, in view of the evidence, that his greatest failings were an unwavering and sometimes unreasonable loyalty to his friends, and an equally unwavering and unrelenting animosity toward his enemies . . . plus an intuitive genius for raising hell and selling newspapers.

George Vanderveer, meanwhile, had joined with his old

friend, Bud Cummings, to establish the firm of Vanderveer and Cummings, with offices in the Hoge Building. Their practice was largely confined to criminal law, and the demand for their services was abundant and almost instantaneous. Men who had faced the grueling cross-examination of George Vanderveer were eager to have him represent them in court, and attorneys who had faced him as opposing counsel displayed a sudden ambition to bring him in as associate counsel in handling their more difficult cases. There were, however, two definite drawbacks: clients accused of crime were not always able to pay well for the legal services they required; and Vanderveer, from the start, demonstrated a complete lack of business efficiency.

He would accept cases that appealed to him without regard to the financial responsibility of his client. He would devote days to the planning of a defense, and often spend money out of his own pocket to subpoena witnesses or to gather information, when he knew from the outset that he could never collect for his services or even recover the money spent. In the opinion of his wife, he was still playing a game of cops-and-robbers, but on the other side of the fence. He gloried in his courtroom triumphs; but too often he came home broke.

Even when a client was able and willing to pay, he demonstrated an amazing lack of efficiency in collecting his fees. His interest in a case ended when the verdict was rendered, and almost invariably he would brush aside Cummings' frequent demands for a final accounting in order to close the books on any particular case. "Aw hell, Bud, we'll get around to that later." The offices of Vanderveer and Cummings were constantly besieged by witnesses demanding their fees, and the frustrated secretary in the front office offered apologies almost as a reflex action: "Mr. Vanderveer has been very busy, but I'm sure he'll attend to it the first thing in the morning."

The lack of a regular monthly income brought new problems to his private life and continuing crises within his home.

He appeared hurt and bewildered and confused when Ellinor called his attention to an accumulation of bills past due, or passed along information about the latest threat of eviction. He met many an immediate crisis by borrowing from his friends, but all of these things he apparently considered as petty and passing annoyances of no particular consequence. His life and his glory were in the courtroom, and nearly everything else was incidental.

Upon the death of their very good friend, Albert J. Tennant, George and Ellinor moved from the Eulalie Apartments to a small house on Mercer Island so that Ellinor could be near Sena Tennant, who was her closest personal friend and who took her loss exceptionally hard. But from Ellinor's standpoint there was another reason of secondary importance: the small house on the island belonged to another good friend, Herman Frye, who dismissed any mercenary talk about monthly rental payments. "Good lord, Gus," he protested, "I'm tickled to death to have you stay there so you can be near Sena, and letting you use my house is about the least I could do." To Ellinor, it was a refreshing variation from her recent skirmishes in dodging a landlord.

Quite often George Vanderveer's fees were in the form of barter when a client lacked cash but insisted upon expressing his gratitude with some kind of payment. At one time when Ellinor's credit at the larger department stores had been suspended because of unpaid bills, he casually mentioned that he had received a motorboat in lieu of a cash fee and had given it to her younger brother, Billy.

"You *gave* it to him?" she gasped. "Wasn't it any good? Couldn't you have sold it?"

He reached over and patted her hand tenderly. "Do you think I would have given it to Billy if it weren't any good? It's a wonderful little boat and he'll have a lot of fun with it." He looked directly into her eyes and smiled happily. "It's a great thing for a boy to have a boat of his own, and learn to take care of it."

COUNSEL FOR THE DAMNED

At another time when the family finances were not at quite such low ebb, and after George and Ellinor had again moved into the city, he told her that he had received an automobile as a fee, and that he had given it to his partner, Bud Cummings.

"You gave it to Bud?" she protested. "He already has a car, and you know it! Why didn't you bring it home? Why couldn't we have a car? Why couldn't you have given it to me, if you had to give it to somebody?"

He stared at her in obvious amazement. "Why, Gus," he protested, "you know we don't have a garage."

On yet another occasion he received a wristwatch from a client, and he gave his pocket watch to a young attorney who recently had joined the firm. Ellinor was quite perturbed when he told her about it.

"I gave you that watch for your last birthday," she sobbed. "I saved nickels and dimes and quarters from the grocery budget so I could pay for it! For a whole year I always walked downtown and back to save the nickels I would have spent for carfare . . . and then you just gave it away!"

George Vanderveer looked embarrassed. "It was a good watch, Gus. I liked it a lot, but—well—I thought a wristwatch would be handier." He extended his left arm to display the watch on his wrist. "You don't have to be taking it out of your pocket all the time."

"Still, you didn't have to give away the one I gave you."

He looked bewildered. "But what on earth would I do with two watches?"

Their daughter, Barbara Francis Vanderveer, was born on July 26, 1912. And almost from the day she was born, George Vanderveer demonstrated that he could be an indulgent but completely unsentimental parent. Under Ellinor's tutelage, the child learned to swim before she was one year old, and was doing nearly perfect high dives by the time she was five. Her father made no attempt to disguise his pride when newspaper reporters and magazine feature writers came to view the

amazing accomplishments of the child. He delighted in bois-
terous games, tossing his daughter into the air and catching
her while she squealed happily; but he gazed at his wife with
a complete lack of comprehension when she appeared reluctant to leave the child's care to others in order to pursue her
social activities.

George and Ellinor no longer rented a summer home at
Eagle Harbor, but they were neither forgotten nor neglected
by their long-time friends. Their financial reverses were more
spasmodic than acute, and Vanderveer was widely considered
to be one of the most successful attorneys of the Northwest.
Even among close personal friends, there were few who ever
suspected the reason for Ellinor's often stringent economies.
"It must be a little foible of hers," they conceded. "Good
lord, they must be rolling in money, what with all of the big
cases he handles."

Through one of his many involved deals wherein he collected his fee through barter, George Vanderveer came into
possession of two small but heavily mortgaged houses on
Highland Avenue in the Green Lake district. With Ellinor's
help in making curtains and planning the decorations, he had
one house completely painted and modernized; and they made
their plans to move into this house, while the other house beside it would be offered for sale. However, through a last-
minute change of plans because of unexpected sales resistance,
he sold the house that had been modernized and moved his
family into the other one. It was old and battered and in need
of paint. The roof leaked and the porch sagged. But with a
contemptuous disregard of these things, he demanded that
Ellinor entertain many of the prominent people of the city's
social, professional, and civic life.

Within the protection and isolation of his home, he demonstrated a side of his nature that was never revealed to his most
intimate friends. There was seldom a night when he did not
take a book to bed with him and read until the early hours
of the morning. He had no interest in fiction, but he avidly

read history, biography, and philosophy. To his wife he quoted long passages from Ingersoll, and occasionally he would awaken her in the night to read aloud stanzas of poetry which particularly appealed to him—but which seldom appealed to her, after such a gratuitous awakening. He was greatly influenced by the writings of Colonel Charles E. S. Wood, the leading attorney of Portland, whose poems were heralded for their "disgust of tyranny, challenge to injustice, and celebration of bastards." Vanderveer possessed an inner love of beauty and a restless longing for tranquility; a hidden passion which responded to significant poetry and left him almost breathless with admiration. These things he took pains to hide from his acquaintances. He seldom referred to the books he had read, and in his professional life he preferred to present himself as a common man with common tastes; almost to the point of protesting too much.

As a defense attorney, Vanderveer frequently found himself opposing the men who had been his deputies in the Prosecutor's office—men for whom he had the deepest respect and admiration. Frequently he would lunch with them at the Elks Club or invite them to his home, but inside the courtroom he recognized no bonds of friendship and he pulled no punches. His legal battles, like his earlier boxing bouts with Nat Carl in the Stanford gymnasium, were vicious and savage and thoroughly unrelenting. In subtle or sarcastic vein, he might question the intelligence and the integrity of John Murphy or Al Lundin, and broadly imply to the jury that the Prosecuting Attorney's office was enmeshed in a heinous plot to crucify his client.

Knowing him and understanding him, his former deputies accepted these things and generally refrained from carrying their resentment or animosity outside the courtroom, although Vanderveer constantly tested their ability to forgive and forget. His desire to win each individual case was a completely overwhelming force; and there can be little doubt that

he would have sacrificed the friendship of a lifetime to gain
the verdict in the most insignificant case of the moment.

To Ellinor Vanderveer there was something incongruous
about her husband's switch from the prosecution to the defense, and she asked him about it when he first opened his
offices in the Hoge Building: "Won't it seem odd to you,
George, to go into court defending men who are accused of
crimes, after all the years you've spent prosecuting them?"

He nodded his head. "It may seem a little odd at first, but
it's like a baseball player who gets traded in the middle of
the season. First thing he knows, he's playing against the
team he used to play for, but he just gets in and plays the best
he can and doesn't let it bother him. It's the game that's important, Gus—not which team you're on."

Vanderveer went into court defending men accused of
rape, larceny, murder, and nearly every other crime in the
statute books; and he defended them as zealously as he had
prosecuted other men charged with the same crimes, but he
recognized no incongruity. To him, each case was a crucial
battle in the cause of justice; and while he occasionally failed
to convince the jury that justice could best be served by finding in behalf of his client, it is doubtful if he ever failed to
convince himself. He was a victim of his own eloquence
and his own logic.

There were many clever lawyers in Seattle who were excellent actors, and who plotted their courtroom strategy like
a producer planning a stage show. There was James Hamil-
ton Lewis, later United States Senator from Illinois, who
strutted and gestured in frock coat and shoestring black tie,
and who was inclined to address more of his remarks to the
audience than to the court, and whose experienced eye could
judge at a glance just which spot in the courtroom was equiv-
alent to front-stage-center. There was John F. Dore—later to
become Mayor of Seattle and a perennial foe of Vanderveer's
—who was as dramatic and as outstanding in the courtroom as

were the Barrymores upon the stage, and who possessed many
of the same talents.

George Vanderveer was not an actor, he was a fighter.
The courtroom was his stadium, not his stage. His attention
seldom strayed from the jury box, the witness chair, and the
judge's bench; and if he was aware of the audience behind
him, he gave little evidence of it.

The familiar courtroom scowl was not permanent upon his
face. On occasion he would flash judge or jury the same
boyish smile which had captivated Ellinor Hausman; and that
infectious smile, coming in sharp contrast upon his previously
foreboding countenance, became his most powerful weapon
in gaining courtroom sympathy. He was shrewd enough not
to squander his asset recklessly.

He was not a man disposed to humorous comments, and his
sarcasm tended to be more biting than laugh-provoking. And
yet upon hundreds of occasions when it suited his needs, he
produced convulsive laughter throughout the courtroom. He
was a master of the change of pace.

Undoubtedly Vanderveer's greatest single asset in the courtroom, however—and his greatest liability in private life—was
his genius for rationalization. He was able to accept any case,
as a prosecutor or as a defense attorney, consider the facts
before him, and build his own convictions as he built his own
case. Beyond all doubt, his string of legal victories would
have been impossible if he had gone into the courtroom lacking the unshakable conviction that his cause was just and
right and fair, beyond all question—and that a tragic miscarriage of justice must be the inevitable result if judge or jury
found in favor of the opposition. The sincerity of his own
convictions was contagious. A close associate commented in
later years: "Van never had clients, in the usual sense. By the
time he represented you in court and got himself all worked
up with his own arguments, he'd honestly believe you were
the greatest person who ever lived. He wouldn't want to

charge you a fee; and likely as not, he'd want to set you up in business."

His genius for rationalization was well illustrated by his defense of Felix Crane in 1915. Crane, a Negro, was widely suspected of collecting protection money from a number of houses of prostitution and turning it over to the police; but since there was no conclusive evidence of what Crane did with the money after collecting it, he was charged with accepting the earnings of a prostitute. A marked five-dollar bill had been traced from a prostitute to the proprietor of the hotel where she practised her profession, and then to the hands of Felix Crane. It was an open-and-shut case and Al Lundin, handling the prosecution, entered the courtroom with evidence to spare. And yet Vanderveer accepted Crane's defense, fought a highly embittered battle throughout the trial; and when Crane was convicted, he carried the appeal to the State Supreme Court (State vs. Crane 88 Wash. 210). Crane, however, was sentenced to two years in the penitentiary.

Vanderveer was handicapped in his defense by Crane's unwillingness to admit in court that he had been collecting protection money, but Vanderveer was fighting for a principle. Under such an interpretation of the law, he argued, a grocer or a shoe clerk might be found guilty of accepting the earnings of a prostitute. Any man in the courtroom might innocently accept a five-dollar bill which at one time had passed through the hands of a prostitute and therefore represented her earnings. The jury, however, concluded that Crane's acceptance of the money had not been entirely innocent and that, under the particular circumstances, he undoubtedly must have known what it represented.

One of the highlights of the trial was the testimony offered by one of the prosecution witnesses, a prostitute. On the witness stand she admitted to Al Lundin that she had been making regular payments to the operator of the hotel at the rate of one dollar for every three men she accommodated, and that she understood that part of this money was being paid

to Crane for protection. On cross-examination by Vanderveer, she immediately denied everything she had just said, and
blandly contributed to the building of the defense.

Her conflicting testimony was confusing and bordered on
the ludicrous, and she found herself being reprimanded by the
court. When the trial was ended, Lundin laughed about it.
"What have you got on that poor girl, Van? She acted afraid
of you."

"Afraid hell!" Vanderveer snorted. "She was merely a
friendly witness." And he insisted in all seriousness that he
made friends where he needed friends.

Vanderveer appeared greatly upset following the conviction of Felix Crane, but he gained little sympathy from his
wife. Ellinor demanded to know why George had chosen to
represent the man in the first place. During his years in the
Prosecuting Attorney's office some time earlier, he had often
expressed a complete loathing for the whole system of police
pay-offs. He had faced the wrath of Colonel Blethen and the
attacks in the pages of the *Times* as a by-product of his animosity toward Wappenstein, and this animosity had been
based in large measure upon his complete disgust with Wappy's collection of pay-offs. To Ellinor, despite the intervening
years, it seemed preposterous for her husband now to attempt
to defend a man obviously guilty of the same crime.

Vanderveer shrugged at his wife's questions: "You just
don't understand, Gus. Wappenstein had a good job and a
fairly good education. He held a position of trust. He was a
white man, and he had a chance to live in a decent environment and to make an honest living. Felix Crane is a Negro.
All his life he's been kicked around from pillar to post—ordered out of restaurants and hotels because he's colored. And
damn it all, that wasn't the proper charge! Just because a
man may be guilty of one crime, that doesn't mean that he
should be convicted of an entirely different crime!"

Ellinor studied her husband thoughtfully. "But wouldn't
the punishment be just as great, or even greater? And you

knew he was guilty, didn't you, before you ever took the case?"

He shook his head. "It's a question of degree. Nobody is ever entirely guilty and nobody is ever entirely innocent. Should we take it on our shoulders to punish Felix Crane for doing something we practically forced him into doing by not giving him any other chance? And what about your business-men and your civic leaders and your ministers, and all the rest of that holier-than-thou gang? Where were they when I wanted 'em to stand behind me—when I wanted to clean up these places, so things like this wouldn't happen? They wanted to stay home and keep out of it! In their own way, they're just as responsible for the condition as Felix Crane is—so why try to pretend that he's entirely guilty and they're entirely innocent? It just doesn't work that way, Gus. It just doesn't work that way."

Vanderveer had developed a great respect and a deep sym-pathy for Felix Crane, collection agent for a vicious and sor-did protection racket. The feeling was not mutual, however. Ten years later Felix Crane was scooped up with ninety other men as Federal agents cracked Seattle's largest bootlegging ring, and he refused to throw in his lot with a dozen co-defendants seeking Vanderveer's services as defense attorney.

"No suh, not me! Ah had that man once, and you know what happened? Ah wound up in the pen, that's what!"

CHAPTER NINE

When the mind is freely exerted, its reasoning is sound; but passion, if it gain possession of it, becomes its tyrant, and reason is powerless.—JULIUS CAESAR

To AN ENTERPRISING young newspaper editor and publisher related to him by marriage, Colonel Blethen of the *Times* offered a concise bit of advice: "Run a newspaper and raise hell." And in those six words, no doubt, he epitomized his own philosophy of life, secret of business success, and key to personal happiness.

He was a man of strong convictions and unquestioned courage, apparently free from the stabbing doubts which might cause another man to ponder the wisdom of a selected course. He loved the smell of printer's ink and the smell of battle; and to him, perhaps, the two aromas were indistinguishable. He accepted his duty as a publisher to attack and expose everything that was wrong or ridiculous or impractical or unsound, and to champion everything that was right and proper and good. Apparently there was never a moment when he questioned his own infallible ability to choose between the two.

His love for his country, its flag and its traditions, stood above honest question. He insisted upon weaving a slightly distorted replica of Old Glory through the masthead of the *Times*, and the daily flag-raising ceremonies on the roof of the Times Building were carried on with military precision.

He worshipped the Army and the Navy and the Marine Corps, and, to a lesser extent, the Coast Guard.

In the field of politics the Colonel was independent and unpredictable, and subject to fluctuations which often seemed inexplicable to everyone but him. He had his own unshakable convictions, his own friends and his own enemies; and these prevailed over party politics.

In 1912 Seattle voters elected George Cotterill as Mayor; and Cotterill, no doubt, had been a long-time subscriber to the *Times*. He, like Colonel Blethen, had been a man of changing political moods, an avid admirer of William Jennings Bryan, and a critic of the local Republican officeholders, including George F. Vanderveer. From a political standpoint there was every logical reason why Cotterill should have received the blessings of the *Times*. But in winning his election as Mayor, Cotterill had defeated the once-recalled Hi Gill, close personal friend of Blethen and Wappenstein—and this, Blethen could not forgive.

The Colonel's opportunity to strike out at Mayor Cotterill was not long delayed. The soapbox orators were having a field day along Skid Road, and the Industrial Workers of the World—the Wobblies—were growing in numbers and in strength. Many of the same men had been making similar speeches from the same soapboxes two years earlier during Hi Gill's administration—in fact, it had been during Gill's administration that the soapbox brigade had returned to Skid Road in force because of the influx of loggers and seamen to the wide-open district—but Colonel Blethen's alarm at the situation came belatedly; and it came at a very convenient time for him, when he wanted a club to use against the newly installed Mayor Cotterill. So he began his journalistic jabbing at the Mayor for permitting such rabble-rousers to speak on the city streets.

Some months earlier Leonard Olsson, a Tacoma Wobbly and a naturalized alien, had been relieved of his certificate of naturalization in Federal court on the charge that it had been acquired through fraud: an I.W.W. member intent upon abolishing capitalism and the wage system must have been insincere in his promise to support and defend the Constitution of the United States. Q.E.D.

The case had rocketed through the headlines of the nation and set off repercussions in Washington, D.C. The Wobblies were indignant, and they were joined in their indignation by many Socialists, Progressives, Populists, and Freethinkers. The United States Attorney General had ordered the case reopened and, under orders from his superior, the United States District Attorney had moved to vacate and set aside the decree. When this motion was denied by the trial judge, C. H. Hanford, the indignation of the Wobblies rose to fever pitch. They demanded the impeachment of the judge, and charges were filed in the House of Representatives by a Socialist Congressman from Wisconsin. The Attorney General put himself squarely on record as believing that a gross injustice had been done to Mr. Olsson, and a sub-committee of the House Judiciary Committee was dispatched to Seattle to conduct hearings. Judge Hanford, an eminent and respected jurist of unquestioned integrity, termed it an attempt of the executive branch of the government to dictate to the judicial, and he clung to his contention that a fair trial had been held, and a fair verdict rendered. The case was closed, so far as he was concerned.

In the White House, President William Howard Taft was becoming a little frantic. Having served with distinction on the Federal bench, himself, he required no advice from his Attorney General as to the issues involved, but he listened a bit desperately to the advice of his political stewards. Already he had alienated the progressive element within the Republican party by his defense of the Payne-Aldrich tariff act, and soon he would be facing the hazards of an election year. The Olsson case, having blossomed overnight into a nation-wide controversy, offered his administration an opportunity to make a move to placate the progressive voters, but

that effort had been stalled by Judge Hanford's adamant refusal to permit reopening of the case.

Meanwhile, in Seattle, the Wobblies were holding indignation meetings and militant parades, and Colonel Blethen was
skillfully aiming his big guns at the heads of the irate Wobblies so that each blast ricocheted from Skid Road to City
Hall. He upbraided the Mayor for tolerating such demonstrations by avowed anarchists, and he subtly reminded the
Seattle voters that they had disregarded his good advice in
electing such a man to office. He demanded that the police
be used to disperse the meetings and the parades.

Mayor Cotterill lashed back with the reminder that free
speech and the right of the people peacefully to assemble
were guaranteed by the Constitution, and that no existing law
forbade such demonstrations in the city's streets. He charged
that Blethen's demands, if met, would constitute anarchy in
themselves. He pleaded for the people of the city to remain
calm, and not to provoke unnecessary incident.

Colonel Blethen, however, had one great advantage over his
opponent, and that was the circulation of the *Times*. He had
thousands of readers to ponder his arguments and his charges,
while the Mayor had only hundreds. The more conservative
P.I. had seldom missed an opportunity to oppose the *Times*,
and yet its editors were reluctant to be forced into a position
where they must defend the wild-eyed radicals down along
Skid Road—and defend a mayor who was openly and bluntly
anti-Republican. Mayor Cotterill's rebuttal had to be confined largely to the labor papers of smaller circulation. The
people of the city did not remain calm, and the original issue
concerning Olsson's loss of his naturalization papers did not
remain clear.

There were rumblings in the saloons along Skid Road:
"Yah! It's a hell of a thing when they can run a man out of
the country, just because he joins a union!"

There were rumblings at the fraternal and social clubs uptown: "I tell you, it's enough to make a man's blood boil

when those dirty anarchists can come to this country and then hide behind the safeguards of our Constitution while they're plotting to overthrow our government!"

The sub-committee of the House Judiciary Committee completed its hearings and departed without comment, and then just as the tension and the suspense were approaching a breaking point, Judge Hanford submitted his resignation. A feeling of optimism crept along Skid Road. In February of 1913, the decision against Olsson was reversed by the Circuit Court of Appeals, and the issue cooled off. It came too late, however, to benefit President Taft. In his bid for reëlection he had amassed a total of eight electoral votes.

The soapbox orators along Skid Road continued to shout their charges against capitalistic parasites, and Colonel Blethen continued to lambast Mayor Cotterill as a bosom pal of the anarchists; but the fever had passed its crisis.

In July, 1913, Seattle prepared for its annual late-summer festival, designed to attract tourists and dollars from other Northwest cities and extensively advertised as the Potlatch Days Celebration. Potlatch—a term borrowed from local Indian jargon—meant "to give," but Seattle merchants were preparing also to receive. Units of the Pacific fleet were expected in port, and the burlesque theatres were busy putting up their glaring posters as Skid Road made ready to reap its harvest. Colonel Blethen had shifted his interest from Mayor Cotterill to the United States Navy, and the prospects of a big military parade at the start of the festival. Mayor Cotterill was busy with the official duties and social obligations of his office, for Seattle was preparing to play host to many distinguished visitors.

On July seventeenth, Secretary of the Navy Josephus Daniels reviewed the military parade as some two thousand soldiers and sailors marched through the downtown streets. Then, in the evening, he appeared at the banquet hall of the exclusive Rainier Club and delivered a stirring, patriotic address which was greeted with unusual enthusiasm by the as-

sembled guests. It was a rousing speech about eternal
vigilance, the value of preparedness, and the glory of freedom
under the American flag. Mr. Daniels spoke well, and he
spoke largely without notes. After all, he had delivered precisely the same speech on previous occasions, elsewhere about
the country.

Mayor Cotterill was among the many who heard and applauded Secretary Daniels' speech. And he readily admitted
that he was somewhat startled, later, when he read about the
speech in the columns of the *Seattle Times*. In a carefully
worded story, the *Times* described the speech without quot-
ing to any great extent; and to the casual reader the story
implied that the Navy Secretary had unmercifully flayed the
Mayor of Seattle for permitting anarchist demonstrations
within the city. From his position at the head table, the
Mayor insisted, he had heard nothing resembling the kind of
speech described in the *Times*.

What startled and alarmed him even more than the story
of the speech, he announced, was the dramatic account of
how a group of anarchists at a soapbox street-meeting in the
Skid Road district had brutally beaten soldiers and sailors
when the enlisted men objected to the insults being heaped
upon the American flag. The story of the beating was woven
in with the story of the speech, under a series of diminishing
column headings: I.W.W. DENOUNCED BY HEAD OF
NAVY, ATTACK SOLDIERS AND SAILORS. *While
Daniels Arouses Patriotism of Rainier Club Diners by Speech,
Anarchists Attack Wearers of Blue.* The article concluded
with a flurry of anonymous statements, credited to the usual
"reliable sources," intimating that red-blooded Americans
would soon answer the insults heaped upon the American
flag—that various patriotic groups would undertake to do
what the Mayor should have done long ago—and that enlisted
men would soon avenge the beating of their brothers-in-arms.

Mayor Cotterill launched an immediate and full-scale investigation of the incident. His police informed him that the

soapbox orator had been a woman pacifist, Mrs. Annie Miller, having no known connection with the I.W.W. The incident had started, apparently, just as hundreds of similar incidents had started in the past—with heckling from the sidewalk and with name-calling in both directions. It had erupted into physical combat after one of the enlisted men had seized the platform and delivered an extemporaneous address of his own to a thoroughly unappreciative audience. A scuffle for possession of the platform had developed quickly into a free-for-all. Police had arrived in time to rescue the embattled and outnumbered servicemen, and three of them had been given medical attention before being released.

Rear Admiral Reynolds, commander of the fleet in port, reported no complaints and no investigation. Apparently the enlisted men had accepted the fight as one of the frequent and inevitable by-products of shore leave. *The Fleet*, a small Navy publication issued by a servicemen's club in Bremerton, charged the soldiers and sailors had been constantly tormented when passing Pioneer Place by the I.W.W. hoodlums assembled there, who mocked them and taunted them. Skid Road, for some time, had been an unhealthy spot for servicemen to visit. The proprietors of the burlesque houses and the operators of stores and shops generally put up their glaring posters to welcome the fleet, and the streetwalkers joined in the welcome; but the great bulk of the inhabitants of the district, including anarchists and pacifists and bindlestiffs, were generally somewhat less than hospitable. Police officers assigned to the district had come to look upon the breaking-up of street brawls as routine incidents of their daily duty.

At City Hall on July eighteenth, the day after the highly publicized incident, Mayor Cotterill grimly announced that he would uncover the true facts of the case and place them squarely before the public. He intimated that the *Times* had distorted the facts and had attempted to make something sensational and dramatic out of a routine incident which, basically, had no great significance. However, while he was still brooding over his reports and planning his phraseology, thousands of the city's people were moving cautiously and curiously toward Skid Road. They had read in the *Times* that something might be happening and, if so, they wanted to see it. Rumors swept through the streets, and mob spirit began to take form. "What in hell are we waiting for?"

Starting about dusk, a loosely organized mob composed of enlisted men and civilians moved through the Skid Road district and wrecked the I.W.W. hall. They smashed chairs, broke windows, ripped the legs from tables and used them to pound plaster from the walls. They piled literature in the gutter and burned it; and then with enthusiasm mounting and their numbers growing, they moved on in search of further conquest. They demolished a newsstand in uptown Seattle where I.W.W. and Socialist papers were sold. They invaded a Socialist hall and wrecked it and, for some reason never fully explained, they ransacked a Gospel mission on Skid Road.

It was a wild, triumphant, shouting mob, encouraged by the applause of other thousands who had heard the news and who had come to watch—and who joined the procession gradually. The police stood by powerless to stop it without bloodshed, and unwilling to open fire. As a result, the whole thing went off without loss of life and without serious injury to anyone except one wildly swinging Wobbly who was quickly overpowered and left with a broken nose.

Mayor Cotterill went into a hurried huddle with his Chief of Police and then swung into action immediately. He publicly charged the *Times* with deliberately and wantonly inciting a riot, and of engineering the entire story. He proclaimed the existence of an emergency and he personally took charge of the city's police and fire departments and cancelled all leaves. He ordered saloons closed for the duration of the celebration, and he banned street meetings of any and every kind. He reminded the citizens that Saturday night and Sunday would see a heavy influx of I.W.W. loggers into Skid

Road, and that any further incident might set off bloodshed to convert a supposedly festive city into one vast, brawling battleground. And as a climax to it all, he sent a squad of police to the Times Building with orders to prohibit the distribution and sale of the *Seattle Times* within the city limits for the duration of the emergency, unless the editors submitted advance proofs of each edition to the Mayor's office in order that Cotterill might certify it as containing nothing "calculated to incite further riot, destruction of property and danger to human life."

The chips were down, and now it was Colonel Blethen's turn to act. He responded with equal vigor, and within a matter of hours he had a restraining order to prohibit Mayor Cotterill from interfering with the freedom of the press. As an added triumph, he secured a restraining order to prohibit Cotterill from closing the saloons. That evening the *Times* was on the street with its story about the smashing of the I.W.W. hall, and with a bitter attack upon Seattle's Mayor who had attempted to interfere with the inalienable freedom of the press.

But the saloons had been closed for several hours, and Seattle was sobering up from its night before. The *Times* had shifted the brunt of its attack from the Skid Road anarchists back to the person of Mayor Cotterill, and this was hardly the type of thing to capture the man on the street and inflame his imagination. Rear Admiral Reynolds sent squads of shore police into the city to keep a close check on Navy personnel, and Seattle settled down to the business of enjoying the last day of its festival.

On July twentieth, the exultant Colonel nearly outdid himself. The front page of the *Times* carried a replica of the American flag in full color, and a flag-waving editorial which accused Mayor Cotterill of making himself king. It announced that Cotterill would be sued for twenty-five thousand dollars' damages "because of his outrageous, illegal, and unprecedented usurpation of authority." For a full month, the Potlatch Days riot seldom strayed far from the headlines, with the *Times* exploding in anti-climatic indignation when Mayor Cotterill relayed to the City Council an itemized claim for damages on behalf of the Socialists whose hall had been raided during the foray. The Council promptly denied the claim.

Eventually, however, the Potlatch Days riot disappeared from the headlines—but its scars did not disappear. The story seeped out to the lumber mills and the logging camps, and each teller twisted the story to fit his mood. Colonel Blethen and Mayor Cotterill were soon sidetracked. It became the story of lumber barons trying to smash organized labor. It became the story of Organized Capital lashing out in mortal fear of the idea of One Big Union. It became the story of heroic martyrs at the I.W.W. hall facing the wrath of an armed mob. It became the story of the United States Government using its troops to attack the laboring class and to protect the profits of big business. Soon there were few in the woods who recalled that the riot had been the semi-spontaneous by-product of a local political feud. Among the Wobblies, particularly, there grew the conviction that Navy Secretary Daniels had been sent to Seattle for the specific purpose of arousing the people to action, and that the presence of so many military men within the city was part of the coordinated plot which had been worked out in intricate detail, far in advance:

"Things like that don't just happen; see what I mean? There wouldn't just happen to be that many soldiers and sailors in town, and they wouldn't just happen to all get leave at the right time . . . when there was just a handful of men to protect the hall."

In the city the scars remained also, and they didn't heal. They became festering sores of suspicion and fear and frustration. They incited the fear of revolution, and of the destruction of everything clean and decent and wholesome. The initials of the strike-promoting I.W.W. were given a new and taunting and almost-universal interpretation: "I Won't Work."

There were few who visualized any Wobbly as a fellow American working long and grueling hours, striving somehow to survive, risking his life in a frantic race against time, and dreaming desperately of a better day in a better world. And yet the ranks of the I.W.W. were swelled with the ex-grocery-clerks from Chicago, the ex-farm hands from Missouri, the ex-cotton pickers from the deep South—men from all parts of the nation and from all walks of life who had been drawn to the Pacific Northwest by the lure of Klondike gold, who had drifted off into the hills and into the lumber camps with an offer to work cheap—and who had grown weary of the bargain.

The tide of fear and hatred spread through the business, industrial, and political life of the community. It entered the churches, and it encompassed the school grounds where even the children recognized their bounden duty to take direct action against any boy whose father was reputed to be a Wobbly. There were fist-fights on the way to and from school, and taunting debates that echoed discussions overheard at home.

In a sense, it is impossible to view the early Wobblies after a lapse of forty years and behold them as they appeared to their contemporaries. The intervening years have altered the definition and the interpretation of basic terms, and the shadows of later events fall across the distorted picture. The Wobblies carried red cards and frequently waved the traditional red flag of revolutionists, but the red flag of their day was free from Soviet implication. The Russian revolution had not yet taken place, and the term *communism* was generally unfamiliar to the great masses of American people. More than half a century had elapsed since the communistic ideas of Charles Fourier had been expounded by Horace Greeley and the *New York Tribune*. With the exception of the Oneida Community, the Amana Community, and a few scattered re-

ligious communities including those of the Shakers, most of
the communist experiments in the United States had died a
natural death long before; and those remaining were not
widely publicized. The I.W.W. red flag was a replica of the
emblem hoisted on the Harvard campus in 1770 by the Sons
of Liberty; the red flag of Moscow had not yet been un-
furled. However, it becomes difficult in a later day, even
with conscious effort, to separate the red flag from its Soviet
implication. It becomes difficult to visualize the Wobbly of
forty years ago and not confuse him with the Communist of
today; and yet he was a different man, cut to a different pattern.

In a broad sense, there can be little doubt that the I.W.W.
movement in the United States and Bolsheviki revolution in
Russia were ignited by the same spark; but the flames of revolution that swept across Russia differed in many ways from
the smoldering rebellion that crept across the United States
—burning white hot in spots, and often failing to spread to
near-by areas. The Russian Bolshevik, born to servitude and
conditioned to civil obedience, promptly accepted his red
dictatorship as a necessary and supposedly temporary evil.
The typical American Wobbly, born to a tradition of personal
liberty and inspired by a dream of universal equality, scorned
even temporary dictatorship as totally evil and totally unnecessary. There were many Wobblies who later joined the
Communist ranks after watching their own dreams collapse,
but they were a minority in the I.W.W. membership. The
majority held fast, spurning all overtures from Moscow, de-
riding the Communists as "comics," and establishing a record
among the first anti-Communist organizations in the United
States.

Despite the fact that Wobblies were often described as "a
bunch of damn foreign anarchists," their rank and file—particularly in the Pacific Northwest—included a vast number of
second and third generation Americans. Of the six men who
had met in Chicago in the fall of 1904 to lay plans for organ-

izing the I.W.W., five were active in the then-existing American labor unions. The sixth, Isaac Cowen, represented the Amalgamated Society of Engineers of Great Britain. Bill Haywood, the "founding father" of the I.W.W., classified himself among a minority of real Americans and boasted of his Indian blood. However, the German and French and British immigrants who joined the organization generally were more outspoken and more articulate than the mass of American laborers, for they had brought with them far greater experience in fighting labor's battles; and they were more than eager to mount the soapboxes. Wobbly oratory was often decorated with foreign accents.

In their own way, the Wobblies were every bit as radical as the Communists proved to be. They were more intolerant of compromise for the sake of expediency, and their ideology was backed by an often-surprising bravado. Unlike the later Communists holding their secret meetings in dark cellars, the Wobblies preferred to hold their meetings on street corners and at ball parks—openly and defiantly. Their goal of abolishing the wage system was not so different from the avowed goal of Socialists, syndicalists, and Communists; but they had their own unwavering notion of how that goal should be achieved, and an eloquent contempt for those who differed with them as to methods. They scorned the Socialists' dream of patient progress through the use of the ballot, and they spoke of Direct Action which precluded any political efforts. They disdained the Communist approach of boring from within, with plotting and scheming, and the building of a well-disciplined world-wide organization, taking orders from an international steering committee. The Wobblies assured each other and assured the world that they would take orders from no one. As workers, they stood mutually convinced that they would some day inherit the earth, because in their hands rested the power of production.

Pertinent and significant may be the observations of a retired captain of the Seattle police force: "With the Wobblies we would rush right into the thick of the fight and grab the ones doing the swinging. But when it came to the Communists, we soon learned to pick off the boys leaning up against the buildings on the street corners. They were the ones who started it and egged the others on, and then got out of the way; the ones in the middle were nothing but suckers and stooges." The later Communist strategy in the Middle East and in Asia differed little from the Communist strategy on a Seattle street corner, but it was the antithesis of I.W.W. policy. The Wobblies were temperamentally unsuited to such subtle and cunning strategy. They gloried in the defiant and undisguised rebellion which kept them in the thick of the battle, swinging their own punches, until their position became untenable. Particularly in those early days, the I.W.W. walked erect, with the courage of its convictions.

1913 was a time of mounting tension in Europe, and increasing apprehension in the United States. Europe was just a few months away from the opening shots of the first World War, and America was in the midst of an era of isolationism. The American people looked to two broad oceans to protect them from any conflict, and they gazed with a certain amount of disfavor upon anything foreign. Thus, the charge that the Wobblies were "a bunch of damn foreign anarchists" was an important part of the anti-I.W.W. campaign. To many thousands of Americans, the charge that the Wobblies were *foreigners* was undoubtedly more disturbing than the charge that they were *anarchists*.

George Vanderveer, like the editors of the *P.I.*, found himself in an uncomfortable position when the *Times* launched its campaign against Mayor Cotterill on the issue of Skid Road anarchists and soapbox oratory. His animosity toward Colonel Blethen produced an immediate opposition to nearly everything the *Times* sponsored, almost as a reflex action; and yet he was reluctant to take his place on the side of the Skid Road Wobblies.

At the time of the Potlatch Days riot, particularly, he found his position confused. On numerous occasions he had indulged in sidewalk heckling of the soapbox orators, and he was a veteran of many battles as the result of it. This had been one of the tantalizing fascinations of Skid Road, back in the days when he and Bruce Shorts had made their periodic forays south of Yesler Way, and he must have felt a bond of kinship with the servicemen who had indulged the same temptation. At the same time, it must have been difficult for him to permit his sympathies to parallel those of Blethen's.

"It's Blethen's own damn fault," he told his wife. "He was the one who wanted Skid Road opened up, and this is the result of it." But when Ellinor asked him, uneasily, what it would all lead to, he merely shrugged.

"It'll all blow over and be forgotten. You'll find that people have a remarkably short memory, and things that seem important today don't mean a thing tomorrow."

In that, he was wrong, however . . . as the later years proved. The events he dismissed with a shrug of his shoulders were to mold the pattern of his life.

CHAPTER TEN

Let us therefore boldly face the life of strife, resolute to do our duty well and manfully . . .—THEODORE ROOSEVELT

THE APPREHENSION which had taken definite form during the Potlatch Days riot crept slowly and irresistibly across the Pacific Northwest until it had encompassed nearly every region bordering on Puget Sound; and it produced many ramifications and many strange alliances.

The craft unions within the American Federation of Labor, heavily dominated by city dwellers who owned their own homes and who read their newspapers with alarm, felt no bond of kinship with the "anarchists" along Skid Road. Union officials had carried on a long fight toward their goal of a fair day's wage for a fair day's work and they could see nothing promising or appealing in the Wobblies' dream of abolishing the wage system and eliminating capitalism. They shared in the apprehension.

The American Federation of Labor already had set up a working fund of thirty thousand dollars, and sent its organizers into the mills and into the lumbering camps in a belated effort to organize all the lumber workers into one tightly knit A.F. of L. body. There was no attempted deception and union officials stated their aims bluntly: it was an effort to organize the loggers and the millworkers and the shingle weavers into a responsible labor organization that would dedicate itself to reasonable goals in seeking better pay and shorter hours and better working conditions without striking at the very basis of the American way of life. It was an effort to head off irresponsible action which might bring disrepute to all labor organizations in the United States and thus destroy the things which the Federation had achieved through its many years of patient effort. But the attempt came too late.

The Wobblies had their hold, and they also had their arguments. By the militant action of their proverbial "fifty thousand loggers" they had achieved more in a short time than any other organization had ever achieved in a long time. They could (and they did) take credit for every inch of progress in reducing the work day in the lumbering industry from fourteen and fifteen hours to eight hours, with better pay. They could point to the Wobbly loggers who had burned their bedrolls in one great defiant bonfire, and announced that no more timber would be cut so long as accommodations provided for workers were generally inferior to those provided for horses and mules. They could (and they did) take credit for all of the progress that had been made in the fight to secure clean beds in decent bunkhouses for men who worked in lumber camps.

As a timely but unexpected weapon, they utilized the industrial depression of 1914 and 1915. The bottom dropped out of the lumber market and most of the independent operators who had survived up to that time sank slowly into bankruptcy. Mills closed and logging camps shut down. Hordes of desperate men besieged the Skid Road employment agencies; and as they became more desperate they became more radical. With empty pockets and empty stomachs they demonstrated little interest in a program dedicated to slow but steady progress in achieving a better wage scale. They drifted away from the A.F. of L. organizers and they flocked to the I.W.W. hall. Among those who still had jobs, the appeal of the A.F. of L. was stronger, but it was not a final victory either way. Neither side achieved its goal of complete dominance, and neither was driven from the scene.

The Wobblies were blunt and outspoken in their meetings and in their literature. They looked upon the craft unions as their natural enemies—reactionary organizations intent upon misleading the workers into the belief that the working class could have interests in common with the employers. They charged that craft unionism, by signing contracts with employers, fostered the practice of one union breaking through the picket line of another, and they explained that the I.W.W. did not believe in employer contracts. And yet when the craft unions went out on strike the Wobblies were almost invariably there in numbers to lend enthusiastic and often unrequested support. By nature, by disposition and by design, they were solidly on the side of any and all who opposed the employing class.

Meanwhile, Mayor Cotterill's attempt to close the saloons during the Potlatch Days celebration had touched off repercussions. The anti-saloon advocates, like the lumber-workers, had been equally quick in forgetting the Blethen-Cotterill feud which had built up to the hour of the riot, and they placed the entire responsibility upon the Demon Rum. They offered Cotterill's attempt to close the saloons as compelling proof that Seattle's Mayor had recognized the alcoholic hazard, and they broadly intimated that prohibition would solve most of the state's problems. Skid Road without booze would become quiet and docile. Wild-eyed radicals would sober up and listen to reason, and the insolent and shiftless stumble-bums south of Yesler Way would amble off toward saloons in other states and leave the soapbox orators without an audience. Other areas of the state seized upon the same remedy to solve their local problems, and the more rabid prohibitionists were joined by thousands of sober-minded citizens who became convinced that alcohol was costing much and contributing little.

On November 3, 1914, the voters of the state passed an initiative measure to enact state-wide prohibition. Not all were convinced that it would automatically and immediately solve all social and moral problems; and in their bid for wide-spread acceptance, the framers of the initiative had avoided a bone-dry statute that might sound fanatical. The new law would permit drugstores to sell alcoholic beverages upon a medical prescription, and physicians would be permitted to use their own discretion in prescribing it for anything from a common cold to snake-bite.

On January first, 1916, the new law became effective in the State of Washington. It failed to affect the pattern of Skid Road to any appreciable extent, but it produced its peculiar effects upon the lives of many people elsewhere.

To George Vanderveer it brought a host of new clients, most of them affluent—ready and willing to pay substantial fees for the services of a good defense attorney. It transferred crime to the status of big business; and for the first time it afforded the criminal lawyer compensations that might compare favorably with those of the corporation attorney. The more prosperous bootleggers sought the accomplished lawyers, and George Vanderveer felt the passing effects of a belated prosperity. However, at Ellinor's insistence, a large share of the newly enlarged income went toward the retirement of old debts that had been mounting through the years. As each fee was collected, a substantial portion of it moved along to meet seemingly endless demands of creditors, and very little of the belated prosperity remained behind to alter the private life of the Vanderveers.

The enactment of state-wide prohibition undoubtedly had a great bearing upon the profession chosen by Logan Billingsley and his brother Fred, from Oklahoma. They began operating the Stewart Street Pharmacy in downtown Seattle, selling an assortment of items from corn plasters to aspirin tablets, but gaining much of their revenue from the sale of alcoholic beverages "for medicinal purposes," as provided under the new state prohibition act. Liquor which could not be accounted for by medical prescriptions on file, they charged off to "leakage and spillage"; and when enforcement officers became curious about the amount of liquor listed under this heading they attempted to shrug away their problem: "Can we help it if we're the clumsy type?" However, it soon became apparent to the Billingsley brothers that they could use the services of a good lawyer.

To Jack Marquett, former Seattle police officer who had served as Colonel Blethen's personal bodyguard under Police Chief Wappenstein, the state prohibition act brought with it a challenge. He undertook to establish himself as king of Seattle's illicit liquor traffic, utilizing his police experience, political connections, and genius for organization. He resented the encroachment of the Billingsley brothers, and perhaps it was not a matter of business so much as a matter of civic pride. Seattle should be able to produce its own bootleggers from among its own home-town boys, without bringing in outside talent. Tension built up between the Marquett gang and the Billingsley brothers, almost from the start.

To Hi Gill, prohibition brought an opportunity and a challenge. He had returned from political obscurity in 1914 once again to become Seattle's Mayor; but he was an all-new-and-all-different Hi Gill. He sought election as a reform candidate, bluntly informing the voters that he had got religion and that he wanted to redeem himself in the eyes of his community—that he wanted to wipe out the blot against his record so that his grandsons could be proud of him. It was a simple, eloquent, and heart-touching plea that stirred up a city's emotions; and to prove that he was sincere, Hi Gill broke with Colonel Blethen and campaigned against the opposition of the *Times*.

Much to the chagrin of some of his reformist backers, Hi Gill opposed the enactment of state-wide prohibition when the initiative appeared on the ballot several months after he had taken office. It was a quiet, off-the-cuff type of opposition, however, and as soon as the law was enacted, Hi Gill recognized his clearly defined duty. He accompanied his Chief of Police in raids upon speakeasies and, with remarkable foresight, he invited news photographers to accompany him upon most of the forays. Seattle newspapers blossomed with their eternal pictures of Mayor Gill, axe in hand, smashing the wooden whiskey kegs, until his critics charged that he had become confused with Carry Nation.

Gill's critics were not numerous at the outset, however. His new-found reformist friends gloried in his zealous devotion to duty and he became the subject of many a Sunday sermon—living proof that a sinner could be saved, and that a man could arise from the disgrace of political graft to redeem himself in the eyes of his fellow men. His old-time friends were less inspired, but perhaps not less pleased. They were convinced that Hi Gill had undertaken to whip the prohibition nonsense in the shortest possible time, in the best possible way: "He knows what he's doing, boys. He's going to ram it down their throats until the public has had a bellyful of it; just you watch and see."

To Al Lundin, Prosecuting Attorney of King County, the new prohibition law brought a series of problems and frustrations. The backers of the initiative had been content to make progress slowly, and they had feared from the outset that an uncompromising, bone-dry proposal would be turned down by voters who favored moderation but who might shy off from anything hinting of fanaticism. Thus, in effect, the 1916 law emerged as a type of loose net, binding together a series of legal loopholes—designed to reduce the heavy, open flow of liquor, but destined to provide ulcers for nearly all who were charged with its enforcement. It prohibited the manufacture, keeping, sale and disposition of alcoholic beverages . . . but it provided that druggists could secure permits from the County Auditor and handle liquor for medicinal purposes, and it allowed doctors to prescribe such alcoholic beverages for the same use. There was no established quotas or restrictions. The result was a broad and practically unpatrolled highway, ready and waiting to handle the liquor traffic.

Lundin informed the Billingsley brothers that their claims of "leakage and spillage" were ridiculous, and he threatened to crack down. He appealed to legislators and liquor-control officers to set some arbitrary limit upon the amount of liquor a drugstore could sell in the period of one month; and he finally took the law into his hands, writing a letter to the County Auditor and limiting the number of barrels of alcoholic beverages that could be handled by a drugstore in the course of a year. He also grasped one other opportunity for direct action: he wrote to the Sheriff of Garfield County, Oklahoma, explaining that the Billingsley brothers were now living in Seattle and that if Oklahoma legal authorities wanted them for any reason, they were more than welcome to come and get them. He learned by return mail that Logan Billingsley was wanted by Oklahoma authorities, and that the Sheriff was sending a deputy to Seattle to take Logan back with him.

The first attempt was unsuccessful. Logan Billingsley went into hiding. Seattle police were sympathetic but uncooperative, and after a week of fruitless waiting, the deputy from Oklahoma announced that he'd had enough, and planned to board a train and head for home. Al Lundin was not through, however.

"He can hide for a week, or he can hide for a month if necessary," he explained to the deputy, "but it's a sure thing he can't hide forever. Probably he'll show up as soon as he's convinced that you're out of town, so here's what I want you to do: as soon as you get back to Oklahoma you get a requisition from the Governor and then I'll issue a fugitive warrant. As soon as he pokes his head up, I'll have one of my boys serve him."

On the day when he was served with the fugitive warrant, Logan Billingsley knew that his need for a good lawyer had become acute, and he called upon George Vanderveer.

For nearly two hours they were closeted in Vanderveer's private office, and then the two of them made a visit to the

Stewart Street Pharmacy. When Vanderveer returned to his office he announced that he didn't want to be disturbed. There were numerous phone calls, and for a good many hours George Vanderveer paced from his office through the outer office and back into his own office again, pounding his fist into the palm of his hand and apparently oblivious of everything around him.

On the following day Logan Billingsley appeared in the back room of a pool hall not far from Skid Road; and in the presence of a known informer, he handed a packet of powder to a nondescript character who sniffed of the powder and handed over a roll of bills. He was overheard explaining that he would be back in a couple of hours with the rest of the stuff and advising his customer to have the cash. Two hours later Logan Billingsley was arrested by a United States marshal on a charge of illegally peddling narcotics. He was taken to jail, and several packets of powder in his possession were seized as evidence.

Late that afternoon Billingsley was released on bail, and several days later he appeared before Justice of the Peace John Gordon for his hearing on the fugitive warrant. He was represented by his attorney, George Vanderveer, and across the room sat the deputy sheriff from Oklahoma. There were several other men in the room obviously taking a keen interest in the proceedings.

Just as the hearing was about to start, one of the men identified himself to the court. He explained that he was the bondsman for Logan Billingsley, and that under the circumstances he did not wish any longer to be responsible for the bail he had posted to insure Billingsley's appearance in Federal court on a narcotics charge.

George Vanderveer turned to one of the other men in the courtroom, who identified himself as a United States marshal. "This is all very embarrassing," he explained with a grin. "I have no choice now but to turn the prisoner over to your custody."

Justice of the Peace Gordon found it even more embarrassing. The defendant, waiting to appear before him, suddenly had become a prisoner in the custody of the United States marshal. Justice Gordon did the only thing he could do. He bowed to the superior authority of the United States, and he dismissed the Oklahoma fugitive warrant.

With the hearing thus ended before it had begun, the United States marshal and his prisoner, Logan Billingsley, accompanied George Vanderveer to his office. They were closely followed by an irately sputtering deputy sheriff from Oklahoma, giving voice to charges of collusion. Inside his office, Vanderveer invited the marshal and his prisoner to be seated, and then he turned to the deputy sheriff.

"This is a private office," he announced. "If you've got any business here, state it . . . or else get to hell out of here and be quick about it."

"You're damn right I got business here," the deputy sputtered. "I'm not going to let Billingsley out of my sight until I get him back to Oklahoma."

Vanderveer walked forward, fists clenched and shoulders hunched. "I remind you again that this is a private office. I'm inviting you to leave here under your own power, while you're still able."

The deputy left, but he remained in Seattle for two weeks waiting for the hearing before the United States Commissioner on the dope-peddling charge against Billingsley. Vanderveer, through a series of maneuvers, managed to get the hearings continued until the deputy sheriff from Oklahoma left town in disgust.

"To hell with it!" the deputy snorted on his last visit to Al Lundin's office. "It would serve your damn county right if Logan Billingsley stayed here the rest of his life, and I hope to God he does!"

Shortly after the deputy's departure, the hearing was held before the United States Commissioner. The charges against

Logan Billingsley collapsed when an analysis of the powder found in his possession proved to be the pulverized substance of ordinary mothballs—so closely resembling cocaine in appearance that even the experts had been fooled. Any charges of deliberate mischief were skillfully skirted by Vanderveer's placid reminder that Logan Billingsley was the proprietor of a drugstore, that he was licensed to sell such merchandise, and that personal delivery was well within the scope of customary service.

By the dramatic and highly unorthodox series of maneuvers, Logan Billingsley had avoided a reluctant trip back to Oklahoma; and while there might be considerable room for debate as to the ethics of such maneuvering, George Vanderveer had neatly extricated his client from a supposedly inescapable situation without the violation of any law. The Billingsley brothers were impressed and they retained Vanderveer in the nature of a professional guide to lead them from one legal loophole to the next in the loosely drawn provisions of the state prohibition act.

To Vanderveer it was a fascinating series of legal skirmishes. He spent hours with the Billingsley brothers, advising them exactly what to do, and exactly what to say to enforcement officers who were constantly tightening down on the Stewart Street Pharmacy. Frequently he was opposed by Al Lundin, and these two men who were staunch personal friends became professional enemies. In court and out of court, across the bench and across the lunch table, they debated the points of law and the points of ethics involved.

Lundin, by his own admission, was in a highly peculiar position, sworn to enforce and uphold a law so loosely written. Tauntingly, Vanderveer hurled at Lundin some of the same charges that Blethen had once fired at him. He accused his friend of overzealousness in attempting to enforce the law, over and beyond the letter of the law.

When Ellinor Vanderveer inquired of her husband as to

the ethics of his new role, he insisted that the whole prohibition program had been enacted in the nature of a fraud upon
the voting public. "If they'd come right out on the ballot
with an initiative to make the state absolutely bone-dry it
wouldn't have stood a chance, and they know it," he told her.
"And if anybody wants to talk about ethics, let him talk about
the ethics of gradually palming off on the public a set of laws
that they would have turned down at the polls."

At another time he told his wife that he was performing a
valuable service, even for the prohibitionists. "Eventually
the state's going to be all dry, or it's going to be all wet. It
can't go on this way, with a prohibition act that's neither fish
nor fowl. If the state goes wet, I haven't hurt anything. If
it goes dry, they'll benefit from having somebody point out
all the existing loopholes."

Vanderveer's off-the-record debates with Al Lundin were
frequent and involved, but they were more or less irrelevant.
The tensions that had existed between the Marquett gang and
the Billingsley brothers were beginning to erupt in acts of
open hostility. A prolonged battle was shaping up which
would be fought far from the courtroom, and wherein neither
side would pause to question legal precedent.

According to the Billingsley brothers, it was Marquett who
started the hijacking, intercepting one of their large shipments
of liquor from California. According to Marquett, it was the
Billingsleys who touched off the battle. But regardless of
which side started it, neither side showed any inclination to
retire from the contest. Practically all of Seattle knew that
the Billingsley brothers and the Marquett gang were fighting
it out for survival, but the scene of battle shifted constantly.
The Billingsleys, somehow, were able to learn about Marquett's liquor shipments, and to swoop down upon a secret
rendezvous and make off with a truckload of liquor. The
Marquett gang displayed equal aptitude in preying upon the
Billingsleys; but the police, for some reason, seemed incapable
of swooping down on either of them.

Gunplay was frequent, and the battles occasionally left their dead and their wounded. George Vanderveer, closely associated with the Billingsleys, secured a police permit and wore two revolvers in shoulder holsters.

"I'm not going to mix into that part of it," he told his wife, earnestly, "but if any of the Marquett gang comes gunning for me they're going to collect an awful lot of lead." He resumed his target shooting, and he spent hours practising the technique of drawing and shooting with either hand. He informed his wife that in his opinion, he could come close to outdrawing and outshooting any man in the Pacific Northwest.

With a genius for organization and with an increasing operating fund, the Billingsley brothers soon outgrew Seattle and its environs, and the Stewart Street Pharmacy became a minor setting in a major game. Their activities extended to the international scale and they shipped liquor in carload quantities from Cuba to Canada—with unprecedented "leakage and spillage" in transit. They bought large consignments of liquor directly from the Hunt Company in San Francisco, and on one occasion George Vanderveer showed Ellinor a signed check for two hundred and fifty thousand dollars which the Billingsley brothers were forwarding for a single shipment.

"I brought the check home just to show you," Vanderveer grinned. "It isn't everybody who even *sees* that kind of money."

Through all of the trying years of scarcity he had never parted with his half-interest in the *Imp* and now, once again, he was able to enjoy the longer cruises up into Canadian and Alaskan waters; but his guests were no longer young attorneys. Sometimes one or other of the Billingsleys went along, and paid all expenses. On numerous occasions his passengers included Mayor Hi Gill who, apparently, had grown bored with the company of his more recent, reformist friends and

who scoffed at their admonition that he should not be seen
with known bootleggers.

From Ellinor's standpoint, the task of retiring old debts
became discouraging on many occasions. Despite the size of
the checks he displayed to her, and despite the amount of
money the Billingsleys readily put up to finance cruises and
such, George Vanderveer did not bring home an income in
proportion. "I'm a lawyer, not a bootlegger," he told his wife
rather earnestly one evening. "It doesn't matter how much
money they're making or how they're making it—I still collect
reasonable fees for legal services, and that's all." He intimated
rather broadly that for little more than the asking, he could
share in the fabulous profits of the enterprise; but he assured
her that he would never even consider such a thing.

"You mustn't become impatient, Gus," he told her one
evening. "We've turned the corner now, and we're starting
to climb out of debt instead of sinking into it more deeply.
Before too long we'll have all of the old debts paid and we'll
be on our feet—but I've got to do it my way. Can't you see
that?"

Events were approaching, however, which were to deny
George Vanderveer his opportunity for a leisurely climb back
to financial stability.

Jack Marquett received an anonymous phone call report-
ing that one of his truckloads of liquor was about to be
hijacked in Georgetown, a Seattle suburb, and that if he
hurried to the scene possibly he could prevent it. A few
minutes later the police received an anonymous phone call
informing them of the exact location of a large consignment
of contraband liquor and explaining that Jack Marquett
would be on the scene with many members of his gang, and
that the entire bunch could be rounded up and caught red-
handed.

The two anonymous phone calls paid off. The police
moved in and found Jack Marquett and a number of armed

men guarding a truckload of liquor in Georgetown. It was a master stroke for the police. The story made headlines in the afternoon papers, and for a very short interval the Billingsley brothers were jubilant. Their competitor had been eliminated.

The jubilation of the Billingsley brothers was short-lived, however. The investigation of Marquett's dealings with the Hunt Company in San Francisco brought to light a great deal of correspondence between the Hunt Company and Logan Billingsley; and the Billingsley brothers were soon trapped in the backwash of the investigation. The arrest of Logan Billingsley brought one charge that rocked Seattle politics to its foundation and no doubt caused a hurried change in the text of many Sunday sermons in the process of preparation. Disillusioned reformers had to reconcile themselves to the realization that a sinner's redemption is not always permanent.

As he was being led to his cell, Logan Billingsley protested that it was all grossly unfair; that he had given money to George Vanderveer to pay off Hi Gill, just to insure that this sort of thing would never happen. "I paid for protection, and I paid plenty," he announced bitterly. "Where is it now when I need it?"

"This thing is going to be plenty rough before it's over," Vanderveer informed his wife grimly. "Logan has made up his mind that he's going to plead guilty, and I guess he might as well; they've got an air-tight case against him. Hi Gill will deny everything, and that'll leave me sitting right in the middle." But he hastened to assure her that he had little to worry about, personally.

"Logan is in a tough spot because he's a bootlegger. Gill is in a tough spot because he's a washed-up politician. But all I've ever been is a lawyer, Gus. All I've ever taken is reasonable legal fees . . . and thank God I can prove it!"

Logan Billingsley was sentenced to serve thirteen months

at the Federal Penitentiary on McNeil's Island and his brother Fred was sentenced to six months in the Whatcom County jail. The repercussions of Billingsley's protest were to come later.

CHAPTER ELEVEN

Take care not to lose your lives unavenged; take care not to be taken and butchered like cattle, rather than, fighting like men, to leave to your enemies a bloody and mournful victory.—CATILINE

PROHIBITION in the State of Washington reflected little change in the appearance of Skid Road, and it brought no surcease to the epidemic of soapbox oratory. I.W.W. activity was on the increase, and by early 1916 the Wobblies were feeling the grip of missionary fever. There were few regular visitors to the district who had not heard all of the I.W.W. arguments—not once, but many times—and although the spirit of rebellion had grown white hot at the Wobbly hall on numerous occasions, the flames had failed to spread. I.W.W. organizers recognized the importance of carrying the torch to new areas, and they turned their attention to the city of Everett, approximately thirty miles north of Seattle.

Everett had no I.W.W. hall, and no counterpart of Seattle's Skid Road. It was an industrial city, the center of large lumbering operations, and it cherished its informal title as the "City of Smokestacks." Its lumber mills and shingle mills were large, permanent installations, feeding upon great booms of logs floated in from distant parts of the Sound. Its millworkers and shingle weavers were mostly local residents who maintained their own homes, paid local taxes, and belonged to the more conservative A.F. of L. unions. The

smell of cedar and spruce was heavy in the air, and the whine
of the giant mills could be heard above the sound of traffic
on the streets. The entire city set its clocks and watches by
the mill whistles. In many ways it looked, sounded and
smelled the same as more distant mills and lumber camps, but
in at least one respect it was entirely different: its workers
had put down roots, and they had little in common with the
transient and migratory lumber-workers who drifted from
one job to the next and pursued the ever-receding timberline.

Everett had been peculiarly free from I.W.W. demonstrations, but it had the Wobbly jitters. The large metropolitan newspapers from Seattle were widely distributed
within the city, and Everett citizens had become familiar with
Colonel Blethen's tirades against the wild-eyed anarchists
plotting to overthrow the government of the United States.
Although the Colonel had died the year before, his son, General Clarence B. Blethen, was now publishing the *Times* and
maintaining the same firm stand against "red-flag anarchists."
Like the good people of Seattle, the people of Everett feared
the destruction of everything clean and decent and wholesome; and they looked hopefully to their police and to
Snohomish County's Sheriff, Donald McRae, to protect them
from the menace.

Their fears began to grow acute in May of 1916 when the
International Shingle Weavers' union went on strike in
Everett. It was an A.F. of L. union with a long record of
animosity toward the Wobblies, and the two organizations
had spent years in bitter and often violent competition. The
I.W.W. had attempted to raid the membership of the Shingle
Weavers' union, and had denounced it as a white-livered
organization completely dominated by conservatives and re-
actionaries, and a willing tool of the lumber barons. However, as was their custom, the Wobblies demonstrated a
willingness to forgive and forget, as soon as the strike was
called. Officially, the I.W.W. took no part in maintaining
the picket line; but individual members, carrying Wobbly

red cards and acting upon their own initiative, moved north from Seattle and trickled in from the hills, and stood side by side with members of the A.F. of L. union.

At I.W.W. headquarters in Seattle, plans were made to "open up" the city of Everett. However, the first Wobbly speaker to reach Everett after the start of the Shingle Weavers' strike was arrested by police when he offered I.W.W. literature for sale to members of his audience. He was charged with peddling without a license, and he was given his opportunity to leave town in lieu of spending thirty days in jail. Everett police had won the first skirmish, but they were allowed little time to reflect upon their glory.

The Wobblies moved in and opened a small I.W.W. hall on Hewitt Avenue, and they began their campaign of providing still-unrequested moral support to the striking Shingle Weavers' union. They moved in to help support the picket line which frequently was being tested by squads of strike-breakers, and they wore their Wobbly buttons proudly.

Not until the I.W.W. advertised its first mass meeting did the police and Sheriff move in, but now they wasted little time on formalities. They ripped the posters from the front of the I.W.W. hall, and they ordered those in charge to leave town by that afternoon or go to jail. They moved methodically through the pool halls of the area, and they delivered an ultimatum to every man who could not prove local residence: "Get out of town by this afternoon, or you'll spend the next thirty days in jail." They questioned the men on the picket line, and every man wearing a Wobbly button was escorted to the city limits and told to keep moving.

The police and the Sheriff were aided in some instances by members of the Shingle Weavers' union when it came to the delicate task of weeding out Wobblies not wearing buttons. They identified their own fellow union members and left the others conspicuously unclaimed. "We don't want them damn anarchists here any more than you do," they protested to the police. "This is our fight, and we'll see it through by ourselves."

Despite these things, however, the I.W.W. mass meeting took place as scheduled. Unable to rent a hall, they held the meeting on a street corner at Hewitt and Westmore; and the Wobblies from Seattle brought not only their speaker but also their own audience. They were taking no chance of presenting the dismal picture of a Wobbly speaker on a soapbox haranguing empty air. For the most part the street meeting was quiet and orderly. Even when the police moved in to pick up the speaker and the ring leaders and hustle them off to jail, there was no attempt to resist arrest.

With remarkable self-discipline, the Wobblies marched along to the city jail and asked the nature of the charges to be filed against them. A flustered and irate Commissioner of Public Safety (Everett's title for the chief of its police force) tried desperately to remain calm and talk sense to the Wobbly speaker:

"Let's all be reasonable about this. We don't want to arrest you but, damn it all, we've got trouble here in Everett. We've got labor trouble—all we can handle, and we don't want any more. All we want to do is settle our own trouble in our own way, and we don't want anybody from the outside messing in on it. If you want me to, I'll bring in the head of the Shingle Weavers' union, and he'll tell you the same thing I'm telling you. They don't want you messing in here, either; so now if you'll all get out of town and stay out, that's all we ask. Later on, you can come back if you want to, and you can hold your street meetings. Yes—and by God, we'll even give you police protection. But not when there's a strike on."

The Wobbly leaders flatly refused to depart, and demanded that they be charged or released. They dared the Commissioner to point out any ordinance prohibiting such meetings, and they bluntly informed him that if released they would return to the street corner and continue the meeting. "Everett is still part of the United States," they argued. "You have no right to decide who can come here, and when they can come, and when or where they can meet. If we've broken any law we demand that we be arrested, and if we haven't broken any law we demand that we be released."

The tolerant, let's-all-be-reasonable smile disappeared from the Commissioner's face. "Oh hell!" he snapped at the arresting officers. "Go ahead and lock 'em up!"

On the blotter they were charged with vagrancy, but they were never brought to trial. The next morning those who were unwilling to leave town unassisted were taken down to the dock and placed aboard a passenger ship bound for Seattle. With streamlined efficiency but without a court order, money taken from one of the prisoners at the time of booking was used to pay the fares. The slightly embarrassed Mayor of Everett, when informed of the situation later, wrote a letter to the Secretary of the Seattle I.W.W. promising that the money would be refunded; but according to the Secretary, that promise was never fulfilled.

The Wobblies now had a new cry and a new crusade, and the strike of the Shingle Weavers' union was of secondary importance. The fundamental question was whether the right of free speech could be suspended upon Everett streets, and whether officers of the law could take it upon their shoulders to rise above the law they were sworn to uphold. These were "fundamental questions" which the Wobblies had debated before in many cities across the country, and the technique of their protests had been built up through considerable practice.

Seven years earlier Wobblies from all over the West Coast had closed in on Spokane, Washington, to contest an alleged abridgment of the right of free speech. They swarmed from every incoming freight train until the city took on the aspect of a vast hobo jungle, and still they continued to come. When the frantic police would grab one man from a soapbox and hustle him off to jail, another man would mount his perch several blocks away and begin to speak. At the peak of the contest, the Spokane jails were crowded beyond capacity, following some five hundred or six hundred arrests. It was an impossible situation, for the city could neither accommodate nor feed so many prisoners, and the attorney representing the Wobblies demanded separate trials for each.

The police were frantic and frustrated, while the prisoners were jubilant and singing. Most of the Wobblies were itinerant workers and experienced bindlestiffs, with no date to be anywhere else at any particular time; and even amid the crowded conditions of the jail they found their hardships not much greater than those which they had come to accept as a matter of course. In the Spokane jails they perfected their technique of the "battleship," which sent all prisoners on a noise-making spree at a given signal, producing a din that would test the walls of Jericho.

On a burst of inspiration, Frank Little, an I.W.W. organizer, had mounted a soapbox and begun reciting the Declaration of Independence—and the Wobblies had gained a valuable propaganda weapon when he was arrested in the middle of his recitation. Even conservative newspapers across the country could hardly refrain from taking a pot-shot at Spokane for arresting a man for reciting the Declaration of Independence.

With the issue in Everett now neatly diverted to the fundamental question of free speech, the Wobblies knew exactly what they should do, and they set about doing it. Night after night they returned to Everett and held their street meetings, and for a time they were unmolested; but the rift was slowly widening and new battlelines were being drawn. Wobbly speakers edged their way into meetings of the A.F. of L. unions to tell their side of the story, but now they spoke less of their dream of abolishing capitalism and the

wage system. They quoted Patrick Henry, and they reviewed
the Battle of Bunker Hill; they delivered impassioned pleas
for the Constitutional right of free speech, and they tossed in
random selections from the Bill of Rights, the Declaration of
Independence, and the Holy Bible. They had points to make,
and they made them with telling effect.

The Everett Labor Council passed a resolution condemn-
ing the city and county authorities for taking the law into
their own hands, and the members of the Shingle Weavers'
union welcomed the Wobblies to their picket line and forgot
the grievances of the past. The dreaded "Skid Road anarchists" had now become martyrs in the cause of labor and the
champions of fundamental liberties gained by the terrible
sacrifice at Valley Forge. The harsh and arbitrary handling
of a few Wobblies had transformed earlier apprehension into
a spreading sympathy for the underdog.

Everett police, familiar with the earlier story in Spokane
and with similar stories elsewhere, pondered what course to
take—and finally took none. They made no attempt to break
up the nightly meetings, and they made no effort to oppose
Sheriff McRae and his deputies, augmented by some two
hundred deputized members of the Commercial Club, who
were determined to drive the anarchists out of the city. The
Commissioner of Public Safety welcomed the opportunity to
back out of an impossible situation and to leave the Wobbly
question largely up to the Sheriff.

As an emergency measure, the Everett City Council rushed
through an ordinance banning public meetings at the corner
of Hewitt and Westmore Avenues, but it was passed without
the customary second and third readings and the Wobblies
charged that the ordinance was illegal.

As soon as he realized that the responsibility rested squarely
on his shoulders, Sheriff McRae swung into action. Street
meetings were broken up and speakers were jailed. Deputized members of the Commercial Club met each incoming

train and passenger ship and interurban from Seattle, and all
persons who could not prove residence or legitimate business
within the county were subjected to extensive questioning.
Suspicious persons were denied admittance to the city. His
position was weakened somewhat by the fact that political
candidates frequently addressed open-air meetings at the
Hewitt-Westmore corner in violation of the disputed ordinance without interference from the city's police; but the
Sheriff disclaimed responsibility: "I'll keep the Wobblies out
of town, but I'm not going to take over all the duties of the
Everett police force."

In an effort to break through the Sheriff's militant guard,
a group of Wobblies took the train to Mukilteo—a small town
several miles south of Everett—and there they hired a launch
to transport them to a small private dock on the Everett
waterfront which, presumably, would be unguarded. However, the news reached Everett ahead of the launch. Sheriff
McRae and a number of deputies boarded a tug and met the
launch offshore where, according to the testimony of the
launch's pilot, the Sheriff opened fire without verbal warning.
Several bullets whistled past the launch's bow, and at least
two thudded into the cabin. The pilot shut down the motor
of the launch, and the tugboat pulled alongside. All persons
on board the launch, including the pilot, were transferred
to the tug, taken into Everett, and lodged in the county jail.
They were jailed without charge and nine days later they
were released, but the incident touched off political repercussions in Mukilteo where the launch's pilot, Jack Mitten,
was a respected member of the small community.

On October thirtieth, the Wobblies determined to make
their most concerted effort to date to crash the barrier and
to hold a "free speech" demonstration in Everett. Forty-one
Wobblies left Seattle aboard a regularly scheduled passenger
ship headed for Everett. Many of them were itinerant harvest
hands just returned from the season's work east of the moun-

COUNSEL FOR THE DAMNED

tains; powerful men hardened by long hours in the harvest
fields, experienced in rough-and-tumble battle, and not afraid
to fight. The Wobblies were jubilant for they believed they
could readily overpower the handful of deputized members
of the Commercial Club who generally met each incoming
ship.

It was late afternoon when the ship reached Everett, and
the forty-one Wobblies were met by a group of men
variously estimated from one hundred to five hundred; most
of them wearing white handkerchiefs across the face or
around the neck for mutual identification. Many of them
were armed with guns or clubs or pick-handles, and they
quickly cut off the Wobblies' possible retreat to the ship.
They escorted the forty-one Wobblies to a line of trucks
and cars waiting near the dock, and then drove to a densely
wooded spot beside the highway, near Beverly Park. (Later
evidence disclosed that two of the more active men at I.W.W.
headquarters in Seattle were Pinkerton men employed by the
Everett authorities and instructed to keep Sheriff McRae informed each time a group of Wobblies headed north.)

A drizzle of rain had started and darkness had closed in by
the time the cars and trucks stopped. Then, according to
later court testimony the vigilantes formed a double line leading along the interurban tracks where they angled across the
highway, and each of the Wobblies, at gun point, was
ordered to run the gauntlet. Clubs, pick-handles and gun
butts crashed down upon the head and shoulders and back
of each man as he staggered forward. A spiny cactus-like
plant known as "devil's club" was used by several of the
vigilantes, and a number of the Wobblies were felled by the
blows, and had to be dragged to their feet to continue
the journey. A few made a desperate effort to escape but were
quickly captured and sent through the line. However, one
of the Wobblies—a teen-age boy—was spared the trip through
the double line after he had made an attempt to escape and

had enlisted the sympathy of the vigilantes who captured
him. "We'll let you off this time, kid, but don't ever come
back here again."

The moans and the screams of the Wobblies mingled with
the curses and the threats of the irate vigilantes, until a man
living in a house a quarter of a mile away came running
through the darkness to investigate.

"What in God's name is going on here?" he panted.

"We're beating hell out of a bunch of Wobblies," he was
told. "That's the only kind of language they can understand."

The affair at Beverly Park set off reactions in Everett and
in Seattle. A committee of citizens from both cities visited
the scene and found numerous bits of blood-stained clothing,
plus evidence of blood on the roadway and on the ties of the
interurban tracks. They interviewed the man who had witnessed the scene, and passengers who had arrived on the ship
from Seattle and watched the round-up on the dock. A
number of Everett ministers met to discuss the problem and
adjourned without reaching a decision. Sheriff McRae and
his deputies denied all knowledge of the incident.

There were many in Everett and in Seattle who gloated
over the news, which was widely discussed on the streets but
generally disregarded by the press: "What they should of
done is killed them damn anarchists when they had the
chance!"

There were many in Seattle who were indignant, but for
a specific reason. Most of the Wobblies were transients, and
Seattle citizens resented having the Snohomish County Sheriff constantly sending them back to Seattle. "They don't
live here. What right has he got to keep sending 'em back
to us?"

There were many, particularly in Everett, who felt that
the Sheriff and the Commercial Club had already gone too
far down the wrong road. Printed disclaimers began to ap-

pear in a number of stores: "We Are Not Members of the Commercial Club." Beyond a doubt, the great majority of Everett's citizens felt that they were trapped between the lumber interests on the one hand, and the Wobblies on the other—in a situation which was neither of their choosing nor to their liking. What they wanted most of all was to have the strike end and life return to normal.

There were a great many who insisted that Sheriff McRae was being paid by the millowners to help break the strike, and to keep Everett safe for the "open shop." And yet the facts reveal that he had been a member of the Shingle Weavers' union before becoming Sheriff, and he had offered a substantial contribution to the general strike fund when the strike was first called. Most of his life he had been a staunch supporter of the A.F. of L. He was an avid sportsman, and there is little doubt that he suffered, personally, from attempts at retribution. Two of his hunting dogs were found mysteriously poisoned, and he was a man who hated dog-poisoners even more than he hated anarchists. His home was constantly decorated with the black-cat calling cards of the Wobblies— a type of defiant reminder that the I.W.W. could reach out in the darkness and find its enemies, and strike when and how it chose. Fires of mysterious origin started on numerous occasions on property owned by the Sheriff, and the mail brought anonymous letters with threats against his life. He was a man of unquestioned courage, and there is ample reason to believe that he was inspired by an unflinching devotion to his duty, as he saw it. Fate and politics had singled him out as the man to safeguard Snohomish County from the infiltration of human termites who would destroy the lumbering industry and undermine everything that decent folks held sacred.

In Seattle the Wobblies were marshaling their forces for one more assault at the Everett bastion, bigger and better than ever before. They made no attempt to disguise their aims, and thousands of handbills appeared on Everett streets:

CITIZENS OF EVERETT
Attention!
A meeting will be held at the corner of Hewitt and Westmore
Aves., on Sunday, Nov. 5th, 2
p. m. Come and help maintain
your and our constitutional right.
—Committee

Loggers, millworkers, shingle weavers, harvest hands, fish-scalers—Wobblies from all of the Northwest pledged to be on hand for the task of invading Everett in force. It was designed to be a repetition of the earlier free-speech triumph in Spokane, and the jubilant committee went about its task with confidence and optimism. The one big problem was transportation. Interurban officials explained that they couldn't possibly transport the number expected. Railroads were gazing with disfavor upon those who tried to ride freights and the Wobblies of the Northwest were a different lot from the earlier bindlestiffs who had been experts at riding the rods. The cost of hiring fleets of trucks was investigated and found prohibitive. As a last resort, the committee pooled its money and bought up all the tickets for the Sunday run of the *Verona*, a passenger ship in regular service between Seattle and Everett. To accommodate its regular passengers who would thus be deprived of their usual Sunday passage, the steamship company announced that the *Calista*, a smaller ship, would immediately follow the *Verona*. Primarily, it would have to accommodate the regular Sunday passengers of the *Verona*; but it could also carry a limited number of Wobblies.

This was hardly what the committee had hoped for at the start. The two ships, at best, could not carry more than three hundred—a number hardly sufficient to overrun the streets of Everett and put on a demonstration similar to the earlier one in Spokane. The party would have to be limited to the number of tickets on hand.

Shortly before noon on Sunday approximately three hundred Wobblies left the I.W.W. hall in Seattle and marched four-abreast to Colman dock. Because of a last-minute mix-up, not all of those who got aboard the *Verona* were members of the Wobbly "free-speech party." Several regular passengers, accustomed to boarding the ship at that time of day, strolled on board without tickets and paid their fare to the purser in cash, a practice not without precedent.

Captain Chance Wyman of the *Verona* called a halt when two hundred and fifty passengers had crossed the gangplank, as this was the maximum limit for his ship. The remaining Wobblies joined the somewhat bewildered regular passengers in moving to Pier Three to board the smaller *Calista*.

On the trip north, the *Verona* stopped to discharge a few regular passengers at Edmonds, approximately halfway between Seattle and Everett, and then she continued her northward voyage. Shortly before two o'clock she shut down her engine and began gliding quietly across the last gap of water separating her from Everett's city dock. The day was clear and bright; the water calm. Passengers stood along the rail, and many were huddled in a tight group near the bow with arms about each other's shoulders as they sang "Hold The Fort":

> "We meet today in Freedom's cause,
>   And raise our voices high;
>   We'll join our hands in union strong,
>   To battle or to die."

It is doubtful, however, if many of them grasped the prophetic significance of the lyrics. What the singing lacked in quality, it made up in volume; and other passengers strolling from the cabin to the deck joined in the song. An exuberant young Wobbly, Hugo Gerlot, began shinnying up

the flagpole and waving to the crowds of people assembled
back up on the hillside.

The *Verona* shuddered momentarily as her propeller was
reversed, kicking up a white froth in the wake until the ship
was almost still in the water, her bow swinging in with the
tide. A deck hand nimbly hopped the railing and picked his
way along the side of the ship toward the bow, in order to
avoid the congestion of people on the forward deck. He
picked up the bowline and, with his other hand grasping the
railing, leaned far out over the water, waiting to loop the line
over a bollard. A couple of deck hands released pins from the
railing and began pulling out the gangplank. Even amid the
singing, a number of passengers began pointing toward an
unusual situation ashore.

City dock usually swarmed with people waiting to greet
an incoming ship, but now the dock stood deserted except
for three men, Sheriff McRae, Deputy Sheriff Jefferson
Beard, and Lieutenant Charles O. Curtis of the Officers'
Reserve Corps of the National Guard. Farther back, ropes
had been strung across the dock to keep the public off.

The bowline looped over the bollard, and Captain Wyman
stepped out of the pilot house momentarily to glance along
the side of his ship and observe its position. From a large
warehouse just east of the spot where the *Verona* was land-
ing, a group of armed men moved quietly out onto the dock.
Others appeared from a smaller warehouse to the south.

Sheriff McRae stepped forward, shifted his belt until the
holster hung squarely in front, and held up one hand for
silence.

"Who's your leader?" he demanded.

The Wobblies shouted that they had no leader—that they
were all leaders. The I.W.W. creed denied the existence of
leaders and followers within the organization.

"Well, you can't land here," the Sheriff warned, and he
was answered by shouts and protests and catcalls from the
ship:

"It's a free country, ain't it?" "Damn you! We're citizens just the same as you are, and you got no right to stop us!"

The youthful Wobbly on the flagpole waved toward the crowd. Witnesses could not agree, later, whether he waved a red flag in a gesture of defiance, or whether he waved his cap in a gesture of greeting.

From somewhere a single shot echoed across the water. Whether it came from the ship or from the shore became equally confused amid the later and often-contradicting testimony of witnesses.

For one brief instant after that first shot, the entire tableau seemed frozen, and then it erupted into one seething, brawling, frightening mass of roaring hell. A volley of shots rang out almost in unison. The young Wobbly on the flagpole winced and crumpled and began sliding downward, and then his body convulsed wildly under the impact of additional bullets. He seemed to push himself away from the pole with one violent convulsion as he was falling, and his lifeless body landed with a sickening thud on the deck. Passengers who had stood huddled together on the forward deck staggered and fell, and struggled to pull themselves across the deck which was already becoming slippery with blood. Bodies lurched wildly under the impact of bullets, and men screamed, cursed and groaned.

The confusion aboard the ship was nearly matched by the confusion on the dock. Deputies lay sprawled upon the rough wooden planks; some of them wounded and two of them dying. Sheriff McRae, wounded in the left leg and in the foot, was down on his knees but still firing and attempting to direct his men.

Those on the ship who had escaped the first blast of fire rushed madly toward the lee side of the cabins in search of protection. The sudden shift of its human cargo caused the ship to list sharply. The dead and the wounded rolled crazily across the deck. A section of railing gave way and an unknown number of passengers plummeted off into the water.

Even on this side of the ship the passengers found little safety, for they were now under the direct fire of deputies stationed on the tugboat *Edison*. Splashes of water kicked up about the men struggling in the bay as they became targets, and only one regained the ship.

In the pilot house Captain Wyman sought safety behind an iron safe after a bullet had smashed a spoke from the hardwood pilot wheel directly beneath his hand. Men were swarming all over the ship in panic and confusion, hiding behind lifeboats, scrambling into life jackets, crouching in the main cabin which was exposed to either side by its series of adjacent windows.

The *Verona*, caught in a deadly crossfire between the dock and the tug, echoed the thud of bullets against her side, and her white paint stood flecked and stained with blood. Down in the engine room Engineer Ernest Shellgren thrust the ship into full speed astern and she shivered and shook as her propellers once again kicked up a white froth. The bowline tightened and strained. The dock pilings lurched as the creaking hauser bit into the heavy timbers at the edge of the dock. Someone on the ship took a fire-axe from its wall holder and began edging forward, only to be turned back by a burst of rifle fire. Whether the hauser finally was chopped or whether it parted under the strain or was weakened by someone firing at it remains a moot question, but the *Verona* slowly edged away from the dock.

It had been approximately ten minutes since the bowline had been looped over the bollard, but in those ten minutes seven men had been killed and fifty-one seriously wounded. An unknown number had disappeared into the waters of the Sound never to be seen again—probably men without homes or families to report their disappearance—men without a permanent address. At I.W.W. headquarters in Seattle, six Wobbly cards remained uncalled-for after that fateful Sunday; which is perhaps as close an estimate as any of the number who lost their lives in the waters of Puget Sound.

Of the seven dead, one was Deputy Sheriff Jefferson Beard, and another Lieutenant Charles O. Curtis—the two men who had been standing beside Sheriff McRae as the *Verona* pulled up to the dock, and two of the three closest targets at the time when the shooting started. The other five known dead were I.W.W. members: Hugo Gerlot, Felix Baron, John Looney, Gustav Johnson and Abraham Rabinowitz. Of those seriously wounded, nineteen were members of Sheriff Mc-Rae's vigilantes, and thirty-one were Wobblies. The one remaining wounded man, with seven bullets in his body, was a passenger who had boarded the *Verona* by mistake.

Out on the bay, Captain Wyman intercepted the *Calista* and warned her not to land, and then with his cargo of dead and wounded he began the grim trip back to Seattle. On board the *Verona*, loggers and harvesters and fish-scalers and laborers of many trades attempted, with awkward fingers, to bind up the wounds of their fellows. There were no medical dressings of any kind on board, and they improvised bandages from bits of soiled and torn clothing. By their own admission, they threw overboard such firearms as they had brought with them, and they combed the ship to get rid of every empty cartridge. They steadfastly insisted, however, that only a very few of their number had been armed with pistols and revolvers. Captain Wyman reported that no rifles or shotguns or visible weapons of any kind had been carried aboard the *Verona*, at the time when he was watching and counting all passengers as they boarded.

There was no singing as the ship docked at Seattle. Police stood by with fugitive warrants requested by Everett authorities for the arrest of every passenger aboard, and police and hospital ambulances stood by to take off the dead and the wounded.

Mayor Hi Gill stormed irately through City Hall, and he publicly accused the Everett vigilantes of deliberate and cold-blooded murder. He ordered his police to treat the prisoners with consideration and, in the face of threats of another re-call, he personally distributed tobacco through the cells.

"If the Everett authorities had an ounce of sense," he charged in a newspaper interview, "this tragedy would have never happened. They have handled the situation like a bunch of imbeciles, and they have been trying to unload these men onto Seattle." He accused the Everett authorities of gross inconsistency in permitting political candidates to speak on the streets, and running the I.W.W.'s out of town when they endeavored to mount a soapbox.

"The men who met the I.W.W.'s at the boat were a bunch of cowards," he insisted. "They outnumbered the I.W.W.'s five-to-one, and in spite of this they stood there on the dock and fired into the boat, I.W.W.'s, innocent passengers, and all. McRae and his deputies had no legal right to tell the I.W.W.'s or anyone else that they could not land there."

The *Times*, however, saw it differently. So did the *P.I.* They charged that Hi Gill was morally responsible for the tragedy by permitting the Wobblies to march four-abreast through the streets of Seattle without interference on their way to board the ship, when it was common knowledge that these avowed anarchists were planning an armed invasion of a sister city.

Al Lundin, Prosecuting Attorney of King County, had no personal part in preparing the prosecution against the I.W.W.'s; that would be Snohomish County's responsibility. But he took a grim view of the entire situation, and he offered the Snohomish County Prosecutor the full cooperation of his office. Lieutenant Charles O. Curtis who had been killed on the Everett city dock was the same man who once had been Sergeant Curtis of Company "L"—the man who had been Lundin's second in that memorable boxing match at Fort Worden.

Two hundred and ninety-four Wobblies were arrested upon their arrival in Seattle, but the men who had been aboard the *Calista* were soon released. The remaining men were marched back and forth before a darkened cell where unseen witnesses were allowed to survey them individually and to identify the ones who should be held for trial, and then all but seventy-four were released.

At the I.W.W. hall in Seattle, frantic calls were going out to General Headquarters in Chicago for legal aid in defending the accused men. Attorney Fred H. Moore of Los Angeles, who had gained the acclaim of the Wobblies through his handling of their defense in the earlier free-speech battle in Spokane, accepted the assignment as chief counsel and immediately headed for Seattle.

In Seattle, Judge Donworth received a letter from the General Headquarters of the I.W.W., asking him if he could recommend a Seattle attorney to work closely with Mr. Fred H. Moore of Los Angeles in defending the accused I.W.W. members. The Judge replied that he could recommend only one man who had the courage and the capabilities required:

"He is Mr. George F. Vanderveer, a former Prosecuting Attorney of King County, now engaged in private practice."

CHAPTER TWELVE

Strong in the testimony of my conscience, in the rectitude of my intentions, in the purity of my civic spirit, I want no indulgence, but I demand strict justice.—MARAT

DESPITE THE PLEADINGS of his wife and the urging of his friends that he proceed with caution, George Vanderveer accepted the bid for his services as associate counsel in defense of the accused Wobblies, and he attempted to override the objections of his wife by assuring her that he would be adequately paid.

"Even if they offered you all of the money in the world, it still wouldn't be smart," Ellinor protested. "I don't like to see you get mixed up with people like that."

He smiled at her. "You can't be a criminal attorney and have nothing but Sunday School teachers for clients, Gus."

"But you can't do anything for people like that," she argued. "They'll come to you asking for help when they're in trouble, but they'll turn against you when they don't need you any more. And even if you win the case, every decent person in town will despise you for it. There's an awful lot of public feeling stirred up."

He shook his head. "Someday you're going to realize how wrong you were. This is going to be a big case, important nationally. It's going to be a turning point of my career. Up until now I've had a reputation just here in the Northwest, but by the time this is over I'll be recognized as one of the outstanding criminal lawyers in the entire United States. It just can't miss."

"It's not just a criminal case," she warned him. "It's a political thing, also."

"Political, hell!" he snorted. "It's just a bunch of men in jail who are going to be charged with first degree murder. Actually, it's nothing more and nothing less than another murder trial. That's all it is, and you can't make anything else out of it!" But within two weeks he knew that he had made a mistake in judgment; he knew that the impending trial would not be just another murder trial and that it was beyond his power to limit it to that status.

"I don't understand those men," he conceded to his wife. "They're like a bunch of damned religious fanatics. Even the men in jail don't seem particularly interested in saving their own necks; they're more interested in standing up in court and expounding their Wobbly ideas."

It could be assumed, he told her, that the prosecution would attempt to ring in all kinds of charges against the I.W.W. organization in order to prejudice the judge and the jury, and to play to the press. No doubt an effort would be made to prove that the Wobblies were anarchists, dedicated to the idea of bloody revolution; that their organization was an illegal conspiracy against all levels of government, and that their invasion of Everett had been part of an illegal plot.

"Actually, that's a little bit removed from the basic question of whether these men plotted to kill and actually did kill Curtis and Beard," he explained. "The logical thing to do is to object to all such testimony. That's what I'd do if I had my way. I don't know if I could make it stand up, but I'd fight it every inch of the way. That's the only sensible thing to do."

"But that's not Mr. Moore's idea?" Ellinor asked.

He grinned. "It's not anybody's idea, except mine. Do you know what they're talking about doing, now? They're talking about wrapping up a bunch of their Wobbly pam-

phlets and mailing them to the Prosecutor without any return
address, just to make sure he'll have them in case he wants
to introduce them as evidence."

She stared at him, uncomprehending. "Why would they
do that?"

He shook his head and began pacing the floor. "It's ridiculous! The whole damn thing doesn't even make sense!
My God, Gus, these men are going to be charged with murder
in the first degree! But all they seem to be interested in right
now is getting the prosecution to introduce their pamphlets
as evidence so they can argue the points in open court. I've
never seen a case in my life where everybody is interested in
the arguments, and nobody seems to be particularly interested
in the verdict."

"What about the men who are in jail?" she asked.

He paused in his pacing and looked at her, his eyes puzzled
and thoughtful. "There's something there, Gus, that you can't
just put your finger on. It's hard to explain. It's a sort of
mass hysteria—mob psychology. I don't know how you'd
define it. If you had just one man in jail he'd be worried
sick about saving his own neck; but when you've got seventy-
four of 'em all laughing and singing and sticking together,
nobody seems to give a damn about what's going to happen
to him, personally. It's something you can't quite understand."

He refused to estimate how much or how little the defense
would be jeopardized by permitting and even encouraging
the introduction of I.W.W. literature, but he assured her that
these things would not improve the defense. He continued
his pacing, pounding his fist into the palm of his hand and
scowling darkly at the floor.

"Damn it all!" he exploded suddenly. "I think our best
chance to win this case would be by keeping it anchored
down to the Everett city dock! If they're going to turn it
loose and let it wander all over the seven seas, God only
knows where it will wind up!"

During the weeks that followed, George Vanderveer spent much of his time in the city of Everett. He spent many hours with the men in jail. He prowled the Everett city dock, taking exact measurements and drawing numerous sketches. He interviewed persons who had witnessed the scene from the hillside and he traced numerous rumors of hidden evidence. He spent many days attempting to locate a number of small boys who, reportedly, had combed the dock after the battle searching for souvenirs. He located nine of them, and he took for evidence the wide assortment of empty cartridges they had picked up from the dock and from the water's edge beneath the dock—revolver, rifle, and shotgun shells, rifle clips, and a number of unfired rifle cartridges. He examined the *Verona* with meticulous care, and he gathered voluminous notes about the weather and the tides and the drifting currents of the harbor.

He joined Attorney Fred H. Moore in presenting demands for a change of venue because of alleged prejudice existing in Everett, and he carried on a prolonged battle for the disqualification of Judges Bell and Alston of Snohomish County; demanding and ultimately being granted the assignment of an outside judge. The final skirmish of that battle was fought in the office of the Governor, in Olympia; and it ended with Governor Lister's selection of Judge J. T. Ronald of King County to hear the case.

On March 5, 1917, exactly four months after the battle and the bloodshed at the Everett city dock, Thomas H. Tracy was placed on trial in the King County Courthouse in Seattle, charged with murder in the first degree. He was the first of the seventy-four Wobblies to be brought to trial and he was accused, specifically, of "having assisted, counselled, aided and abetted and encouraged some unknown person to kill Jefferson Beard on the fifth of November, 1916."

The prosecution disclaimed any attempt to prove that Tracy had fired the particular bullet that had struck and mor-

tally wounded Jefferson Beard. It conceded that Tracy probably had not fired that particular bullet; but that he had fired
the first, or one of the first shots fired from the steamer *Verona*. The course of the bullet that killed Jefferson Beard
had followed a downward angle through the body and apparently had been fired from the hurricane deck of the steamer,
the prosecution explained. It promised to produce a succession of witnesses who had seen and recognized Tracy firing
from an open window on the main deck. Under the law, it
would be unnecessary to prove who had fired the fatal bullet.
All who had participated in the alleged plot would stand
equally guilty, if convicted.

Prosecuting Attorney Lloyd Black of Snohomish County,
in his opening statement, charged that an I.W.W. committee
had threatened the invasion of Everett to flood its jails and to
tie up and overwhelm its court machinery; that I.W.W.
members had threatened to burn the city and that a number
of fires of mysterious origin had followed the threat. He
charged that Mayor Merrill of Everett, Sheriff McRae of
Snohomish County, and other peace officers had received
anonymous letters threatening them with death; and he
charged that the tragedy at the Everett city dock had begun
with a fusillade from the decks of the *Verona*, fired without
warning—wounding Sheriff McRae, mowing down the two
men on either side of him, wounding and dispersing approximately one hundred and forty regular and special deputies of
Snohomish County who had been assembled to maintain law
and order, and about half of whom were unarmed.

As anticipated by the defense, he also charged that the
I.W.W. organization was an unlawful conspiracy designed to
effect an absolute revolution in society and in government,
"not by organization as the labor unions hope to get higher
wages, not to get into effect their theory of society by the
ballot, as the Socialists hope, but that they expressly state that
the election of a Socialist President will accomplish no good,
and that sabotage should be employed against government

ownership as well as against private production, so that directly they might put into effect their theories of government and society."

The charges of the prosecution screamed from headlines across the nation, but at the defense table in Judge Ronald's courtroom on the fourth floor of the King County Courthouse, there was little pessimism. A special table had been installed in the courtroom to accommodate the unprecedented number of reporters representing the various wire services, metropolitan newspapers from all over the country, national magazines, and a wide variety of labor papers of local and national circulation. As a number of reporters converged on the defense table at the conclusion of the first day's hearing, Attorney Moore smiled confidently. He reminded the reporters that they shouldn't start predicting the final score, when his team hadn't yet had its first turn at bat.

The defense declined to make an opening statement, reserving that privilege until the conclusion of the prosecution's case. Attorney Moore and the I.W.W. defense committee, wise in the ways of propaganda, chose not to scatter their fire. Public opinion swings like a pendulum, they assured each other. "The farther we let them push it off center to start with, the easier it will be to swing it back our way later on."

The story that streamed from the courtroom to the headlines was largely the prosecution's story, in the opening days of the trial. Witness after witness identified Tracy as the man seen firing a revolver from an open window on the main deck of the *Verona*. Without defense objection, the prosecution offered into evidence a copy of the I.W.W. constitution and by-laws, a number of I.W.W. pamphlets and booklets, and the Joe Hill Memorial Edition of the I.W.W. Song Book, while Prosecuting Attorney Black and his associates built up their picture of a vast, illegal conspiracy.

There were occasions, however, when the prosecution's case was jarred by Vanderveer's cross-examination of wit-

nesses. This was his specialty, and during the opening phase
of the long trial, Vanderveer represented the defense almost
single-handed. Chief Counsel Fred Moore and the other defense attorneys could be seen, occasionally, engaged in whispered conversations; but generally they were content to leave
this part of the battle to a man who was acknowledged to be
a master of this art. With the prosecution planning its own
strategy, there was little opportunity at this point to steer the
course of battle away from the charge of first degree murder
and to open up the involved issues of the class struggle. Attorney Moore was content to bide his time.

. Owen Clay, a special deputy who had been injured during
the battle on the Everett city dock, was called by the prosecution to describe the scene as he had witnessed it. He told
of being wounded in the right arm at the outset of the firing,
and he explained that he had flung himself around the corner
of the ticket office to get out of the line of fire. There, with
his right hand useless, he had taken his revolver in his left
hand and fired blindly around the corner in the general direction of the ship.

On cross-examination, Vanderveer fired two questions at
the witness, from close range:

"Who shot Jeff Beard in the right breast?"

The witness shook his head. "I don't know."

"Did *you* do it?" Vanderveer thundered.

Once again the witness shook his head, and then ran a hand
across his eyes. "I don't know," he said weakly. To nearly
everyone in the courtroom that simple, agonized answer
hinted of sleepless nights and taunting uncertainties, following
those few desperate moments of irrational behavior when he
had fired blindly around the corner of a wooden building.

George Vanderveer glanced significantly toward the jury,
nodded his head, and then turned away. "That's all." But the
first great shadow of a reasonable doubt had begun to spread
across the carefully prepared case of the prosecution.

Mayor D. D. Merrill of Everett was called to the stand by

the prosecution to tell of anonymous letters he had received, threatening his life; and to tell of the fire loss in Everett since the I.W.W. threat to burn and pillage the city. He estimated a fire loss of $100,000 during the latter part of 1916.

By adroit cross-examination, Vanderveer succeeded in getting Mayor Merrill to name Everett's Fire Chief, W. C. Carroll, as the city's most reliable authority on the subject of fires. He then offered into evidence an official report of Everett's Fire Chief, and he called the jury's attention to the fact that the year 1916 had produced fewer fires than any previous year in Everett's civic history; and that of these, only four were of incendiary origin. He demanded that the Mayor state whether, of his own knowledge, the incendiary fires had not been set by certain Everett officials in order to turn public opinion against the I.W.W. members, and he pointed out that the incendiary fires all had been discovered and extinguished promptly—a coincidence hardly to be expected if the fires had been set by men earnestly intent upon causing destruction. The allegations were promptly denied, and strenuous objections came from the prosecution; but the seeds of a nagging thought had been planted in the minds of jurymen.

There was an interruption in the presentation of the prosecution's case, following the testimony of Mayor Merrill. George Vanderveer asked for a court recess in order that he might appear in behalf of Mayor Hi Gill in a separate case being heard in Federal court. Judge Ronald granted the request and then he, too, moved on to Federal court to sit beside the court as an honored guest while Vanderveer assumed the unaccustomed role of a witness, and a possible defendant in a later action.

Logan Billingsley's earlier charges that he had paid money for protection in his bootlegging operations had touched off a chain reaction which had brought a grand jury indictment against Mayor Hi Gill, Police Chief Charles L. Beckingham, King County Sheriff Robert T. Hodge, and a number of

others including the Billingsleys—but not including George
Vanderveer.

Certain correspondence copied in the indictment was addressed to the Jessie Moore Hunt Company of San Francisco,
California, and signed by one "Joe Bush." It referred
obliquely to "Old Boss," and the task of the prosecution was
to convince the jury that "Joe Bush" was, in reality, Logan
Billingsley; and that "Old Boss" was none other than Mayor
Hi Gill.

Mayor Gill's actions in distributing tobacco to the Wobbly
prisoners in the King County jail had in no way endeared
him to the voting public, and his now-revealed association
with the Billingsley brothers came as a sobering shock to his
reformist backers. Petitions for his recall were already circu-
lating through the streets.

On the witness stand in Federal court, Vanderveer spoke
quietly, earnestly, and at considerable length. He was not on
trial, but he knew that he was under suspicion, and subject to
possible indictment because of his close association with the
Billingsley brothers during the course of their illegal operations.

He welcomed the opportunity to deny that his association
with the Billingsleys had been anything but an entirely proper
relationship between a lawyer and his clients. He denied any
financial interest in the activities of his clients and he offered
conclusive proof that his fees had been moderate and in ratio
to professional services rendered. He insisted that a lawyer,
by the nature of his relationship to his client, held an inviolate
trust and that he had no legal or moral right to make public
any information provided him in confidence by his client. He
answered questions readily, dispassionately, and with apparent
honesty; and by the time he stepped down from the stand he
had the respect of every person in the courtroom. Vanderveer was dismissed as a witness, and he was never indicted.
Mayor Hi Gill was acquitted, and the petitions on the street
slowly disappeared while still lacking sufficient signatures for

action. Legally, Hi Gill was innocent; but politically he was dead. Police Chief Beckingham and Sheriff Hodge were acquitted also.

Vanderveer returned to Judge Ronald's courtroom as an attorney for the defense. Repeatedly in his cross-examination of witnesses, he inquired as to the position of the *Verona* at the time of the shooting, and of the location of the witness upon the dock. There was almost unanimous agreement that the *Verona* lay with her stern jutting out into the harbor, and with her bowline fastened to the wharf.

The purpose of Vanderveer's persistent questioning about the position of the *Verona* in the water became evident toward the close of the prosecution's case, when he lined up a scale model of the *Verona* before a scale model of the dock, and demanded to know how Tom Tracy could have been seen in the position described by the identifying witnesses. The curved contour of the ship and the regular spacing of the window casings on the main deck combined to present a solid screen to obscure any man from view if he had been in the position repeatedly described by the parade of prosecution witnesses!

It is inevitable that amid any scene of disorganized action and wild confusion, there will be discrepancies among the honest report of witnesses. There had been such confusion among witnesses early in the trial, when they had repeatedly contradicted each other regarding the actions of Sheriff Mc-Rae just prior to the shooting. One witness had described the Sheriff as standing with his right hand raised and his left hand resting near the butt of his gun in a hip holster. Another witness, on cross-examination, had insisted that the Sheriff had raised his left hand, and that it was his right hand that had rested on the holster. Yet another had testified that to the best of his recollection, the Sheriff had held both hands aloft, and then brought them both down together.

Such contradictions as to details reasonably could be expected from any group of witnesses under similar circumstances; and yet as each contradiction had appeared in court, Vanderveer had smiled and nodded significantly toward the jury. It was an eloquent and meaningful gesture and the prosecution, no doubt, had smarted under the skillful technique which slowly was impugning the veracity and the accuracy of witness after witness.

There is no real evidence that the prosecution coached its witnesses in advance to agree upon the approximate position of Tom Tracy aboard the ship, but it is significant that upon this point there was no contradiction. The establishment of this point was vital to the prosecution, and time after time the witnesses placed Tom Tracy in the same spot, firing from the open window on the main deck . . . and not until the position was irrefutably established by the careful compounding of testimony did Vanderveer call the jury's attention to the fact that all of these witnesses had sworn under oath to something that was a physical impossibility.

It was a triumphant blow as the prosecution was completing its case, and Tom Tracy whispered audibly to his attorneys: "As far as I'm concerned, you could let the case go to the jury right now!"

However, Chief Counsel Fred Moore and the I.W.W. strategy committee undoubtedly would have been quite unhappy to have the case end at that point. Up until now, the prosecution had been calling all of the plays and the defense had quietly awaited its turn. Newspapers all over the nation had carried the prosecution's anti-I.W.W. arguments on the front page, under glaring headlines. The only points the defense had made to date had been those which Vanderveer had been able to sneak in while cross-examining the State's own witnesses. Starting the following Monday morning, the defense would have its say. It could present its arguments, deferred from the opening of the trial, and it could call its own witnesses; and the nation would begin to hear the other side of the story.

There was, however, one point that had not been consid-

ered by the strategy committee: Fate, by a bit of unique timing, chose to upset all of the carefully prepared plans.

On Monday morning, April 2, George Vanderveer stood
in Judge Ronald's court and opened the case for the defense.
He reviewed the evidence presented by the prosecution, and
he charged that it had failed to produce any evidence of a
conspiracy, any evidence that the defendant had been a party
to a conspiracy, or evidence that the defendant had been directly involved in causing the death of Jefferson Beard.

At approximately the same hour, on the same day, President
Wilson was addressing a joint session of Congress, requesting
that Congress declare a state of war existing between the
United States and the German Empire.

For the first time since the trial started, the jostling crowds
no longer filled the corridors of the King County Courthouse.
For the first time, there were empty chairs at the large table
reserved for the press; and empty seats in the back of the
small courtroom. For the first time there was no room on the
first page of even local newspapers for the story of the dramatic trial.

The case for the defense wasted little time in wading into
the propaganda field. Its first witness was Herbert Mahler,
Secretary of the I.W.W. in Seattle, who reviewed the events
in Everett leading up to November fifth, and who explained
the ideas and the ideals of the I.W.W. in combatting "the
atrocities of the lumber barons."

It was but a warm-up for the appearance of the second
witness, James P. Thompson, one of the intellectuals identified with the I.W.W. movement, who was called in to explain
the various pamphlets and documents that had been submitted
by the prosecution. He led off by reading the I.W.W. preamble: "The working class and the employing class have
nothing in common. There can be no peace so long as hunger
and want are found among millions of the working people
and the few, who make up the employing class, have all the
good things of life. . . ."

He launched into a discussion of the history of trade unions in America. Overriding the objections of the prosecution, he delivered a fiery oration on the subject of free speech; branched out into a discussion of economic distribution, explained the meaning of industrial democracy, and he wound up some two days later analyzing the cause of war and explaining that the I.W.W. was dedicated to universal peace, prosperity and equality.

Thompson spoke fluently and earnestly. He was guided by questions from Attorney Moore, who ran legal interference in blocking out the prosecution's frequent objections by pointing out that the various documents and pamphlets and topics under discussion had been introduced by the State.

From a propaganda standpoint it was a masterful oration, but the avenues of distribution had broken down completely. Judge Ronald's courtroom had become a nearly deserted sideshow while the attention of the world was focused upon events at the national capital. The Senate and the House of Representatives were debating the issue of declaring war and attending to the technicalities involved. The nation was shifting to a wartime footing. Representatives from a number of metropolitan newspapers were hurrying home to new assignments. But on the fourth floor of the King County Courthouse, the case droned on.

During much of this phase of the trial, Vanderveer remained seated at the table reserved for defense counsel and peered endlessly through his notes. The Wobbly strategy in court was based on a two-platoon system, using Moore on the offense, to spread the I.W.W. philosophy, and using Vanderveer on the defense, to rip apart the State's charges of first degree murder. Temporarily, Vanderveer was on the side lines.

On Wednesday, April 18, the jury was transported to the Everett city dock. The steamer *Verona* was tied with her bowline while her stern was swung out into the harbor in approximately the same position she had held on that bloody

Sunday more than five months earlier. Jury members were escorted to the various spots where witnesses claimed to have seen Tom Tracy shooting from an open window on the main deck, and each in turn was permitted to verify the claim that Vanderveer had made in court: the curved contour of the ship and the angle from the dock would have made it impossible for Tom Tracy to be seen in the position described.

The prosecution had presented a succession of witnesses claiming that the first shots had come from the men aboard the *Verona*. The defense now produced its witnesses in equal number, claiming that the first shots had come from the men on the dock.

Several defense witnesses, I.W.W. members who had been on the *Verona*, acknowledged that they had carried loaded revolvers on the way to Everett, and that they had thrown the weapons overboard on the return trip to Seattle. Under questioning, each explained that he had been bruised and beaten on previous occasions when he had visited Everett unarmed.

Questioned by the defense as to why he had carried a gun on the fifth of November, James Francis Billings replied: "I took it for my own personal benefit. I didn't intend to let anybody beat me up like I was beaten on October thirtieth, in the condition I was in. I was in bad condition at the time."

The defense attorneys all through the trial had insinuated to the jury that powerful lumber interests were pushing the prosecution of the case, that officials of Snohomish County had been unduly influenced by the wealthy lumber operators, and that the entire courtroom drama was part of a heavily financed plot to thwart the demands of organized labor in Everett.

In a sudden and daring move, Vanderveer called Attorney H. D. Cooley to the stand—associate counsel for the prosecution. As soon as the witness had been sworn in, Vanderveer stood spread-legged before him and after a quick glance at the jury, asked significantly: "By whom are you employed in this case, Mr. Cooley?"

"Objected to as immaterial!" The protest came from counsel for the State as if by reflex action. With the objection sustained by the court, Vanderveer shrugged his heavy shoulders in a helpless gesture and once again turned to the jury to nod his head as if in mutual understanding.

Had the prosecution chosen to permit Mr. Cooley to answer the question, he could have explained that he had been employed by the County Commissioners of Snohomish County to assist Prosecuting Attorney Black on this particular case, and such an answer could have contributed little to either side. By its prompt protest and its refusal to permit the question to be answered, the prosecution left the jury with ugly doubts which could hardly be wiped away, regardless of any instructions from the court. Vanderveer had gambled on that immediate protest, and he had won the gamble.

Years later, in his defense of another action, Vanderveer found himself the victim of somewhat similar strategy employed by opposing counsel and his indignation was extreme. Before the court and in front of the jury, he upbraided the opposing counsel with eloquent rebuke—and undoubtedly he erased any advantage the opposition had hoped to gain, and turned it to his own favor.

He objected to a question propounded by opposing counsel, and his objection was sustained by the court; but Vanderveer was not content with this. He charged that an improper question had been asked, for the sole intent of deceiving the jury, and that the action of opposing counsel was venal. He objected to opposing counsel standing before the jury with a formal-looking paper in his hand which had not been offered into evidence. By his improper question, opposing counsel had intimated that the paper contained information harmful to Vanderveer's client.

"The court says that this paper has not been offered into evidence and therefore there is nothing before the court to pass upon," Vanderveer protested, "but I say this paper *was* introduced into evidence! Everything that goes on in this courtroom that the jury can see or hear or smell is evidence! Can the sight of that formal-looking paper be removed from the minds of the jurors who saw it? Can a bell be unrung, so that the hearing of the listener is operated upon—and a part of his memory removed forever from his mind? The mere record of the evidence is what the court passes upon, but the actual evidence is what a jury comprehends! That is why counsel's act was so venal; he was introducing into actual evidence something that he could not introduce into legal evidence!"

There can be little doubt that in his defense of Thomas H. Tracy, Vanderveer was ringing many bells which he knew could never be unrung; and that in his significant glances toward the jury, he was submitting into evidence many things which would never appear in the written record of the trial.

Apparently impressed by the manner in which Vanderveer had so often upset the prosecution's case through his relentless and often savage cross-examination, Prosecuting Attorney Black attempted frequent cross-examination of defense witnesses. However, he was a young man who had assumed his first term of office shortly before the case had come to trial. Later, he was to become a respected Federal court judge, but at that time he lacked Vanderveer's experience and mastery of trial technique; and many of his efforts backfired with devastating effect.

In his cross-examination of one of the men who had cleaned up the *Verona* after her arrival in Seattle, Black attempted to force the man to admit that he had found empty cartridges or evidence of other weapons aboard the ship. Failing to get anywhere with his specific questions, he finally asked in desperation: "Didn't you pick up anything at all from the deck?"

The witness nodded, and a horrified gasp came from the jury box as he answered: "I picked up an eye. A man's eye."

At another point, striving to shoulder the tremendous job that had been thrust upon him, the young Prosecutor asked a defense witness to recall any conversations he had heard aboard the ship on the way to Everett. "What were they talking about—or not talking about?" he demanded, but his question was interrupted by a comment from the bench:

"There might be two or three million things they were not talking about."

For nearly nine weeks the case droned on; dramatic and sensational at times; dreary and monotonous at others.

In his arguments, Prosecutor Black offered to the jury an apology for his youth and his lack of courtroom experience. He called attention to the great amount of conflicting testimony that had been presented during the trial, and he stressed the fact that prosecution witnesses had been substantial, respected members of society—men with jobs, and homes, and reputations for honesty and integrity. He described the I.W.W. witnesses for the defense as "men—some of them boys—flitting here and there from job to job, with never more than a dollar or two in their pockets." The jury would be safe, he assured them, in accepting the statements of the good, substantial prosecution witnesses as being the truth; and in discarding as falsehood most of the claims of the irresponsible, unstable I.W.W. witnesses presented by the defense.

He admitted that mistakes had been made by law enforcement officers in Everett prior to November fifth, but these things, he pointed out, were beyond the scope of the present trial and served only to prove the State's charges—that the I.W.W. members had converged on Everett in great numbers; many of them armed and seeking revenge for real or fancied grievances of the past—thus proving beyond doubt that they were the aggressors. Tom Tracy, he charged, was one of the instigators of the plot, having greatly exaggerated the minor disturbances Everett had experienced prior to November fifth, and purposely inflaming these misguided men to irrational action which ended in appalling tragedy. He repeated the charge that Tracy had been seen by a number of reliable witnesses; and he pointed out that witnesses, at such a time as that, don't stop to measure the angle of a boat in the water and all of that sort of thing. The witnesses might have forgotten exactly where they were standing, he conceded, or they might be mistaken about the position of the ship, but they were not mistaken in their identification of Tom Tracy. "If there is anything in the world that would impress itself into the memory and recollection of a man it is the remembrance of a face filled with venomous hatred, the eyes shooting daggers at you while he is gazing at you over the muzzle of a gun—and you are not going to forget that!"

He demanded that Tom Tracy be found guilty of murder in the first degree.

In presenting the closing arguments for the defense, Vanderveer led off with a simple charge to the jury: "We do not ask in this case for mercy; we do not ask for sympathy, but it is essential—absolutely essential—that we have cold, stern justice."

He reviewed the history of Everett's trouble with the I.W.W. He reminded the jury that the Sheriff's deputies had begun by taking the Wobblies one or two at a time, and beating and abusing them—in violation of all Constitutional law. Later, they had taken them five or six at a time; then eighteen, and finally they had taken forty-one and beaten them unmercifully at Beverly Park. He paused and wiped at his brow, and when he spoke again his voice was calm and deliberate but rising toward a crescendo as he spoke:

"But I ask you, would you believe it possible that they could take two hundred or three hundred people in broad daylight and do to them what had been done to the others? Yet the evidence in this case shows convincingly and conclusively they intended to do substantially that thing. They intended to run those men into a warehouse; they didn't intend to let one of them get away. And had they gotten them

COUNSEL FOR THE DAMNED

208

into that warehouse you don't know and I don't know—nobody knows—what would have happened!"

Why else, he asked, had the mass of deputies remained hidden in the warehouse until the *Verona* had docked? Why else had Sheriff McRae waited until the bowline had been made fast? Why else had one of the deputies admitted, in court, that he had fired repeatedly at a man aboard the ship who was striving to get that line loose from the bollard?

He reminded the jurors that they had stood on the dock at Everett and had seen that it would have been impossible for a number of the State's witnesses to see Tom Tracy in the position which they, under oath, had sworn they had seen him; and he charged that many of the State's witnesses, in good faith or in bad faith, had sworn to numerous things they had not seen at all.

Attorney Fred Moore concluded the defense's case with a long and eloquent plea for social justice. He reviewed the long struggle of man's climb from serfdom and slavery.

"Your verdict means much," he reminded the jury. "The wires tonight will carry the word all over this land, into Australia, New Zealand, and throughout the world. Your verdict means much to the workers, their mothers, their children, who are interested in this great struggle. We are not in this courtroom as the representatives of one person, two persons or three persons; our clients run into five or six hundred thousand. We are here as the mouthpiece of the workers of America, organized and unorganized, and they are all behind our voices."

It was shortly before noon, May fourth, when the jury retired.

Twenty-two hours later Judge Ronald hastened to his courtroom upon receiving word that the jury had reached a verdict. The word swept through the city and all up and down Skid Road. By nine o'clock in the morning the corridors of the Courthouse were jammed solid and the courtroom was packed to capacity. A hush of expectancy fell over the room as the jury members filed in and stood before the seats they had occupied for two months to the day.

The foreman of the jury, James R. Williams, stood frowning at a piece of paper in his hand as he answered the preliminary questions of the Judge and then, with a quick glance toward the defendant, he passed the paper to the waiting bailiff. The clerk after getting it back from the court, read it out loud:

"We, the jury, find the defendant, Thomas H. Tracy, not guilty!"

CHAPTER THIRTEEN

So many worlds, so much to do, so little done, such things to be.
—TENNYSON

To FINANCE THE DEFENSE of Thomas H. Tracy, the Wobblies had carried on a national fund-raising campaign seeking contributions from individual I.W.W. members and locals from coast to coast. Wobbly speakers had poured forth from Seattle to address meetings all over the country; to recite the Wobbly version of the "Everett Massacre," to enlist public sympathy, and to take up contributions for the defense. In Seattle they had sponsored a series of dances, picnics, prize fights, theatrical benefits and other entertainments to raise money. Local unions of the American Federation of Labor had been solicited for funds, and many had contributed. Thousands of embossed imitation-leather membership-card-holders had been sold to I.W.W. members as souvenirs of Everett's Bloody Sunday and memorials to the "martyred dead."

Through these combined efforts the Wobblies had raised a total of $37,835.84. All but five hundred dollars of it had been poured into the defense of Thomas H. Tracy, and the remaining dollars had been designated for a special fund to benefit three of the most seriously wounded Wobblies who had been aboard the *Verona*.

On the evening of May fifth there was wild jubilation but little cash on hand at the I.W.W. headquarters in Seattle. The

Wobblies had won the most sensational and most widely publicized case in their short but dramatic history, and victory celebrations were held at I.W.W. halls all over the country. Spontaneous parades got under way in some of the major cities; and in hobo jungles along the railroad tracks there were songs by jubilant bindlestiffs—songs from the Little Red Song Book which had become the hymnal of Wobbly fervor.

In Seattle, I.W.W. members swarmed in from the hills and the fields and the logging camps and the canneries to join in the celebration, and to greet Tom Tracy and the other prisoners when they were released from jail. However, the jail doors remained closed and the Seattle celebration began to wane in the absence of the intended guests of honor. A sobering rumor swept along Skid Road.

The trial of Thomas H. Tracy had been the trial of one man, on one charge of murder. The jury had found him not guilty of the murder of Jefferson Beard, but the State, if it cared to do so, could now charge him with the murder of Charles O. Curtis, and another lengthy trial would begin. Each of the remaining seventy-three men in jail could be brought to trial . . . and where would the Wobblies get the money to defend them? Could they go back to their members and ask a duplication of the original contributions? Could they show up time after time asking sympathy and financial help from other labor organizations? Could they expect even the most loyal Wobbly to buy seventy-four embossed membership cardholders?

A similar rumor swept down from Everett: the prosecution was determined to give the Wobblies a dose of their own medicine, and do precisely what the I.W.W. had done in Spokane some seven years earlier. This time it would be the State demanding separate trials for all of the accused, while the Wobblies would have to turn in every dollar they could collect, abandon rent payments on their halls and publication

of their literature—or abandon their fellow members, still in
jail.

At I.W.W. headquarters in Seattle, all of the ramifications
were being considered. If the remaining prisoners were unable to hire defense attorneys, the court would be obliged to
appoint counsel for them; but without men like Fred Moore
and George Vanderveer, could an acquittal be expected?
Prosecution witnesses, for the most part, were citizens of
Everett who maintained permanent homes and who would
be available to testify during the months ahead. Many of the
defense witnesses were itinerant workers who could no longer
remain in Seattle. They had to be off to follow the harvests
and the seasons—thinning lettuce in California, shearing sheep
in Utah, picking cotton in the deep South, harvesting apples
in eastern Washington. There could be no assurance that a
second trial would repeat the verdict of the first. Never again
would the prosecution wander into the traps which Vanderveer had sprung with such telling effect.

Attorney Fred Moore might be prevailed upon to remain
in Seattle for another trial, despite the fact that he had labor
cases in California awaiting his return. There were grave
doubts among the Wobblies, however, that George Vanderveer would accept a second assignment without the promise
of payment. In the lengthy trial of Tom Tracy he had received something less than a hundred dollars a week; and during his testimony in Federal court he had reviewed his
personal finances and acknowledged that he was heavily in
debt.

There was a general feeling among the Wobblies that Vanderveer's sympathy for the "cause" was open to serious question. He had argued vehemently against making Tracy's trial
a propaganda trial. At one time when he was unable to draw
some needed money from the defense fund because of involved complications with the defense committee, he had
demanded to know how in hell the I.W.W. ever expected to
run American industry when it couldn't even handle its own

affairs with any slight resemblance to intelligent operation. One of the Wobbly journalists, Walker C. Smith, expressed it subtly and politely by writing: "It was only with evident effort that Attorney Vanderveer kept on the unfamiliar ground of the class struggle, his natural tendencies being to try the case as a defense of a pure and simple murder charge."

The gathering gloom along Skid Road dispersed suddenly and unexpectedly, after it had spent several days building up. All of the accused Wobblies were released from jail, and talk of a second trial died instantly. The liberated prisoners assembled at the I.W.W. hall in Seattle and then, in a body, they visited the Mount Pleasant cemetery to view the graves of their dead compatriots.

Attorney Fred Moore departed for Los Angeles, and two days later George Vanderveer returned to his home on Highland Avenue. His clothes were soiled and an ugly bruise showed on the side of his jaw. His face was haggard and his eyes were bloodshot. He smelled of alcohol, and he brushed aside the anxious questions of his wife who had spent several days telephoning all over Seattle to locate him.

"Don't ask questions, Gus," he told her. "Just forget it. Forget it ever happened." He trudged wearily toward the bedroom and sank into bed.

The next morning at the breakfast table he was humble and contrite. "Don't ask me where I've been because I don't even know. I've never been that drunk before in my life, and I hope I never am again."

For nearly two hours he sat at the breakfast table talking earnestly, trying to tell her how he felt. He hadn't started out to celebrate the victory, he assured her. He had been pleased with the verdict, naturally, but there was far more to it than that.

The Wobblies, he insisted, were largely the victims of circumstance—men who had been maligned by false accusations. Most of them were decent and loyal and honest men under the hard calluses of abuse and, like Felix Crane whom he had defended earlier, they could not help being what they were. The world hadn't given them any other chance.

"My God, Gus," he almost sobbed, "you ought to see how those men live! You ought to see some of the flophouses on Skid Road. When you force people to live like that, you're just asking for trouble! There's bound to come the day when they'll rise up and say to hell with it! It's happened all through history, since time began."

He reviewed some of the evidence of the trial, and he charged that the Everett authorities had doubled and trebled the threat of revolution in the United States by taking the law into their own hands; by persecuting an entire class of people, and by handing out punishment without trial. "People wouldn't tolerate that, way back in the thirteenth century," he insisted, "and it's a sure thing they won't tolerate it today. You can't take a bunch of red-blooded men and treat 'em like that, without having all hell break loose. My God, they should know that!"

He told her that in his six months' association with the Wobblies he had come to know them and understand them to a certain extent. "The more they get kicked around, the bigger they grow and the tougher they get!" He explained that I.W.W. membership in the Pacific Northwest had increased steadily since the start of the trouble in Everett. When he had been called into the case there had been two I.W.W. officials under pay in Seattle, and now there were more than twenty of them—busy processing the thousands of applications for I.W.W. membership. Just about the same thing was going on all over the country, the Wobblies had informed him. At the peak of the trial when it was in headlines from coast to coast, the I.W.W. Agricultural Workers Organization had been taking in members at the rate of five thousand a month, all through the South and the Middle West. He insisted that Sheriff McRae and his deputies had done more to swell the rolls of I.W.W. membership and to promote the threat of revolution than had all of the organizers and soapbox orators in Wobbly history.

However, despite his insistence that the Wobblies were the victims of vicious circumstance, it became evident to Ellinor that he was not entirely happy about his courtroom victory, and that he was troubled with grave doubts. Indirectly, in the days that followed, she learned that he had been halted in the corridor shortly after the announcement of the verdict, and had been accused of giving aid and comfort to the enemy in time of war.

"That was a vicious thing for anybody to say," she told him. "After all, the country wasn't at war when you took the case."

He shook his head. "What in God's name is a man supposed to do? What way do you turn, when every way is the wrong way? You can go out and get drunk and forget about it for a few days, but you can't stay drunk forever. What do you do then, Gus? What do you do then?"

For the next few days he spoke to her very little. Usually he came home late from the office and spent his evenings in thoughtful contemplation, playing countless games of solitaire.

It was nearly a week later when he told her that he had decided to join the Army. He was just a few months short of being forty-two years old, which was above the most desirable age for recruits without military training; and yet he pointed out that he was in excellent physical condition and that he was confident that he could outfight, outmarch and outshoot most of the younger men.

"I've thought it all over very carefully," he told her. "The only thing that worries me is how you and Barbara will get along. There won't be much money and we're not in very good shape. Probably you'll have to go stay with your mother."

His announcement did not come as a complete surprise to Ellinor. She, too, had done considerable thinking during the quiet days just past, and she had guessed her husband's thoughts as he sat with his endless games of solitaire. "I knew that was coming," she said, simply.

He studied her quizically. "I've got to do it, Gus. It's the only way." He told her about the Wobblies seeking legal help who now besieged his office every day, because he had helped to bring about the acquittal of Tom Tracy and because few other attorneys would represent them. He assured her that he would find life simple in the front line trenches, compared to the struggle he had been going through in recent days.

"Just think how simple it would be! You're in a trench here, and the Huns are in a trench over there. You try to shoot them, and they try to shoot you—and that's all there is to it. You're not out in the middle of no-man's-land, wondering which side you ought to be on. And if you go over the top and wipe out a machine-gun nest, your buddies don't tap you on the shoulder and accuse you of giving aid and comfort to the enemy. You don't wake up in the middle of the night and wonder if you're in the right trench!"

For two days, his plans to enlist formed the main topic of conversation between them. To Ellinor, the whole thought of it was rather terrifying. She knew that they would lose the modest little house which she cherished as the only symbol of security her marriage had produced during eleven turbulent years; and even though it was still heavily mortgaged she could not face the thought of losing it. Her daughter, now five years old, would soon be starting to school and there would be the need for school clothes and shoes and all of the other inevitable expenses involved. Her mother, now retired, had won her hard fight to raise and educate her own children without financial help but it seemed unfair, now, to ask her to take in a grown daughter and a granddaughter. And yet there was little that Ellinor could say to her husband; little that she dared trust herself to say.

However, the days slipped past and he mentioned his enlistment plans less and less. Once again he became deeply absorbed in his law practice. Fearful of starting the chain of thought again, Ellinor avoided asking him any questions about it and she was content to leave the subject closed. Her only real hint came from overhearing his side of a telephone conversation in which, to some friend, he upbraided the government unmercifully and charged that the Army was being run by a bunch of near-sighted nincompoops who would gladly take in a twenty-one-year-old walking cadaver and give him a uniform, but would get picayunish about a man in his forties, and just in the prime of life. She assumed that George's first tentative offer to serve his country had been met with something less than wild jubilation; but never in their years of married life did he discuss it with her and never did she ask him about it. Surely life could hold no deeper chagrin for George Vanderveer than being rejected because of physical condition.

Vanderveer's office, during the summer of 1917, took on a slight resemblance to the I.W.W. headquarters on Skid Road. The outer waiting room frequently was crowded with coarsely dressed men who sat with quiet self-discipline, and eyed with suspicion those better-dressed clients who appeared with diminishing frequency. Bud Cummings had left the firm to join a partnership in New York and to practise his one true love, international law. His departure had left Vanderveer without the influence of a steadying hand which had helped to maintain a reasonable ratio of paying clients.

Individually and in groups, the Wobblies of Skid Road were becoming involved in all manner of brushes with the law, ranging from drunk and disorderly to the inciting of riot; and generally they took their troubles to the already heavily burdened George Vanderveer. Time after time he told them that it would be impossible for him to accept any additional cases for defense, and time after time he relented and took the cases, regardless. Few of the clients were able to pay for his services, either in cash or in barter, but the volume of business was staggering.

The summer of 1917 saw mounting bitterness in the anti-I.W.W. campaign across the nation, and it saw increasing activities on the part of the Wobblies who opposed the war, protested the draft, stepped up the tempo of their strikes, and continually increased their membership. No longer was the Wobbly orator a harassed man on a soapbox, haranguing a handful of men on a Skid Road street corner. Wobbly speakers had moved into the ball parks and the open arenas to address audiences numbered in the hundreds of thousands. Millions of Americans felt they had been betrayed into war after voting for Wilson and expressing a desire to stay out of war.

Thomas J. Mooney, who had been convicted of planting the dynamite which had exploded during San Francisco's Preparedness Day Parade, was sentenced to death by hanging on May 17, less than two weeks after Tom Tracy's acquittal in Seattle. This latest development in the Mooney case touched off turbulent demonstrations throughout the ranks of American labor; and generally, the Wobblies were the most militant of all. The anti-German propaganda in the press was matched, almost inch by inch, by the anti-I.W.W. propaganda; and there could be little doubt that the United States was fighting a war on two fronts. There were repeated charges that the I.W.W. was being financed by funds smuggled into the country by the Kaiser.

On June 26 the first American troops landed in France, while American industry was being hamstrung by strikes. War orders piled up on desks, while mines and factories closed down; and the American people pondered the fate of their armed forces overseas if they should be left without weapons or ammunition or supplies, or adequate ships to meet the increasing demand. Bitterness built up and battle-lines shifted until there was little trace of the original struggle between capital and labor. It had become a personal thing touching nearly every American home.

Copper had become a critical item on the day that war was

declared, but spreading strikes in the copper mines of Arizona had throttled the nation's major source of supply. As usual, the I.W.W. was actively involved in the strikes.

On July 10, approximately seventy I.W.W. strikers from Arizona's United Verde Copper Company mine were rounded up by armed guards and vigilantes. They were placed aboard cattle cars and exported to California with a warning not to set foot in the state again. Word of the maneuver had leaked out, however, and the Wobblies were met at the California border by an armed posse and driven back across the boundary into Arizona. It was an inter-state battle with the disarmed Wobblies trapped between, milling like cattle and seeking some way of escape. At Bisbee, two days later, more than a thousand Wobblies were rounded up and placed aboard cattle cars, but this time no attempt was made to export them to California. The cattle cars were shunted out into the desert, and there the Wobblies were dumped without food or water. Later, they were shifted on to New Mexico.

Frank Little, a Wobbly organizer who had first gained national attention in Spokane, Washington, when he had been arrested while reciting the Declaration of Independence from a soapbox, once again produced headlines. In late July he went to Butte, Montana, to direct the organization of a miners' strike, and to help organize an I.W.W. unit on Anaconda Hill—another important source of American copper.

The crippling strikes in the Butte area had followed a mine tragedy in which nearly two hundred miners had lost their lives. There were wild charges hurled in both directions. The miners charged that the tragedy was due to the company's neglect of safety regulations—that the doomed men had been trapped and burned to death while seeking escape hatches required by law but not installed in the Butte Speculator Mine. The Wobblies, experts at exploitation and dramatization, followed up their natural advantage. They portrayed the picture of trapped miners clawing with bloody fingers at the concrete bulkheads far underground—seeking the steel hatches which would have offered them safety and escape—but which the mineowners had failed to install because, to them, dollars were precious and lives were cheap. The horror of that picture stirred up the already-unstable emotions of the bereaved, and it played upon the fears of all miners' families. The strike spread to Anaconda Hill, and the union demands for a six-dollar-six-hour day in the mines became secondary to the widely publicized demand for increased safety regulations.

Mineowners and company officials accused the Wobblies of moving in—mostly as outsiders—to exploit a tragedy and to hinder the Allied war effort. The dead men could not be brought back to life, they pointed out, but additional American men might be slaughtered by the thousands if the Wobblies were permitted to upset war production, thus leaving American boys on the field of battle without weapons or ammunition. Their arguments helped to build the spreading conviction that strikes in time of war were tantamount to treason—morally, if not legally.

As feeling continued to mount, it centered more and more against Frank Little, Wobbly organizer and a member of the I.W.W. General Executive Board in Chicago. On the night of July 31, he was taken from his hotel room in Butte, tied with a rope, and dragged through the streets behind a speeding automobile. His lifeless body was left hanging by the neck from a railway trestle on the outskirts of town.

On September 5, 1917, agents of the U.S. Department of Justice closed in simultaneously on every I.W.W. hall in the country, seizing office records and files and membership lists. On September 28, indictments were returned against one hundred and sixty-six I.W.W. leaders, including all of those associated with the General Headquarters in Chicago.

Meanwhile, George Vanderveer in Seattle was pondering an urgent plea that he hurry to Chicago to represent the

I.W.W. as chief counsel in the impending trials to be held there.

"What do you think I ought to do?" he asked his wife. He explained that a General Defense Committee was being organized, that pleas for funds were going out to I.W.W. locals, and that he had been offered ten thousand dollars, above expenses, if he would take the case.

"It's going to be a long trial," he conceded, "and it's going to be pretty rough going all the way; but if I could come back to Seattle with ten thousand dollars in my pocket we could pay off the mortgage on the house and clean up most of our old bills."

For two days they discussed the idea and all of its various ramifications, while telegrams continued to pile up at the office, each demanding an immediate reply.

"I can't put it off any longer," he announced at last. "I've got to tell them what I'm going to do, one way or another. What's your final thought, Gus?"

She refused to take the responsibility for the decision. She admitted to him that it would be a glorious thing to climb completely out of debt, but she expressed the fear that the acceptance of such a case might ruin his entire career.

He shook his head. "I'm not worried about that part of it. If you're going to be a criminal lawyer, you can't have clients who always smell like roses." He reminded her, however, that never before in his life had he been influenced to accept a case merely because a nice fat fee had been dangled in front of his nose.

"Before I took the Tom Tracy case I had a chance to look into it, and I took it because I was pretty sure I knew how I could win it. This is like buying a pig in a poke. I'd have to agree to take it, first, and then go back there and look into it afterwards. I don't like to do things that way."

He explained that in accepting the Chicago assignment he would be lining up against the legal strength of the Federal government, and that it would be far different from opposing a Snohomish County prosecuting attorney. "It's not that I'm afraid of their lawyers," he insisted. "I'll face any lawyer in the country if we can meet on even terms—but good God! In a case like that, you're lining up against the men who write the rules and pay the referee!" In time of war, particularly, he told her, the Federal government takes unprecedented powers.

"Then you don't think you ought to accept it?" she asked.

"I'm afraid not."

Her shoulders wilted slightly, but she tried to smile. "It's maybe just as well, anyhow. I hate to see you get mixed up with those men any more than you are now, and we'll get along somehow. We always have."

For a long time he sat studying her, and then his face broke into a grin. "Aw, to hell with it!" he snorted. "We can use that ten thousand dollars just as well as anybody else can, and I've sort of got it coming after all the free work I've done for the local Wobblies this past summer!"

He reached for the telephone, called Western Union, and sent a wire to Chicago saying that he would accept the post. However, he did not send the telegram collect.

"That's one of the handicaps," he told his wife uneasily. "I'll more or less have to finance myself until they get their committee organized and a little money coming in."

CHAPTER FOURTEEN

*I have been accused, Your Honor, of being an enemy of the sol-
dier. I hope I am laying no flattering unction to my soul
when I say that I don't believe the soldier has a more sympathetic friend than I am. If I had my way, there would be
no soldiers*—EUGENE VICTOR DEBS

THE ENTRY OF the United States into the war in Europe
had brought its perplexing problems to the members of
the General Executive Board of the I.W.W. in Chicago. The
emergence of a common enemy overseas had served to weld
many of the rifts in American society. Almost overnight, the
American soldier had become a national hero, and a rising
patriotic fervor swept across the nation.

For approximately a decade the Wobblies had used the
industrial strike as their major weapon. Many of their battles
had been long and bloody and hard fought, with final victory
uncertain. It had been a rough-and-tumble battle between the
employers and workers, with no holds barred. And while it
was true that an entire community might suffer in the region
of a strike and that the deepest economic scars might be borne
by the innocent bystanders, still, the basic lines had been
clearly drawn.

Now, in a nation at war, the old familiar weapon had become so lethal and so devastating as to alarm the men who
had used it in the past. Conflicts between employers and
workers had taken on international significance; and resent-

ments smoldering in a mine shaft in Arizona could affect the fighting on the battlefields of France.

As experts in propaganda and dealers in human passions, the Wobbly leaders could not fail to see the dangers ahead of them. An aroused nation might turn upon them in wrath if I.W.W. strikes interfered with war production, and a ten-year struggle to gain public sympathy could be lost in a few short weeks. Inversely, if they should surrender their right to strike for the duration of the war, they would be left unarmed at the very hour when greater victories appeared in sight, and all of their achievements of the bygone years might be wiped away as they stood defenseless. The more militant and the more impatient members would pull away from an organization that had "gone soft" on the eve of victory, and all of the martyrs to the Wobbly cause would have died in vain. ———

The I.W.W. membership could not be depended upon for solidarity, for each man's loyalty was an individual thing, woven from the total of his own experiences. In recent months, particularly, the expanding Wobbly ranks had taken in many new members who would have to be classified as an unknown quantity. For the first time in its history, the I.W.W. had been able to offer something more than a desperate dream of some distant tomorrow. Agricultural workers in the Midwest had found that life was simpler for those who carried the red card, for a vigilant and sometimes violent picket line had been strung from eastern Missouri to North Dakota, to turn back any migrating non-Wobblies. I.W.W. membership had become an inexpensive type of health insurance for those who attempted to follow the harvests. Brakemen on freight trains generally gazed with disfavor upon those who attempted to ride the rods or who swarmed aboard the empty boxcars, and who did not carry Wobbly cards; and more than one non-Wobbly had been forced to jump from a moving train, or had been left stranded at some isolated prairie junction. Beyond a doubt there had been men who had applied for I.W.W. membership in recent months who had been inspired by motives of convenience rather than devotion to the class struggle.

Older workers, for the most part, were fervent and militant Wobblies dedicated solely to the class struggle and recognizing no other allegiance. They had joined to fight the long battle, and not to share in the crumbs of the first partial victories. I.W.W. membership, to them, was a philosophy, a creed, a dedication—an unwavering goal of life and the key to immortality. To those men, the war in Europe represented little more than a symbol of capitalistic failure and a possibly fatal weakening of the opposition. They demanded an increase in the tempo of the struggle, convinced that the employers would give ground in their fear of losing everything in one vast social and military catastrophe. They did not fear persecution and, apparently, some of them did not fear death.

Even among the older Wobblies, however, there were some who had sons and brothers going into military service, and who placed their allegiance to their country above all. There were men who felt the tingling rebirth of patriotism as Old Glory passed down the street and the stirring music of a military band reached out to touch the soul, for they had been American citizens much longer than they had been Wobblies. There were others who had fled to America ahead of the German sweep across Europe, and whose dedication to the class struggle was diluted by hatreds and fears left over from an earlier day.

Within a week of the United States' entry into the war, it had become impossible to fit the I.W.W. membership into a common mold. Without an actual caucus, it would have been impossible to judge the temper of the rank and file. And yet the hard core of the Wobbly movement courted no compromise, and the General Executive Board in Chicago represented the hard core of the organization. Despite the hazard of arousing public wrath, it was decided to carry on with the program of industrial strikes—and to aim, particularly, at those vulnerable spots where a prolonged strike and stalemate could not be endured by the employers or by the nation. Immediate efforts were made to stem the wrath of the American public and to channel the bitterness back toward the factory-owners and the mineowners, and others of the employing class. The I.W.W. charged that these capitalists had betrayed their country into war and were responsible for sending young men into a senseless slaughter merely for the sake of increasing their sordid profits. It was a bold and desperate effort at counter-propaganda, but it failed to make any substantial impression.

An even more perplexing problem, faced by the General Executive Board, was the matter of the draft. More and more, since the outbreak of the war in Europe, the Wobblies had screamed their anti-war propaganda. It had provided unending ammunition for the Wobbly orators, as they used the European conflict as an object lesson in capitalistic folly. Time after time they had charged that the war was an ill-disguised plot to build up the profits of the munitions-makers, and to thin the ranks of the world's proletariat by letting them kill off one another in wholesale numbers. Regardless of whether the Wobbly orators had influenced others by their arguments, there can be little doubt that they had convinced themselves. Individually and in groups they besieged the Chicago headquarters with demands to know the official I.W.W. stand on the matter of registering for the draft.

In Chicago the board met in emergency session. The executive members knew that they would be damned by their own followers if they recommended a policy of registering for the draft and going off to fight a "capitalistic war." They knew that their organization would be damned by the American public if they endorsed a policy of refusing to register and refusing to fight. Of the two alternatives, they could agree upon neither; and after several days they adjourned without offering any recommendation at all. It was almost unanimously conceded that the I.W.W. held an untenable

COUNSEL FOR THE DAMNED

position with no possible avenue of retreat or escape. Meanwhile, around the country, some of the Wobblies were being drafted. Some of them were hiding out in hobo jungles and waiting from day to day for official instructions. Some of them had registered as conscientious objectors, opposed to war, and others had marched into police headquarters of their respective localities to state their refusal and to demand mass arrest.

The "surprise" raids on the I.W.W. halls all over the country on September fifth had been no surprise at all. Somehow the Wobbly grapevine had tapped the Department of Justice time schedule, so that Wobbly leaders knew not only the date but the approximate hour of the impending raids. In many of the local halls, the executives were ready and waiting, with all of their books in order.

Among the members of the General Executive Board there was a sharp conflict of opinion as to the selection of a defense attorney for the trials that lay ahead. Clarence Darrow was widely conceded to be the best trial lawyer in the United States and he had amply demonstrated his sympathy to the cause of labor. However, George Vanderveer had captured the imagination of many of the Wobblies by his smashing triumph in the Tracy case. There were some lingering questions as to his personal sympathy for the class struggle, but those who had observed him in the courtroom insisted that he was without equal.

The question resolved itself quickly, however, when it was learned that Clarence Darrow would not be available because of his heavy burden of war work at the national capital. He wired his regrets, asked that he not be considered for the assignment, and offered the services of his investigating staff in Chicago. His prompt refusal after the tentative inquiry was followed by an embittered and totally unconfirmed rumor that swept through the Wobbly ranks, charging that Darrow was in Washington helping to tighten the espionage law under which the I.W.W. leaders would be tried.

Herbert Mahler, former Secretary of the Seattle I.W.W. local, was placed in charge of the General Defense Committee and assigned the task of raising funds for the long legal battle ahead. He had rendered conspicuous service in the Everett case, and he promptly set about organizing local defense committees to raise money in every section of the country. However, Mahler and his immediate associates were also picked up by the Federal agents and lodged in the Cook County jail.

The General Defense Committee had determined to make the forthcoming Chicago trial a propaganda trial, and George Vanderveer's first instructions, when he reached Chicago, were to defend the men not as individuals but as disciples of a great cause—to seek not only liberation for the prisoners, but justification in the eyes of their fellow men. The courtroom was to become the sounding board for Wobbly arguments so that the prisoners, when released, would be hailed as national heroes by the great masses of the people who do the world's work and who, belatedly, must be made to realize that in the I.W.W. lay their hope and their salvation. Ideas, not men, would be on trial. Vanderveer had been summoned to Chicago as chief counsel for the defense; but according to the Committee, that was a mere technicality and a misnomer. Propaganda wise, the I.W.W. would remain on the offensive.

The Espionage Act, under which the men were to be tried, had been passed as an emergency measure after the outbreak of the war and was specifically restricted to the duration of hostilities. It was a broad, all-inclusive act, covering sabotage as well as espionage, and like many wartime measures, it had been drawn upon the theory that the security of a nation in time of war is of greater importance than the traditional safeguards of the individual which are recognized in time of peace. Of necessity, however, the crimes charged under the act would require proof of commission after the act had become effective.

At the preliminary hearing each of the accused prisoners

pleaded not guilty and was led back to the Cook County jail, and Vanderveer began his fight to have the court establish bail.

At the time of Vanderveer's arrival in Chicago there was little money available and he was asked to continue to finance himself until such time as the Defense Committee could begin to acquire funds in substantial amounts from the various local committees. There were multitudinous demands for the first small amounts that began dribbling in, but he pointed out that he was not in a position to finance himself and that arrangements would have to be made to meet his expenses from day to day.

The prosecution offered vigorous opposition to all efforts to have the court set bail, insisting that the security of the United States was involved. The prisoners did not help their own cause when, on November seventh, they touched off a wild demonstration within the jail as they heard the first news of Bolshevik revolution in Russia, and taunted their guards with the assurance that this was but the first step in a worldwide upheaval that would liberate the downtrodden masses, destroy the masters, and establish the world's first true democracy. The prosecution assured the court that in due time it would offer conclusive proof that the American I.W.W.'s and the Russian Bolsheviki were directly financed by the Kaiser.

By early spring, 1918, Vanderveer succeeded in getting the court to set bail at thirty thousand dollars for each of the principal prisoners, but the achievement served to undermine his own financial interests for the assets of many sympathizers were promptly signed over to guarantee bail, and all such assets became unavailable to the general defense fund, from which he was to be paid. Exercising its prerogative to the maximum, the court demanded iron-clad guarantees, with the result that approximately one hundred thousand dollars' worth of securities had to be pledged before the guarantees were considered fully met in each individual case. Real and personal property offered as surety, generally was appraised at approximately one fourth of its current market value, and few of the Wobbly sympathizers had any substantial amounts of cash. Many of them pledged everything they owned in order to meet the bail, and they stood helpless in the face of pleas for direct contributions to help carry on the legal fight.

In preparing the defense, Vanderveer was assisted by Attorneys Otto Christensen of Chicago, William Cleary of Arizona, and Caroline Loew of Kansas. At Vanderveer's suggestion, wives and sweethearts of some of the accused men were sent out to work in factories in the Chicago area, to enable them to testify as to hours and wages and working conditions. He insisted that the basic question involved was the right of labor to strike in time of war, while industry was permitted to operate at a profit, and to bargain over prices.

The trial of the accused Wobblies opened on April first, 1918, in the courtroom of Judge Kenesaw Mountain Landis, in Chicago's Federal court. There were other trials pending, within the jurisdiction of other courts; but here in Chicago, the prosecution was aiming for the very heart of the organization. Among the one hundred and one defendants were nearly all of the key men of the national organization, all of the members of the General Executive Board—all of the leaders of an organization that denied that it had any leaders. However, insofar as the press was concerned, one hundred of the men were incidental; it was one man who claimed the attention. Newspapers frequently referred to it as the trial of Bill Haywood—Mr. I.W.W., himself.

Big Bill Haywood, former General Secretary-Treasurer of the Western Federation of Miners, had been selected as the permanent chairman of the first I.W.W. convention in 1905, at the time of its organization, and in the intervening years he had become the most prominent of the I.W.W. leaders. He was a huge man, strangely soft-spoken; blind in one eye and marked by the battles of the years. He was impressive, even in the white marble courtroom with its massive furnishings, and at almost any given hour during the long trial it would have been possible to find several persons within the courtroom sketching his somber countenance.

Judge Landis, a slender man dressed in an ordinary business suit, generally disdained the usual pompous dignity of the court. Much of the time he sat quietly on the bench with his chin in hand, listening to the arguments with apparent interest. At other times he would leave the bench and perch canary-like on the steps of the jury box. Upon his invitation, many of the defendants removed their coats on warm days and lounged languidly in their shirt-sleeves. Upon occasion, snores could be heard as a defendant stretched himself out on a bench and dropped off to sleep during the delivery of monotonous and detailed testimony, but Judge Landis appeared unperturbed. He ordered brass cuspidors placed beside the prisoners' seats when he learned that many of them chewed tobacco, and he requested that persons in the courtroom refrain from rising as he entered or departed. The judge had his own emphatic ideas about everyday democracy.

Jack Reed, an ex-Wobbly newspaper reporter and a Bolshevik sympathizer, conceded: "It takes some human understanding for a judge to fly in the face of judicial ritual as much as that." However, Reed's written description of the Judge was somewhat less than flattering: "Small on the bench sits a wasted man with untidy white hair, an emaciated face in which two burning eyes are set like jewels, parchment skin split by a crack for a mouth; the face of Andrew Jackson, three years dead."

As in the trial of Thomas Tracy, the prosecution charged that the I.W.W. was an illegal conspiracy, dedicated to the overthrow of the United States Government by violence and sabotage; and that I.W.W. members were intent upon abolishing the wage system and destroying the property of private citizens as well as the property of the government.

During the presentation of the prosecution's case, numerous witnesses were called to tell their stories of I.W.W.

sabotage—of spikes driven into saw logs, of copper nails driven into fruit trees to kill off entire orchards—of wanton destruction of many kinds, including widespread arson and the dynamiting of factories and farm buildings.

Vanderveer, on cross-examination, generally was able to rip such testimony apart, forcing witness after witness to concede that he had not seen I.W.W. members actually commit the alleged acts of sabotage and that he did not know, of his own knowledge, exactly who was responsible. Once again Vanderveer brought forth the concession that such acts *could* have been performed by those who were opposed to the I.W.W. and wished to see its members blamed.

The prosecution introduced into evidence a number of I.W.W. pamphlets, including one titled "Sabotage" by Elizabeth Gurley Flynn—a concise little document listing the types of sabotage recommended by anarchists and syndicalists in Europe, while adroitly refraining from any direct recommendations.

Vanderveer, in his turn, reminded the jury that Elizabeth Gurley Flynn's book listed the methods of sabotage recommended in Europe as a matter of historic record, and that it did not recommend or suggest that these methods be used in the United States. He argued that a news reporter may relate the incidents of a murder for the enlightenment of his readers—but it should not be assumed that the reporter is urging his readers to duplicate the crime.

The term *sabotage* had recently been borrowed from the French, and the slow-down strike had not yet been designated as such. In the Wobbly lexicon, all types of slow-down on the job were classified as sabotage. At one point of the trial, Judge Landis asked Jim Rowan, an I.W.W. defendant: "Mr. Rowan, what is sabotage?" The defendant pondered the question for a moment and replied, "Well, I'd say it's giving bum work for bum pay." The prosecution, however, charged that I.W.W. sabotage also included the wanton destruction of property, and there can be little doubt that the parade of prosecution witnesses left its impression upon the jury. Obviously, a man committing such acts of sabotage would not perform them before an audience . . . but should he be permitted to go free and to further endanger a nation at war, merely because of a technicality in the law? And why would the I.W.W. leaders approve the publication and distribution of the "Sabotage" pamphlet if they did not intend to pass along the ideas to members in the field? Why would they go to that expense, merely to distribute information of historic record?

The first really damaging blow against the defense, however, came at the start of Vanderveer's case when Judge Landis refused to permit the introduction of evidence concerning wages and hours and working conditions in American industry.

In the absence of the jury, Vanderveer argued eloquently and passionately for the right to introduce such evidence. He charged that the basic issue of the trial was camouflaged by the prosecution, and that the only real question concerned labor's right to strike in time of war. He argued that the attitudes and practices of employers were directly pertinent to the basic question and should be submitted to the jury. He cited historic precedents where men accused of violence had been permitted to state their provocation.

Judge Landis ruled that the precedents cited did not fit the present situation; that American industry was not on trial in the case before the court, and that the indictment did not charge the I.W.W. members with conducting illegal strikes. The prosecution had produced no such charges, and the defense could not now offer such rebuttal.

To George Vanderveer that ruling was devastating. He offered his apologies to the women who had worked in the various factories near the Loop and whose testimony could not now be presented; and that week-end, for the first time in his life, he began drinking in the midst of an important trial.

It was early Sunday morning when he returned to his hotel to find a note in his box, informing him that his wife had been attempting to reach him by long distance from Seattle. He went up to his room and placed the call for the Seattle operator.

"What's wrong, Gus?" he demanded as soon as he got his wife on the phone. "Are you all right?"

Ellinor explained that she could no longer stall off some of the creditors, and that she had no money to pay them; that there had been a threat to attach the furniture, and she was completely desperate. "You haven't even answered my last three letters," she added.

He hesitated. "I've been awfully busy."

"What shall I do, George? I can't live here in an empty house."

Again he hesitated. "I don't know. Good God, if I had the money I'd send it to you. I can't send you what I haven't got; can't you understand that?"

Ellinor was crying now. "What am I supposed to do? Just tell me. . ."

Once again there was a long pause. "Well, I guess you could go live with your mother if they take the furniture. That's all I can think of."

She tried to speak but she couldn't quite make it. She was sobbing.

"Damn it, Gus, listen to me!" he commanded. "You've got to be tough. You've got to learn to take these things! Good lord, do you think you're the only one who's left alone? What about these women whose husbands are in jail? They've got children, too—some of them—and they're getting along the best they can, and you don't hear them complaining about it."

For a moment longer Ellinor continued crying and then she hung up the receiver without saying goodbye. Several days later he received a short note informing him that she had sold the diamond ring he had given her, and had made payments on the most pressing accounts.

The trial dragged on amid constant shouts of objection from opposing counsel, and almost as many questions were ordered stricken from the record as were allowed to remain. The lines of the battle had been carefully chosen by the prosecution and restricted by the ruling of the court. George Vanderveer and his associate counsel were never permitted to take the offensive, or follow through with the avowed intention of placing the capitalistic system on trial. Of necessity, theirs remained a defensive battle all the way, raging over the legal grounds where defense was the most difficult.

A seething and unrelenting anger seemed to have encompassed Vanderveer—augmented, perhaps, by the complications of his personal life and intensified by his wife's tears. For the first time in his life he had accepted a legal assignment without advance investigation because of the inducement of the proffered fee, and by now he knew he would never receive the money. His examination of prosecution witnesses became more savage and his sarcasm became more cutting than ever before; but the infectuous smile which had been his most reliable weapon of the past appeared almost not at all. He seemed far more embittered than any of the defendants.

Red Doran, who had been the first man to see him before the trial of Tom Tracy, took his place on the witness stand in Chicago. For a full five hours, Doran reviewed the struggles of the itinerant workers and explained the dreams of the I.W.W., and he held the attention of nearly every person in the courtroom through every minute of the time. When he concluded, he smiled affably at the members of the jury. "It is customary with I.W.W. speakers to take up a collection but under the circumstances, we will dispense with it today." A roar of laughter went up from the spectators. Judge Landis permitted himself an audible chuckle, and a couple of the members of the jury were convulsed.

George Vanderveer, however, presented little more than a strained and mechanical smile. He was not in the mood for levity.

On the question of denouncing and opposing the war, the Wobblies had no possible defense for their record and their pamphlets offered proof beyond all doubt. The only course open to them had to be unflinching agreement: "If this be treason, make the most of it!"

Big Bill Haywood took the stand, and his intense sincerity was sufficient to rouse the jurors from their lethargy which had been building up during the long trial.

"Mr. Vanderveer," Haywood said in answer to a question, "I don't want the jury and I don't want these defendants to get the idea that I am in favor of war. I am very much opposed to war, and would have the war stopped tomorrow if it were in my power to do it. I believe there are other methods by which human beings should settle any existing difficulty. It is not only the murdering of men; it is the suffering of wives and children, and it is what this war means to society after it is over . . . that is the terrible part of war." He expressed the hope that the conflict would last just long enough to drive all of the hatred and all of the bitterness out of men's souls, and that it would prove to be the last war in the history of the world.

The sincerity of the man was impressive, and he may have gained the sympathy and respect of the spectators but, at best, he had merely pleaded guilty to the prosecution's charge that he opposed the war in Europe, and had denounced his country's participation in it.

When not in court, Vanderveer spent hours pawing through his notes and searching legal precedents, seeking some possible avenue to get the defense off the restricted ground where it had been confined. He talked to the men on trial who had been liberated on bail, but he was not close to any of them. He discussed the various ramifications of the case with his associate counsel, but he avoided all personal conversations. He drove himself relentlessly, and often he appeared in court haggard from the lack of sleep, and with nothing to show for his night's devotion to legal research. He was like a fighter backed into a corner and unable to get out, too closely confined to throw punches of his own, but unwilling to accept the defeat that appeared inevitable.

He was a desperate and lonely man when he met Kitty Beck, head of the defense committee in Portland, Oregon, who had stopped off in Chicago to observe the progress of the trial. She was small, dark, attractive, and extremely feminine. She was a woman of considerable wealth, but perhaps the thing that impressed Vanderveer most of all was the fact that she did not consider wealth, of itself, particularly important. She spoke earnestly of Justice and Equality and the Brotherhood of Man, and he was delighted to discover that she was the ward of Colonel Charles E. S. Wood, the Portland attorney, whose poems Vanderveer had particularly enjoyed. They spent much time together during her visit to Chicago.

Unconsciously, perhaps, George Vanderveer had found in Ellinor a physical resemblance to the hidden memories of his mother; for Ellinor was tall, attractive, blessed with an enviable complexion, and her luxuriant dark hair which hung to her waist had once evoked comment from David Vanderveer: "You know, George's mother had hair like that."

In Kitty Beck, there was no physical resemblance to George's mother; but in her, perhaps, he found a similarity of spirit and a duplication of his mother's philosophy of life. She was perfectly at home in the world of literature and art, where Vanderveer had trespassed only as a curious alien. She had read nearly everything he had read, and a great deal more, in the fields of philosophy and biography, and yet she had retained an almost childlike love for the imaginary world of gallant knights and deadly dragons. Like Joan of Arc, she had heard the clear call to her mission in behalf of the persecuted and the downtrodden, and she was a woman dedicated

to an ideal. Undoubtedly her influence upon George Vanderveer was great.

In Kitty Beck he found solace for his loneliness and reassurance for his lagging faith. In the reflection of her
admiring eyes he could see himself not as a failure in the
world of economic competition whose family was clinging
precariously to a mortgaged home and whose wife had been
forced to sell her diamond engagement ring because of his
failure to provide, but rather as a modern gladiator whose
lightning thrusts of legal debate were holding an oppressive
dragon at bay.

The dragon, however, was by no means at bay. During
the last week of August, 1918, the defense completed its
case, and prosecution began its closing arguments. Jurors
were reminded that the United States depended upon them
to do their duty to their country, just as other Americans
were doing their duty in the trenches of France; and that
the clear, unquestioned duty in the present case was to find
the defendants guilty. The prosecution arguments were long
and sometimes eloquent, but the members of the jury sat
wearily and apparently unimpressed. The five long months
of the trial had inured them to oratory and perhaps they had
long since passed that point where they could remember the
hundreds of exhibits and the testimony of many scores of
witnesses.

After a hasty conference, the defense attorneys decided to
rest their case without a summation, and the judge began his
detailed charge to the jury. As the jurors filed out to weigh
the great mass of evidence and to consider their verdict, the
courtroom audience thinned. Reporters strolled out through
the corridors of the Federal Building to smoke cigarettes and
to make routine calls to their respective papers, but within an
hour they were called back. Already the jury had reached
a verdict!

A hush fell over the room as the foreman waited to give

their verdict to the court. "We, the jury, find the defendants guilty as charged in the indictment."

Pandemonium broke loose all at once. Reporters raced frantically for the exits. Shouts echoed through the building, and a band in the lobby blared forth with "Hail, Columbia." For the most part, the defendants stood stoical and expressionless while spectators in the back of the courtroom slapped each other on the back and grinned happily.

At one corner of the defense counsel's table, with his back turned toward the defendants and with his fists clenched, George Vanderveer stood with tears streaming down his cheeks. It was the first major defeat of his legal career, and he took it hard.

CHAPTER FIFTEEN

You have collected a band of profligates and worthless men,
*   abandoned not only by all fortune but even by hope.*
                                              —CICERO

THE VICTORY of the prosecution in Chicago touched off
nearly as much jubilation as had the victory of the Allies
in the battle of the Marne some weeks earlier. The first
bright rays of hope were breaking through the clouds of
war, and success appeared almost within grasp for those who
had dedicated their lives, their fortunes, and their honor to
make the world safe for democracy. The conviction of the
one hundred and one Wobblies fitted nicely into the bright-
ening pattern.

In his courtroom in Chicago, Judge Landis passed sentence
on the convicted men amid angry shouts of protest from the
prisoners, and demands for the traditional right to make a
statement to the court. Time after time the prisoners demanded their prerogative and started their recitation of
Wobbly oratory for the benefit of the press. Time after
time they were silenced by the impatient rapping of the
judicial gavel, and the reminder that any statements offered
must have a direct bearing upon the case and upon the
evidence submitted.

It was a grim process, but in remarkably short time all of
the sentences had been passed. A couple of the routine employees of the I.W.W. headquarters who had been scooped

up in the Justice Department's net received sentences of ten days in the county jail. Rank-and-file members received sentences ranging from one to four years. Three different groups drew sentences of five years, and a fourth group was sentenced to ten years in the Federal penitentiary at Leavenworth.

Last to be sentenced were big Bill Haywood, Ralph Chaplin, Vincent St. John, and some seven others closely associated with the Chicago headquarters and members of the General Executive Board, as the court demonstrated a conviction that the leaders shared the greater responsibility and that their followers may have been victims of bad advice. Each of the remaining prisoners was brought before the court and sentenced to twenty years at Leavenworth.

The convicted Wobblies were handcuffed and marched down Austin Avenue while police held back the jeering throngs. A special train waited at the LaSalle Street Depot to carry the convicted men to Leavenworth, and as the procession moved on, the cross-traffic once again filled the street. Police officers on special duty returned to their regular stations; and in the days that followed, the headlines reverted to the big news overseas. Allied troops were moving into position for the impending battle of St. Mihiel; and at Camp Devens, Massachusetts, an enlisted man was just coming down with a yet-undiagnosed illness that was to touch off the great influenza epidemic across the nation. The big story of the Chicago trial was ended, and there were too many other big stories shaping up to permit conversational or journalistic post mortems.

In Wobbly headquarters throughout the country, the Chicago decision demonstrated its immediate effects. The great masses of new members drifted away from the organization; leaving a cold, hard skeleton of resistance robbed of its flesh and driven underground. The red membership cards no longer served as unofficial passes for those riding railway freight cars, and thousands of the memorial cardholders issued at the time of the Everett trial were never seen again. Those who continued to carry their red cards generally secreted them within the lining of a jacket or beneath the innersole of a shoe so that the damning evidence could not immediately be found if a man were picked up for routine examination by the police or were given a preliminary working-over by vigilantes.

The more conservative unions of the American Federation of Labor which had given financial support to the Wobblies at the time of the Everett trial demonstrated no continuing sympathy. The I.W.W. carried no official recognition at Central Labor Councils, and a number of locals made concerted attempts to purge their ranks of suspected Wobblies or former Wobblies. Those who continued, openly and defiantly, to visit I.W.W. headquarters were mostly hard-bitten men with a universal contempt for social approval and an unyielding dedication to a lost cause and a fading dream.

To George Vanderveer, the Chicago defeat was cataclysmic. He returned to Seattle embittered and disillusioned. He had received but a small fraction of the ten thousand dollar fee which had induced him to undertake the Chicago defense in the first place, but he now demonstrated an increasing conviction that money, of itself, was unimportant.

There was a new restraint between Vanderveer and Ellinor. They remained polite, but reserved, and their relationship did not regain the warmth of understanding that had existed prior to the Chicago trip.

There were other changes, too, and they became apparent as Vanderveer met old friends and acquaintances in Seattle, as he attempted once again to pick up his practice. Possibly the sharpest jolt came when he met his long-time friend and former deputy, Al Lundin.

The two men shook hands and exchanged personal greetings. Briefly Vanderveer reviewed the highlights of the Chicago trial, and he explained that the legal battle was far from ended; that an appeal was going up to the United States

Supreme Court. "By God, they haven't seen the last of me," he announced bitterly.

For a moment Lundin stood shaking his head. "It hurts me to say this, Van," he said quietly, "but in my opinion, you're a traitor to your country."

Vanderveer drew back as if trying, physically, to dodge the unexpected blow. "Why do you say that?" he demanded.

"Those men you're trying to defend—they're not worth it," Lundin argued earnestly. "I've seen some of the orchards they've ruined; tree after tree dying off, and always the copper nail driven into it. I've seen some of the fires they've started, because they haven't even got the guts to come out into the open and fight like men. My God, Van! You can't throw your life away on men like that!"

Vanderveer stood with his fists clenched and his shoulders hunched, his eyes belligerent. "You can't prove that! You can't prove a damn word of it! You round 'em up and pull 'em into court, and I'll defend 'em! I'll show you that you haven't got a God damned ounce of evidence that'll stand up in court!"

Lundin continued to shake his head, and he spoke without anger. "It's true, and you know it. You know it as well as I do; as well as anybody does. You can't be sincere in defending men like that."

"Oh, horse manure!" Vanderveer snorted. "You can't stand here on the sidewalk and decide that men are guilty, when you can't prove it in court! This will be one hell of a country when the newspapers and the sidewalk jury can find men guilty of things that can't be proved in the courtroom."

To his old friend, Bruce Shorts, Vanderveer unburdened even more of the rising bitterness within him. He argued that the Wobblies were a persecuted minority, denied the fundamental rights guaranteed by the Constitution; many of them driven from their homes and brutally beaten without

any pretense of legal procedure—denied the rights of free
speech and peaceful assemblage, convicted in the kangaroo
court of public opinion, and condemned to the legion of the
damned. He charged that the people of the United States
were destroying at home the very liberties they were fighting
overseas to defend.

"I don't say that the I.W.W. is one hundred percent right
in everything that it does, and I might not argue with you
if you say that it's one hundred percent wrong," he told
Bruce Shorts. "I do say, though, that these men are human
beings, and they've got a right to live like human beings!"

He reminded Bruce Shorts of the time when a mob had
attempted to drive the Chinese out of Seattle, and Judge
Burke had faced that mob and demanded that law and order
be respected.

"Damn it all, it's no different now," he argued. "If these
men had yellow skins or black skins and they were being
treated the way they are, then every decent person in the
United States would rise up and demand a halt to it. By God,
nobody would stand by and let a minority race be treated
like that—not even in the South. Why should everybody feel
that it's all right, just because most of the I.W.W.'s happen
to be white men?"

Despite the earnestness of his arguments, however, Vanderveer found little sympathy and little understanding among
his friends of the legal profession, and even less from those
outside the profession. At the Elks Club he was treated with
cool reserve, and eventually he was asked to surrender his
membership in that organization. He responded with a bitter
blast of contempt, but those close to him knew that it was a
severe blow.

During his close association with the Wobblies in Chicago
he had acquired the habit of rolling his own cigarettes, and
now he disdained any other type. There seemed to be a
contemptuous defiance behind his choice, as if the loosely
rolled brown-paper cylinders were a badge of some secret

pledge of austerity. In the presence of men smoking expensive cigars, he appeared to relish the conspicuous contrast as he whipped out his bag of Bull Durham, measured out the tobacco, and rolled the cigarette with dexterity. His contemptuous glance spoke of something more than simple pride in acquired skill. It was as if he had just delivered a significant editorial, enacted in pantomine—a rebuke to those who sought prestige in material things.

His habits of dress also began to show the effects of a social rebellion in many little ways, and his casual conversations became increasingly sprinkled with off-color expletives. In another man, the occasional slips in grammar might be charged to habits of carelessness; but in George Vanderveer they had to represent purposeful design and an unspoken challenge to the world: By God, I can speak as I damn well please! Unlike many of the crude and coarsely-dressed habitués of Skid Road who seldom ventured beyond the limits of this unofficial reservation, Vanderveer seemed to take a special pride in flaunting his shabbiness and his austerity in the most refined circles.

Elmer Todd, who was one of Seattle's leading attorneys before he became publisher of the *Seattle Times* following the death of General Clarence B. Blethen, (and, incidentally, who, together with the three grandsons of the Colonel, built the *Times* into a nationally respected, Pulitzer Prize winning newspaper) recalled seeing Vanderveer in New York during one of his labor defense battles. Together with a half-dozen poorly dressed, obviously embarrassed and reluctant laboring men, Vanderveer entered the dining room of the Waldorf-Astoria. He was as shabbily dressed as any man in the group and somewhat more disheveled in appearance, but he lacked the attitude of self-consciousness which characterized the men with him. His expression was one of haughty and semi-belligerent contempt as he gazed about the large dining room, and it was obvious that he was enjoying his role immensely. Throughout the meal, his companions seldom let their gaze wander from the dishes before them, except for furtive and apprehensive glances at one another. Vanderveer, however, continued to glance about the room like an alert tennis player surveying the court—watching for any look of scorn, and a chance to return the service. His was a peculiar type of snobbishness-in-reverse.

He had given up his offices in the Hoge Building before his departure for Chicago in order to save the monthly rental, and his application for office space upon his return to Seattle met with the announcement that there were no available vacancies. He turned his attention to other office buildings in the business district with the same results. The classified ads carried long lists of offices available, but it soon became apparent that the Wobbly-defending Vanderveer was not welcome to any of the office buildings in uptown Seattle.

Despite his frequent and vitriolic threats to bring suit against various property-owners on a charge of conspiracy, Vanderveer did not follow through. He found desk space in the offices of Attorney Ralph Pierce, in the ancient shell of the Collins Building at Second and James, not far from the fringes of Skid Road. Later, he leased a suite of offices in the same building, under his own name. The steps of the building were steep and the hallways dark and gloomy. At times the entire building quivered as the heavy presses of a printing plant on the upper floor went into action, and the peculiar odors of the printing room mingled with the smell of tobacco smoke and damp plaster, to permeate the building. The adjoining rooms of his office suite were small, with cracked plaster walls and dark woodwork ornamented with the fancy scrollwork of a long-forgotten glory. The ceilings were high, and the windows tall and narrow.

He seemed reluctant to have his name printed on the office door. On the day when he moved in he placed a small business card in the corner of the opaque glass of the door, and it remained there until it was yellow with age. Later, he had a sign painter print the impersonal designation: LEGAL DE-

PARTMENT—SEATTLE CENTRAL LABOR COUN-
CIL. And when he ordered the names of his associates printed
upon the glass, he refrained from having his own name
included. Even those closest to him never knew whether his
reticence was inspired by wounded pride or by some peculiar
quirk of belated professional modesty. Certainly the dismal
setting was not one to add prestige to his name.

From a business standpoint, the location of his offices in
the Collins Building proved better than he may have anticipated, for he was close to his potential clients. For the first
time in his legal career he began branching away from the
practice of criminal law, as he plunged into a series of personal
injury suits, seeking compensation for workmen who had
been injured on the job; and his personal finances improved
as he hammered out a succession of court victories. The war
years had brought vast ship building projects to Seattle and
had stimulated activity in other heavy industries. In the
stepped-up tempo of war production, injuries were numerous
and the demand for Vanderveer's legal service was almost
unending.

At home he seldom discussed his professional problems
with his wife, nor did he discuss matters of family finance.
For the most part, his conversations were restricted to polite
and reserved comments about the physical things within the
home, and he closely guarded his innermost thoughts. And
yet from conversations overheard, and from little remarks
offered from time to time, Ellinor realized that his dwindling
interest in criminal law was but a part of the change that had
encompassed him, and that any interest in financial gain was
purely incidental. In pressing the personal injury claims
in behalf of injured workmen, he was helping to fight the
cause of the laboring man and he was tapping the profits of
big business. In his own peculiar way, he was driving the
copper nails of retribution, and gaining a vast amount of
personal satisfaction.

He had acquired a blunt and impersonal procedure of

extracting his fees from amounts awarded by the court, and
no longer did he need to engage in barter because a client
was unable to pay cash. And yet under no possible interpretation could Vanderveer be classified as a good businessman, nor did the financial phase of his practice approach
anything resembling efficiency.

Reasonable attorney costs were generally added to the
amount of compensation demanded for a client, and he
frequently boasted that he was working for the poor and
being paid by the wealthy; and yet in a great many cases
he instructed that a draft for the entire amount be directed
to the claimant.

He succeeded in winning a substantial judgment for an
injured musician, a flute player who was slowly dying of
cancer of the mouth. It was a long and hard-fought case
that had brought a parade of professional medical witnesses,
and although Vanderveer had paid expenses out of his own
pocket, he instructed that the entire amount of the judgment
be assigned to his client. When the musician insisted that
Vanderveer should take out his expenses plus a reasonable
fee, he shook his head. "I'll tell you what we'll do. We'll
put all of the money in the bank and you draw out two
hundred dollars a month as long as you live. We'll both hope
to God that you use it all up; but if you don't, I'll take what's
left as my fee."

In his own mind, no doubt, his position was not so different
from that of a modern Robin Hood; levying his toll upon
the wealthy and giving to the poor—utilizing his skill in the
courtroom in lieu of the longbow and quarterstaff.

He considered himself a man completely devoid of sentiment, and yet he was perhaps one of the most sentimental
men who ever lived. His complete disregard of Christmas,
birthdays and anniversaries was more than indifference; it
was a conscious rebellion—a defiant insistence that mere
circumstance should not dictate his generosity. He once
explained to an associate: "When I give a man something,

COUNSEL FOR THE DAMNED 249

it's because I want him to have it; and it's not because of any special date on the calendar. To hell with that sort of thing!"

He was equally unorthodox in his contributions to charity, and he seethed at any suggestion of a quota. "Nobody, by God, is going to tell me where to give money, or how much!" On a later occasion he irately returned the sheets of Christmas seals that had been sent to him unrequested, refusing to use them or pay for them; and yet, month after month, he fed almost as many of the hard-bitten men of the Skid Road district as were fed by some of the established mission houses. He would part with his last dollar to help out some human derelict who was down on his luck, but he did not take kindly to direct solicitation; nor did he encourage the notion that he was an easy touch. He was becoming known as a hard-drinking man, himself, but he demanded sobriety of those whom he helped. At one time he was halted by the police while administering a severe beating to a man on First Avenue South. "He's a dirty son-of-a-bitch," Vanderveer told the officers. "I gave him twenty dollars to eat on, and to buy some clothes—and he went out and spent it on rot-gut!" Ironically, in the opinion of the police, Vanderveer was the more inebriated of the two; and for this he offered no apology. He had accepted no contribution.

Despite the fact that his legal practice was yielding substantial revenue, Vanderveer was making little headway against the accumulation of bills that had piled up from the past and this was due, in large measure, to his eternal contributions to the ceaseless parade of poverty-ridden men with whom he daily rubbed shoulders. In compliance with court orders or in the face of threatened suits, he would pay some of the older accounts while current expenses drifted on to become delinquent. He was short-tempered and intolerant when collection agents called upon him, and generally he threatened them with physical violence rather than entering into any serious discussion of how to meet the situation. However, he gave no indication of being deeply concerned about the ever-pressing debts, and when Ellinor reported her occasional encounters with bill collectors who came to the house he offered the casual advice that she should tell them to go away and quit bothering her. To him, apparently, it was as simple as that.

Previously in their married life he had discussed with her those legal assignments that sent him away from home, much as he had discussed the call to Chicago to defend the Wobblies. Now, however, he remained noncommittal. Occasionally he would pack his suitcase and inform her that he had to be out of town for several days, while offering no explanation of where he was going. Sometimes she would chance upon a news item which mentioned his name in connection with a legal action in Spokane, or Butte, or Portland.

Ellinor told herself that it was time for a showdown, that much could be lost and nothing could be gained by maintaining the status quo indefinitely while hoping for a miracle. But before she could quite get up courage to discuss the matter with her husband, the miracle appeared.

James Hoge, Seattle capitalist and owner of the building where Vanderveer had maintained his offices with Bud Cummings, offered Vanderveer a twenty-five-thousand-dollar annual retainer if he would return to civil practice in uptown Seattle. The bid, coming within a few months of Vanderveer's return from Chicago, was something more than a financial offer to a skilled attorney; it was an invitation back into the folds of respectability, with a suite of offices in the Hoge Building. It was a twenty-five-thousand-dollar olive branch, signifying that all would be forgiven and forgotten, and that George Vanderveer could claim his rightful place as the outstanding lawyer of Seattle. It was a major concession by James Hoge, who held a high regard for Vanderveer's legal ability and who offered thus to alter the current of hostility which had driven Vanderveer from uptown Seattle. Perhaps, too, the offer was based upon a familiar adage about trapping more flies with honey than with vinegar—for

Vanderveer's incessant buzzing through the courtrooms of the
Northwest was becoming annoying and expensive to the
owners of industry.

For the first time in weeks, George Vanderveer returned
home without a chip on his shoulder; and the once-familiar
boyish eagerness shone in his eyes as he discussed the offer
with his wife. For the first time since his return from
Chicago, there was warmth and understanding.

The next morning Ellinor was up early, and she went to
visit her mother to pass on the good news. The day was crisp
and clear and cool, and she rode downtown on the streetcar
and spent a couple of hours browsing through the stores.
She hadn't remembered that Seattle could be so beautiful.

Because of her husband's highly irregular hours, she had
got out of the habit of preparing dinner for him until he
reached the house; but now she prepared a special meal and
had it ready by six o'clock. In the center of the table, to add
a festive touch, she placed a long-treasured bottle of sparkling
wine. However, at six o'clock, George had not arrived.

By ten o'clock most of the sparkle was gone from the wine
and from the day, and Ellinor knew that her husband had
been drinking when she heard him let himself in the front
door. She hurried in from the kitchen and for a moment he
stood in the middle of the living room staring at her.

He shook his head. "I can't do it, Gus. I can't walk off
and leave all of those men. I can't let them down."

Her hand crept up to her throat. "What did you tell Mr.
Hoge?" She already knew the answer. She had known it,
somehow, since a little after six o'clock when he had failed
to return and failed to telephone.

"You don't understand, Gus. I couldn't expect you to
understand. But, damn it all, I just couldn't do it! I couldn't
walk off and leave those men when they need me—no matter
what. . . ."

CHAPTER SIXTEEN

*His rash, fierce blaze of riot cannot last, for violent fires soon burn out themselves.—*Shakespeare

On November 11, 1918, after one false start, Seattle ripped loose with an almost-hysterical celebration of the signing of the armistice. The great whistle atop the Times Building blasted its prearranged signal, and special editions were on the street within a matter of minutes. People swarmed through the downtown business district buying noise-makers of all kinds to help swell the cacophony of jubilation. Men in uniform were swept from their feet and carried upon the shoulders of a shouting throng. Strangers embraced one another; and a gala pyrotechnic display set off from the roof of the Times Building in the late evening surpassed anything that had been seen in the Pacific Northwest. Seattle had embarked upon an emotional binge that stood without parallel in its civic history, and it lasted far into the night.

The days that followed brought their sobering reactions. Some forty thousand men and boys had streamed into the city during the war years to take up the jobs in the shipyards and most of them had been earning good money—approximately five dollars a day for unskilled labor—and they returned to their jobs with morbid speculations about the future. Surely there would be no need, now, to keep on building ships at the wartime pace. Men soon would be returning from overseas, and there would be fewer jobs with

COUNSEL FOR THE DAMNED

ever-increasing applicants. It was sobering to realize that the era was ended, and labor agitators lost no time in moving into the fertile field and sowing their seeds of discontent.

Even before the signing of the armistice, rumors of fabulous wartime profits had begun to sweep through the ranks of the workers: ships were being built that never could be used—merely to add to the profits of the shipbuilders; the Army had bought ten times as many saddles at it had horses, and high government officials were splitting the profits with the saddle-makers; somewhere on the East Coast there were a dozen warehouses filled to the rafters with hand-knit sox that American women had knitted and contributed to the "boys overseas." There were rumors about the Red Cross and the Salvation Army—vicious and ugly rumors that were passed along by men who knew they were false, as well as by men who believed they were true.

Those who had retained their membership in the I.W.W. made their voices heard, but they had a new technique. The anti-I.W.W. sentiment had made their soapbox perches practically untenable; and now they used the weapon of other agitators, which was proving even more effective—the whispering campaign. The formal haranguing of an audience was a luxury they seldom could afford, and so they spread their propaganda with embittered comments across a pool table, or with apparent casualness in a hiring hall or on a streetcar loaded with working men. It was a new game that any number could play, and it was played by Wobblies, Communists, Socialists, syndicalists, and an unknown number of individual, free-lance cynics and malcontents.

Together, they helped to hatch a new era of cynicism among American workers. They painted a picture of wartime profiteering, sapping the wealth and the strength of a nation. They played upon the inevitable fears of those who faced the shift to peacetime production and the end of their wartime jobs. They planted a thousand rumors and sent them on their way; and not all of them were entirely without foundation.

They pointed to the hulls of ships lining up in Lake Union, just a stone's throw from downtown Seattle, and they charged that each had added its fabulous profits to the capitalist who had built it. They added a sarcastic inflection to the wartime slogan about making the world safe for democracy, and they helped to produce the mood of cynicism which was to distinguish the Roaring Twenties.

The first morbid mood of apprehension on Seattle's labor front was allayed somewhat by the announcement from the government and from the shipbuilders that existing contracts would not be canceled and that ships already under construction would be completed. For the thousands of shipyard workers, it was a temporary reprieve from impending unemployment, but their jubilation was short-lived. The Shipbuilding Adjustment Board announced a uniform nation-wide wage scale, and the members of the seventeen unions affiliated with the Seattle Metal Trades Council were immediately up in arms. All during the war, workers in the West Coast shipyards had received wages fractionally higher than those paid on the eastern seaboard to compensate for the slightly higher cost of living, and the new edict of the board eliminated this.

The Metal Trades Council presented its protests to the employers and to the board and, failing to get satisfaction, called for a strike vote among its affiliated unions. On January 21, 1919, the thirty-five thousand members of the seventeen affiliated unions walked off the job.

The strike was crippling to the shipbuilding industry, and it immediately affected thousands of other workers affiliated with other unions; and yet it lacked any note of urgency. The ships under construction were being completed for no obvious reason, to meet no known deadline. The pressure of wartime necessity was gone. Transports no longer needed replacement because of enemy action. Already the United States Government had more ships than it could use, and many would have to be sold as surplus. It was reported that the Seattle shipbuilders stood ready and willing to pay the increased wages demanded, but were prohibited from doing so by the Shipbuilding Adjustment Board. The men on strike were eager to win the concessions and get back to work and back to regular paychecks. The government, obviously, felt no such pressing urgency. So far as the Shipbuilding Adjustment Board was concerned, apparently, the strike could last indefinitely.

The members of the Metal Trades Council surveyed their unenviable situation and sought some answer to the dilemma. They didn't need long to ponder, for the simple answer had been recommended years ago by the I.W.W., and there were Wobblies who made certain that it was not overlooked in this hour of crisis. From its inception, the I.W.W. had fostered the idea of the general strike as the ultimate and irresistible weapon of labor. That was the basic premise of its formula for one big union: ". . . an organization formed in such a way that all its members in any one industry, or in all industries if necessary, cease work whenever a strike or lockout is on in any department thereof, thus making an injury to one an injury to all." And thus, on the second day of their strike, the delegates of the Metal Trades Council asked the Seattle Central Labor Council to call out all of its unions in sympathy, to bring about the first general strike in the history of the United States.

The Wobblies had no official recognition at the Central Labor Council, but their members were there to lend moral support—technical experts who had spent years planning the strategy of the general strike. They had all of their time-tested arguments at their finger tips: "Don't let 'em sit and starve you out while their bellies are full and yours are empty! Tie up the whole damn city! Let some of the capitalist bastards miss a few meals themselves, and they'll come crawling to you on their bellies and give you everything you ask!"

Many of the conservative labor leaders of Seattle were not present at the Central Labor Council, having recently departed to attend a national meeting in Chicago seeking the release of Tom Mooney, whose death sentence had been commuted to life imprisonment. Their absence from the city was coincidence, and the more rabid agitators made the most of it. Without the quieting voices of those who generally interpreted the national policy of the American Federation of Labor, the radicals enjoyed an oratorical field day.

Within the Central Labor Council, one hundred and ten unions voted to strike, and their balloting touched off its repercussions throughout the nation and throughout the world. At I.W.W. headquarters in every section of the country, the hard-core Wobblies made ready for the climax of their long class struggle. Undoubtedly there would be fighting and bloodshed in the streets of Seattle—clashes between armed troops and masses of laboring men. The general strike would spread like a creeping paralysis across the nation until, within a matter of days, all business and all industry and all commerce would be at a standstill. Not a train or a truck or a wagon would move; and in the major cities, particularly, the crisis would come quickly. Without food, without water, without lights, without sanitation, there could be no prolonged resistance. Revolution might be an accomplished fact within a matter of days and, with any kind of luck, it might be carried through with a minimum of bloodshed. Hard-core Wobblies studied the pattern of the successful Russian revolution and hastened to be ready.

Bolshevist Russia followed the trend of the story, with dispatches from Seattle going directly to Moscow, establishing the conviction that the second major proletariat uprising was already taking form. It was later charged that the blame for the general strike rested squarely upon Bolshevist organizers sent to Seattle and operating under assumed names.

At Washington, D.C., the potential of the impending strike was being soberly considered, and the deployment of troops throughout the nation analyzed. Major General Morrison, in command of the Western Military District, was dispatched directly to Seattle to take command of the local situation there. He moved fifteen hundred armed troops into Seattle from Fort Lewis, near Olympia, and reported that additional troops could be moved in within a matter of hours if the trouble remained localized in the Seattle area. Industrial centers elsewhere in the nation, considered potential danger spots in case the strike should spread, required special consideration with armed troops held in readiness. It had been less than fourteen months since the successful Bolshevist revolution in Russia, and nobody could be sure just what to expect.

In Seattle, a Committee of Fifteen had been appointed by the General Strike Committee to take complete charge of the impending walkout which had been scheduled for Thursday, February 6, and hardly a member of the committee was permitted an hour's uninterrupted rest. Details seemingly without end had to be attended to. Matters of policy had to be decided. This was to be an act without precedent in American history, and there was no one to point the way. In a city of 300,000 people, a single day can bring problems of many kinds. There would be births and deaths and emergency operations—fires, accidents, and possibly riots. It had sounded simple enough to "close down the whole damn city," but what about ambulances and hearses and grave diggers, and fire trucks? What about food and fuel for hospitals, and electric lights for the operating rooms? What about milk for the city's children? Food and care for the aged and the infirm? What about vehicles handling United States mail? What about life-and-death calls if telephone service were discontinued, and what about medical prescriptions with drugstores closed? Under the weight of the terrible responsibilities that had been placed upon their shoulders, each of the fifteen became progressively more conservative and increasingly conscious of his duties toward his fellow men in all walks of life.

They were plagued by radicals who demanded that milk

be provided only for the children of union members: "Them damn capitalists don't care whether our kids starve when times are tough, so why should we worry about theirs?" By the same arguments, they insisted that food and medical care should be restricted to union members and their families; but the committee was responding to its new responsibility. Under a flood of executive orders, exceptions were made to permit certain union members to carry on the crucial work of civic survival.

Hospitals would remain fully staffed, and the various unions would cater to their needs for light and fuel and transportation. Drugstores would be permitted to remain open, but for the filling of prescriptions only. Telephone operators would remain on duty for restricted service. City light would remain in full operation. Service unions such as plumbers and electrical workers would maintain staffs to meet emergencies but would make no new installations. Elaborate plans were rushed through to establish and operate emergency kitchens that would feed the hungry, and after fiery but short-lived debate it was announced that they would feed any and all, with but one concession to those who opposed the feeding of "damned capitalists": union members would be entitled to a special discount.

Mayor Ole Hanson, who had succeeded Hi Gill in the spring of the year, went into a huddle with his Chief of Police, Joel F. Warren, and two thousand volunteers were sworn in to aid the city's regular police officers in maintaining law and order. Intricate battle plans were drawn, including the massing of defense forces at strategic spots, courier service, and the distribution of arms and ammunition. However, the Committee of Fifteen was busy with similar plans to establish its own highly disciplined labor guards dedicated to the same cause—to patrol the streets, to quell riots, to check hooliganism, and to aid the regular police force in every way possible. In the final hours before the strike deadline, the efforts of the supposedly opposing forces were running strangely parallel.

In an impassioned statement to the press, Mayor Hanson announced that the seat of government was still at the City Hall. But despite his eloquent contention, nearly everyone realized that the city's destiny rested in the hands of the Committee of Fifteen. Through its control of labor it had the power to shut off food, light, power, water, transportation, communications—everything that enables a city to exist from one day to the next.

On Thursday morning, February sixth, 1919, the first general strike in American history got under way. Streetcars returned to the carbarns, where special labor guards waited to patrol them. Taxicabs returned to their garages. Elevators stopped operating and the heavy industries shut down. Stores closed their doors as the clerks walked out, and within an hour Seattle was strangely quiet. The downtown business district was almost deserted and hardly a door was open. Ships lay idle in the harbor and the cross-Sound steamers stood at their berths. Policemen patrolled their beats like caretakers in a deserted village. Newsboys left their corners and went home, for there were no papers to sell. With the exception of a small tabloid put out by the strikers, every press in the city was silent. Restaurants were closed, and hotel proprietors informed their guests that they would have to make their own beds. It was a strange and awesome silence in the first hours of the strike, and mothers kept their children off the streets.

Rumors spread as the day progressed, but still the quiet lingered over all. There were fantastic stories about rioting and bloodshed and dynamitings—always on the other side of town—or in some distant city, for there were reports that the entire nation was gripped in revolution. As darkness fell across Seattle, it proved to be a strange, unfamiliar darkness. The long lines of street lights glimmered in incandescent chains up over Queen Anne Hill, Capitol Hill, out toward

Ballard and angling up the long streets of Beacon Hill; and
yet many of the houses were dark. Cautious homeowners
were providing no illuminated targets for irresponsible rioters
who might come storming down the streets. Inside their
darkened windows, people sat staring out at their city—watching for flames against the darkened sky—watching for evidence of the violent upheaval that had been widely predicted
—listening for the rattle of machine guns and the roar of expected battle. They saw nothing and they heard nothing.
The awesome quiet continued.

The second day was almost like the first, but now more
people appeared upon the streets, and they did not glance
around so anxiously. Mothers let their children out into the
yard to play. Neighbors gossiped over the back fence. Nothing had happened; probably nothing would happen. Seattle,
generally, breathed a sigh of relief; but for many there appeared an undercurrent of disillusionment or disappointment
that was difficult to understand. It might be compared, perhaps, to the feelings of a man who hastily puts up his storm
windows and barricades his doors in the face of frantic storm
warnings, only to face continuing days of balmly weather
without so much as the rippling of a gentle breeze. Seattle
had prepared for violence and excitement. It had witnessed
two of the quietest days in its civic history.

At City Hall, Mayor Hanson put aside his intricate plans
of battle strategy and issued a formal proclamation. He assured citizens of complete protection and absolute safety. He
urged people to go back to their jobs, confident in the knowledge that any law violators would be prosecuted, and that the
city government would guarantee its people all of the necessi-
ties of life including food, transportation, water, light and
gas. He took occasion to announce that "the anarchists in this
community shall not rule its affairs."

In the industrial districts, particularly, the labor guards
with their identifying armbands strolled the streets in pairs,
nodding pleasantly to the regular police officers on duty, ex-

changing greetings with the people they met, but generally discouraging any loitering or assemblage. The shipyards had never been so completely guarded during the war; and despite the early rumors to the contrary, the first two days of the general strike had witnessed the loss of not a single drop of blood or the destruction of a nickel's worth of property.

Among many of the strikers, too, there was disillusionment and discouragement. They had been led to believe that this ultimate stroke of labor's united power would bring quick and overwhelming victory; but so far it had brought nothing except the quiet ticking of the clock and the orderly passing of time. How long would it last, and how could you tell who had won? Collectively, the strikers were losing something in the neighborhood of a million dollars a day in wages, and what were they getting for it? A view of a city marking time on a road that led to nowhere.

Perhaps the greatest gloom of all settled over the I.W.W. headquarters, where disillusioned Wobblies sat viewing the effects of their secret weapon. This was a general strike. This was America's first glimpse of labor's "irresistible force" and a demonstration of the power that would be inherent in One Big Union. This was the technique the I.W.W. had counted upon for the smashing victories that would deliver the tools of production into the hands of the workers. Disillusionment could hardly have been greater if scientists gathered in New Mexico to test the first atom bomb had been forced to concede that the weapon was compounded upon a false premise and generally less potent than an air rifle.

During the early hours the Wobblies had waited eagerly for the first news of the spreading strike and the impending revolution. They had perfected their grapevine to filter in information from various parts of the city in case of a complete breakdown of regular channels of communication, and they had pondered the problem of how to relay information to other Wobbly headquarters as the strike spread across the nation. However, there was no problem. There was no information to pass on. The strike had not spread; and the second day they knew that it would not spread. Their long-cherished weapon was a dud, and they promptly charged that the Committee of Fifteen had rendered it impotent by making it too highly organized.

On the third day, the Committee of Fifteen recommended that the strike be called off. It had achieved nothing and it proved nothing. Labor leaders who had rushed back from Chicago agreed almost unanimously that the calling of the general strike had been a mistake. It would jeopardize the agreements held by many of the individual unions, and it was contrary to the national policy of the American Federation of Labor. More than a hundred unions had walked out in sympathy, while conceding that they had no grievance with their respective employers; and the whole thing was decried by returning labor leaders as an ill-fated junket in political adventuring which hardly could be improved by prolonging the folly.

By now, some of the workers were straggling back to their jobs. The streetcars began running on haphazard schedules, and the newspapers were able to recruit enough workers to get out special editions. At the Central Labor Council, a number of unions failed to provide delegates even to answer the roll call. In one final effort to preserve some semblance of solidarity, the General Strike Committee urged all union members to stay away from work until February twelfth when the strike would officially end and labor would return voluntarily. Some of the individuals who had returned to work on their own initiative once again left their jobs, but the awesome quiet failed to return. Streetcars continued to run, and presses continued to roll. Newsboys shouted the headlines from street corners, and private automobiles rolled down the streets. Neighborhood food stores were operating and some of the restaurants opened their doors.

One week after the start of the general strike, Seattle was back to normal. The troops returned to Fort Lewis without a shot having been fired. Once again ships were loading at the docks, and steamers were shuttling back and forth across the Sound. However, Seattle's general strike left its imprint upon the lives of many individuals and, for all practical purposes, it shattered the recurring dream of One Big Union. The strikers were almost unanimous in their agreement that the big strike had been a mistake and they gazed with mounting suspicion upon those who had started the stampede. In a broad sense, the influence of the radical labor leaders died amid the quiet hours of the strike and a new era of conservative leadership was born.

Mayor Ole Hanson was saluted in editorials across the nation because of his firm stand, and a number of Eastern editors suggested him as a likely Republican candidate for President of the United States. Reporters besieged him. Writers for national magazines converged upon Seattle to get his life's story. A speaker's bureau urged him to go on a nation-wide lecture tour. The general strike had achieved at least one thing: it had made Ole Hanson America's man of the hour.

He resigned his office as Seattle's Mayor and he informed huge audiences in New York and in Boston how he had conquered the threats of Bolshevism on the streets of Seattle. He was a dynamic speaker who knew how to make a good story sound even better, but somehow the interest in Seattle's completely uneventful general strike seemed to wane with the passing weeks; and by the time the Republican National Convention got down to the task of selecting a Presidential candidate, Ole Hanson was not seriously in the running.

To George Vanderveer, although he took no personal part in it, the Seattle general strike proved disillusioning in many ways. At considerable sacrifice he had dedicated himself to the task of defending a persecuted minority which he felt had been denied the basic rights guaranteed to all men by the Constitution, and in the days immediately prior to the strike he was appalled at the contemptuous disregard these same men held for the rights of others. In Chicago he had learned to respect and admire many of the I.W.W. leaders whom he considered men of unquestioned personal integrity, inspired by a dream of social justice, and completely uncompromising in their dedication to an ideal. It was difficult to envision many of the same qualities in some of the embittered rabble-rousers who were making their voices heard in Seattle and who professed to represent the radical element of organized labor. It was as if the Department of Justice had skimmed off the cream in its round-up of I.W.W. leaders, and what was left was of dubious quality.

Even more disillusioning to him was labor's failure to maintain a solid front for more than three days, once the strike had become a reality. He watched in amazement as the strike disintegrated and workers began streaming back to their jobs, and he listened to the arguments that swept through the ranks and influenced many who had joined the sympathy walkout: "What do we get out of it, even if they win their raise at the shipyards? Not a damn thing! We've already lost three days' pay and, by God, that's enough!"

George Vanderveer did not discuss these reactions with his wife at the time, and he displayed no particular interest in the progress of the strike. Years later, however, he discussed them with an associate, Sam Bassett.

"I was never so God damn disgusted in my life," he recalled. "Imagine yourself listening to those bastards belly-aching about the fifteen or twenty bucks they'd lost in a sympathy walkout, when you'd just given up twenty-five thousand dollars a year in a sympathy walkout of your own! By God, Sam, it makes a man stop and think!"

Despite his disillusionment and mounting cynicism, however, he continued to defend Wobblies who were being imprisoned all over the Northwest. I.W.W. halls were being raided by groups of vigilantes, and known Wobblies were ordered to hit the road. Occasionally there was opposition and violence, and violence generally was followed by the arrest of one or more Wobblies. Defense funds were limited, for men who held steady jobs often drew away from the organization and failed to pay their dues. Appeals for financial help sometimes went to Chicago, but they were futile. The Chicago headquarters was equally hard pressed.

There was little reason now for the type of Wobbly jitters that once had gripped the city of Everett, for the I.W.W. no longer was a growing, militant organization. It was ripped with internal dissension and falling apart, and its days of influence were ended. Wobbly halls were haunted by a dwindling number of desperate men; and when they sang "Hold the Fort," it was lacking in both conviction and volume. The meeting halls had become a refuge for those who had no jobs, no money, no friends, and no place else to turn; but the anti-Wobbly fervor grew as the opposition dwindled. The fire of Wobbly rebellion had all but burned itself out, and an aroused public was intent upon stamping out the last spark.

Efforts to reorganize and revitalize the I.W.W. generally were unsuccessful. Even the remaining skeleton of the once-powerful organization now began to fall apart because of dissension over the question of Communist affiliation.

Big Bill Haywood came out of Leavenworth in the fall of 1919 failing in health and embittered in spirit; no longer convinced that the I.W.W. could stand alone and bring about the realization of his ancient dream. He followed reports of Wobblies being imprisoned in all parts of the country, and glumly he read the frantic appeals for financial help. Weakened with diabetes, blind in one eye and rapidly losing the sight of the other, he had lost faith in himself as a leader, and he turned his remaining strength to the effort of building up the exhausted defense fund. With uncontrolled jubilation, he announced that an offer of financial help had come directly from Moscow, thus solving all of the pressing problems and paving the way for the I.W.W. to assume its proper place as an integral part of the world-wide proletariat revolution. He was shocked and chagrined to learn that his jubilation was not

shared by other members of the General Executive Board and
that his attitude was not acceptable to the rank and file. It
was a shock from which Haywood never completely re-
covered.

Much had gone on during the months of his imprisonment,
and a change had come over the Wobblies since that day
when they had cheered the first news of the Bolshevik revolution. As a group, the Wobblies were perhaps as well informed about communism as any similar group in the United
States.   They had followed each development in the
"Worker's Fatherland" since the day of the revolution, and
many of them had grown progressively disillusioned. Lenin's
arguments in favor of a "necessary dictatorship" rankled in
the majority. To them, the Moscow version of communism
symbolized much that they were struggling against, and very
little that they were struggling for; and with typical Wobbly
disdain, the rank and file referred to the Communists as "comics." Bill Haywood, behind the bars at Leavenworth, had not
followed the transition and now he could not understand it.

Grudgingly, at Haywood's insistence, the board consented
to send an emissary to Moscow to investigate the offer of
financial assistance, and to determine whether it was to be a
forthright gift or whether there would be strings attached.
When the emissary returned with the advice not to touch the
money, the General Executive Board refused the offer, and
big Bill Haywood withdrew more and more into himself.
Often he sat staring into space, isolated from the world around
him. The shadow of Leavenworth still hung over the very
men who had turned down the offer, and pleas for financial
help were coming in almost daily from all parts of the country, where individual I.W.W. members were being imprisoned upon every charge imaginable. The refusal to accept
Moscow's offer of direct financial help was more than Haywood could comprehend.

There were others who agreed with Haywood. There

were some in Chicago, and there were others scattered around
the country—enough of them to split the organization apart.
Later, when big Bill Haywood jumped his bail and was lured
to Moscow with the promise that he would become Lenin's
adviser in organizing the Red International labor unions and
would be placed in charge of the Kuznets Basin project, the
bitterness became acute. Wobbly sympathizers who had
posted bond for Haywood faced financial ruin, and the anti-
Communist Wobblies charged that it would become almost
impossible for I.W.W. members to find bondsmen in the future. In its appeal to Haywood, reportedly, Moscow had
promised that the bondsmen would be reimbursed with
money to be raised from the sale of the Russian crown jewels,
but the promise was never fulfilled.

Wobblies who favored Communist affiliation withdrew
from the I.W.W. following the Haywood flight to Russia,
but the newly purged I.W.W. was unable to erase the stigma
or to alter the public conception that the Wobblies were
"just a bunch of damned Bolsheviks." Just as the Wobblies
once had moved into the A.F. of L. picket lines unwanted and
uninvited, so now the Communists move in uninvited to take
their place beside the Wobblies and to call public attention to
the similarity of their aims. Having refused the helping hand
from Moscow, the I.W.W. had been selected for the kiss of
death.

Aside from George Vanderveer, with the frequent assistance of Ralph Pierce who had shared his office with him,
there were few attorneys in the Northwest who demonstrated any eagerness to defend the Wobblies who were land-
ing behind bars in increasing numbers. The voluntary
acceptance of a Wobbly defense might be interpreted by the
public to indicate a certain amount of I.W.W. sympathy, at
a time when I.W.W. sympathizers were receiving as much
scorn as the Wobblies themselves.

Certainly there was small inducement for a lawyer to accept

a case which offered neither profit nor glory, and which might send him into court at the jeopardy of his own career to defend men for whom he felt a deep personal loathing. And yet George Vanderveer on numerous occasions expressed his contempt for fellow attorneys who were somewhat less than eager to defend the accused Wobblies. He was widely quoted as describing the members of the King County bar as "a bunch of kept women." He reminded some of them of the oath they had taken, never to reject the cause of defenseless or the oppressed because of any personal considerations, and he charged that the oath was being violated by all of those who refused to defend the Wobblies for fear of damage to their own reputations. All of his bitter words served little purpose, except for such personal satisfaction as he may have found in uttering them. He remained almost alone in the Seattle area, fighting the battles of the accused Wobblies; and he had less and less time to press the personal injury suits which had given promise of solving some of his own financial problems.

A succession of courtroom victories in his defense of the Wobblies through the early twenties added nothing to Vanderveer's popularity as far as the general public was concerned. He was feared, hated, criticized and condemned, but the legend of his wizardry in the courtroom continued to grow. Actually, he told an associate in later years, the press gave him credit for many miracles he never performed. "They were picking these men up on the damnedest charges you ever heard of, and without a damn ounce of evidence against them. You didn't have to be a genius to win those cases, because lots of times the prosecution would go into court without a leg to stand on." Public opinion, however, had already tried them and found them guilty; and the newspapers generally refrained from hinting that any of the Wobblies had been found not guilty because they had been wrongly accused. The impression spread that all of the men

were invariably guilty as hell, but spared from conviction by
George Vanderveer.

Law enforcement officers had borrowed a page from the
I.W.W. book of strategy, for they discovered that they could
arrest Wobblies much faster than Vanderveer could move
around the area to defend them. He was kept hopping from
one city to the next, all through the Northwest, defending
men charged with everything from vagrancy to crimes in-
volving moral turpitude; from syndicalism to contempt of
court. And few cities welcomed him as an honored guest.

Ellinor Vanderveer knew by now that there could be no
complete reconciliation. The future offered no promise, and
the present was intolerable. She attempted to jack up her
courage for a final showdown; but that, in itself, would require something in the nature of an emotional revolution.
Since the day when he had selected their first home, practically every final decision had been his, and he was not a man
who reacted calmly in the face of an ultimatum. She realized
that the force of his anger would be sufficient to overwhelm
her, and so she went on from day to day enduring those things
which were almost unendurable.

It was while her husband was out of town on one of his
many trips that she found her avenue of temporary escape.
She was invited to go along as a guest on the shakedown
cruise of one of the surplus government ships that had been
purchased by a large industrialist who was a friend of her
family. She could sign on as a member of the crew, but make
the trip as a guest and visit several ports of call on the west
coasts of North and South America. She backed away from
the invitation at first, convinced that George would never
stand for it; but in a final burst of emotional rebellion she
agreed to go.

To Ellinor, the trip was a revelation. For the first time
since her marriage she found herself free from the encompassing shadow of her husband, and recognized as a person-

ality in her own rights. When it was time for the ship to start its return trip northward she rebelled. The respite had been altogether too brief. She talked it over with another woman who had made the trip as a guest, and they decided to stay over for a while longer; to see a little more of the country, and to make the trip back north on one of the many freighters that carried a few passengers, stopped at many of the smaller ports, and returned via the Panama Canal. She wrote her husband telling him of her decision, and together the two women began their spontaneous and unguided tour.

It was more than a month later when they arrived in New York, and despite their careful calculations and frugal habits, the trip had cost a little more than they had anticipated when adjusting their itinerary to their budget. Ellinor arrived in New York without sufficient money to pay her train fare back to Seattle, and she immediately got in touch with her old friend and George's former law partner, Bud Cummings. From Cummings' office she attempted to reach her husband by telephone, first at the office and then at the house, but without success. In fact, her attempt to reach the house brought the disturbing news that the telephone had been disconnected.

"You two gals go out and see the town," Bud Cummings urged. "I'll keep on trying to get in touch with Van and tell him that you're here."

When Ellinor returned to the office late in the afternoon, Bud Cummings looked grim. "I'm afraid I haven't got very good news for you," he told her. "Apparently somebody was holding a mortgage on the house and they foreclosed a couple of weeks ago. I didn't get hold of Van, but I understand that he's got a room in the Butler Hotel, and he hasn't got a dime. John Savage is letting him sign for his meals in the hotel dining room, and I guess he's as flat as it's possible to get."

Ellinor sank into a chair and Bud Cummings tried futilely to console her. "Don't you worry, now. I'll see that you get

home all right, and this'll all blow over. Maybe it's not as bad
as it sounds."

However, when Ellinor reached Seattle she discovered that
it was even worse than it had sounded. The house was gone
and the furniture was gone. Nothing of value remained to
commemorate the many years of struggle against the ever-
present and ever-growing debts. She was informed that
George had been drinking more in recent weeks than ever
before, and there were reports that some woman was sharing
his room at the hotel, at least on occasion. Without attempting to reach him, she moved into a small guest house adjacent
to her mother's home. Not until they were completely settled did she call him and tell him that she was back. It was a
polite, noncommittal conversation, and both agreed that they
would have to get together soon to talk things over. No definite plans for such a meeting were offered by either of them.

At the Butler Hotel, Vanderveer was able to live well at
moderate cost under the terms of an unspoken agreement
with his long-time friend, John Savage. The complete hospitality of the hotel was his, and he had merely to sign his name.
No accounts were kept, and no bills were submitted. He was
treated as an honored guest, and no eyebrows were raised
when he invited friends to dine with him and then merely
signed his name to the check with no thought of ever paying.
He was welcome without limit to the best Savage had to
offer. On all legal matters, Vanderveer represented John
Savage and here, too, no accounts were kept and no statements submitted. Each man gave his best to the other, and
neither attempted even a rough appraisal to see who was getting the better of the exchange. Between them there was
complete understanding.

To reëstablish his sagging faith in himself and in everything he had been fighting for, George Vanderveer sent for
Kitty Beck. He needed her quiet courage, her reassurance,
her unfailing idealism; and he needed her understanding. He
needed someone he could talk to, and someone who could

talk to him . . . someone who could gaze upon his poverty
and behold it as the achievement of a martyr rather than the
ultimate dissolution of a man who had proved himself a
failure.

Kitty Beck rushed to Seattle, and she moved into the Butler
Hotel with him. With her she brought understanding and
admiration and respect for the man she loved, but she brought
one thing in addition; she brought her checkbook with its access to substantial funds in a Portland bank. And Vanderveer's pockets no longer remained empty. He was even able
to send money to Ellinor so she could repay Bud Cummings
for her train ticket home.

A few weeks after her return home, Ellinor met her husband at the hotel, and they had lunch together in the coffee
shop. She asked him to arrange the legal matters of securing
a divorce, but he brushed her suggestion aside, and he refused
to discuss the matter of a divorce further.

Through the remainder of the summer and into the early
fall she saw him only rarely, and there was no more mention
of divorce. In mid-October they met accidentally on the
street and he insisted upon taking her to the Copper Spoon
for lunch. He had been drinking, but he was not drunk.

For a long time after he had given their order, he sat
studying her, with a peculiar smile upon his lips. "You're like
a lot of people, aren't you, Gus?" he asked at last. "You think
you can judge whether a man is a success or a failure, just by
how much money he's got in the bank. That's your yardstick, isn't it? If he's got a lot of money, he's a big success; if
he hasn't got any money, he's a big failure."

She could feel her face redden. "Do you think that's a fair
thing to say, George, after all the years I stood by you when
we couldn't ever get our heads above water? Do you
think . . ."

He waved a hand uncertainly to halt her. "I don't mean
anything personal by it. I mean, that's the way people are.

You aren't any different from anybody else, as far as that goes. There's a big, important man; he's got a lot of money. There's a no-good bum; he hasn't got a dime. Isn't that the way it is?"

"What are you trying to say, George?"

He shook his head and grinned crookedly. "I'm saying to hell with it! I'm tired of taking it on the chin for men who haven't got enough guts to fight their own battles. I'm tired of being the one who always sucks the hind tit. I'll show you, by God, that I can make money better than the best of them!"

She stared at him. "Do you mean to say you're going to quit defending the I.W.W.'s?"

"Hell no!" he snorted. "I'll defend anybody, any time, anywhere, on any charge, and do a damn good job of it! But it's going to be cash on the line. I'm going to start playing the game the way everybody else plays it—just to prove to myself that I can do it!"

He handed her a twenty-dollar bill, and he assured her that there would be regular and substantial payments in the very near future.

"Those damn Wobblies pay cash to the landlord when they rent a hall, and they pay cash to the printer," he told her with a grin. "They can damn well pay cash to their lawyer, too, or learn to get along without him!"

It was just a few weeks later, however, on November eleventh. 1919, when George Vanderveer bought an extra from the newsboy on the street because of the shouted headlines: "I.W.W. SHOOTS UP LEGION PARADE." Hastily he read through the story of an I.W.W. mob in Centralia, Washington, which reportedly had opened fire on members of the American Legion marching in a parade to observe the first anniversary of the signing of the armistice. Actual details of the shooting were confused among the first garbled reports, and he wasted little time attempting to digest them. He dashed to the hotel and telephoned Kitty Beck from the lobby:

"My God!" he gasped. "Throw some stuff in a suitcase and get ready to go to Centralia! All hell has broken loose, all at once!"

CHAPTER SEVENTEEN

The mob is man, voluntarily descending to the nature of the beast.—EMERSON

D ESPITE HIS EXPRESSIONS of cynicism to Ellinor and similar expressions made occasionally to others, Vanderveer had no sympathy for those Wobblies who had favored accepting financial help from Moscow, and he demonstrated an almost-belligerent animosity toward an emissary from Moscow who later was dispatched to Seattle, under an assumed name, to make a bid for his support. Attorney Leslie Sulgrove, who not only knew of the incident but who also met the Communist emissary, described Vanderveer as "far too much of an individualist to submit to dictation or discipline." And he added: "I think he was too intellectually honest to accept any philosophy which was not open and above board in its objectives."

Superficially, Vanderveer was an enigma; completely baffling to many who had known him for years. He demonstrated certain chameleon-like qualities—an ability to take on the appearance and the political coloring of his immediate associates; and yet, beneath the surface, there were many consistencies of his nature which apparently never changed at all. And these things precluded any interest in Communist affiliation.

Basically, his admiration for the Wobblies was not unlike his earlier admiration for Al Lundin or Judge Burke, or Bruce

Shorts, or any other of a long list of personal idols. He admired them for their willingness to stand up and expose their own chins, and to fight their own battles, with a disregard of the odds against them. He measured other men as he measured himself—by the ability to get up from the canvas and keep on fighting. He admired the slugging type of fighter who throws each punch with his heart and soul behind it, and he held much less regard for the clever boxer who feints and backs away and wins his victory through strategic retreat.

As an athlete, he had mastered the technique of "follow-through," but to him it was a moral thing as well as a physical thing. He had been an excellent tennis player, and even when playing against someone who offered little opposition, he would smash each drive down the court with all of the power and accuracy of which he was capable, taking consecutive love sets. For him, there was no other way to play the game.

He admired the Wobblies for the same type of uncompromising drive; for their belligerent and often ill-advised bravado which sent them scrambling to their soapboxes in the face of almost certain arrest or persecution. His legal battles were restricted largely to the defense of those hard-bitten, uncompromising, rugged individualists who would look an arresting officer in the eye and announce: "You're damn right I'm a Wobbly, and proud of it! What in hell are you going to do about it?" For such a man, any strategic retreat behind the Fifth Amendment would have been incompatible to his nature.

He displayed little admiration for the later Wobbly strategists who deserted their soapboxes, disguised their identity, hid behind a cloak of anonymity, and resorted to the whispering campaign. They may have been wiser strategists than their predecessors, but they lacked the one quality which Vanderveer admired. That quality was even more lacking in the Communists with their technique of boring from within and planning their battles to expose someone else's chin; and he looked upon them with undisguised contempt.

At the time, in November, 1919, when he accepted the assignment to defend the accused Wobblies of Centralia, Vanderveer was assured at the outset that there would be adequate funds. Some of the I.W.W. leaders released from Leavenworth were busy barnstorming the country and breathing a little new life upon the dying embers of rebellious fire, and also collecting funds at every meeting. There could be little question that the I.W.W. was making its last-ditch stand, and hardly a Wobbly dollar in the United States was considered too precious to go for such a cause.

Probably never in the history of American courts of law was there ever a spectacle to rival the trial of the twelve I.W.W. members and their local attorney, Elmer Smith. They were jointly tried on a charge of murder in the first degree for the killing of Warren O. Grimm, Commander of the Centralia Post of the American Legion. Two of the men on trial were not present at any time, for they had disappeared immediately after the tragedy and never had been apprehended. They were listed in the information as John Doe Davis and Ole Hanson (no known relationship to Seattle's ex-Mayor of the same name). The remaining I.W.W. defendants were Britt Smith, O. C. Bland, Bert Faulkner, Ray Becker, James McInerney, Loren Roberts, Eugene Barnett, Mike Sheehan, Bert Bland and John Lamb. All submitted a plea of not guilty; and in behalf of Loren Roberts, a special plea was added: not guilty by reason of insanity.

Because of alleged prejudice existing in Centralia and its sister city of Chehalis, Vanderveer demanded a change of venue. The scene of the trial was shifted to Montesano, in Grays Harbor County—approximately forty miles distant— but no discernable change could be noted in the mood of the public. According to the reports in newspapers of general circulation, the Wobblies had fired upon the Armistice Day parade without warning or provocation, mowing down the young American men who had returned safely from the battlefields of France—mortally wounding at least three of them,

COUNSEL FOR THE DAMNED

and inflicting such serious wounds upon others that they might never recover. Throughout the entire Northwest there erupted a demand for immediate and final retribution. This was more than the public could stand. There were front page editorials to dramatize the horror of the "Centralia Massacre," and there was open talk of lynching.

One of the Centralia Wobblies not on trial was Wesley Everest, who had been captured by an enraged mob immediately following the tragedy. He had been beaten senseless, clubbed, bayonetted, castrated, and left hanging by the neck from a bridge that spanned the Chehalis River. Newspaper reports generally omitted reference to the fact that Wesley Everest, also, was a former serviceman.

During the course of the trial, State Guardsmen were encamped on the Courthouse lawn. Few men walked the streets unarmed; and early in the trial, Vanderveer was ordered to surrender his revolver upon entering the courtroom. Because of constant threats against his life, he refused to remain in Montesano when not actually in court. With Kitty Beck serving as his secretary, the two of them daily commuted from Aberdeen, and their excursions both ways often resembled a flight through enemy lines. The trial was held in the courtroom of Vanderveer's old friend, big Bill Campbell —now Judge Campbell—but Judge John M. Wilson had been appointed to hear the case. Judge Campbell, who had become a man of great influence in Grays Harbor County, pleaded with the public for rational behavior and calm deliberation, but he might almost as well have saved his breath.

An enraged public was sick of the leisurely processes of the law, under which the shrewd Wobbly lawyer often found immunity for his clients amid the maze of legal technicalities. For years the I.W.W. had preached the philosophy of direct action in order to achieve its aims, and now the general public had taken its cue from the Wobbly strategists. Irate citizens were in a mood for direct action of their own, and they stated their opinions publicly and bluntly: To hell with courts and

juries and crooked lawyers and legal technicalities! The time
had come, they insisted, for men to act like men—and to crush
this evil once and for all! You don't sit back and operate according to Roberts' Rules of Order when you find a poison-
ous viper in your bed—your life threatened—some of your
sons already dead! You strike out and you crush and destroy
the evil thing any way that you can; and the end justifies the
means.

There were a few of the more radical labor papers that
presented the other side of the story—no doubt with equal
prejudice. According to these reports, the Wobblies had been
victims and the Legionnaires had been the aggressors all the
way. Armed Legionnaires in battle dress had halted their parade and had stormed the I.W.W. hall as part of their Armistice Day celebration. To the Centralia Wobblies, this was
nothing new. Their former meeting place had been raided
by vigilantes and members of the Commercial Club some
eighteen months earlier. Wobblies had been unlawfully
beaten and threatened with lynching; and because their hall
had been so nearly demolished, they had been forced to move
into their present hall on Tower Avenue without compensation for their property which had been destroyed.

For weeks, it was charged, the impending raid on the
I.W.W. hall had been common knowledge throughout the
entire area. I.W.W. leaders had called upon public officials
with demands for protection and had met with nothing but
taunting refusals. In desperation, the Wobblies had called
upon Attorney Elmer Smith and he had advised them that all
men are within their rights when defending themselves and
their property from unlawful attack. Upon his advice, it was
charged, the Wobblies had acted upon their Constitutional
right to bear arms. Even though hopelessly outnumbered,
they had determined to make an effort to defend themselves
when attacked, rather than to submit meekly to the beatings,
the tar-and-feathering, and the possible lynchings so widely
publicized in advance.

There were few people, however, who read both sides of
the story; and perhaps none who weighed the conflicting
accounts impartially. The vast majority of the people
throughout the Northwest never even saw the more radical
labor papers of limited circulation. The subscribers to the
radical papers had freer access to the large metropolitan
papers but if they bothered to read the accounts, it was almost irrelevant. They had learned to look upon the public
press as a means of mass distortion of half-truths, twisted to
suit the desires of the capitalist advertisers and the disciples
of big business. If they read such papers, they read them only
to sneer.

Perhaps the true story of what happened in Centralia on
November 11, 1919, lay somewhere between the two conflicting accounts. Even the Washington State Supreme
Court, in its later review of the vast amount of testimony
from the long trial, conceded that questions of fact lay un-
determined behind the conflict of evidence (State vs. Smith,
115 Wash. 407). Nevertheless, it upheld the decision of the
lower court, and this time the technicality of the law did not
benefit George Vanderveer and his clients (State vs. Smith,
115 Wash. 407). It served the prosecution.

In planning their startegy for November eleventh—whether
for purposes of offense or defense—the Wobblies chose to
deploy their fire power according to the best principles of
battle strategy, guided by the advice of members who had
fought their way through villages of France and Germany.
Rather than concentrating all of the armed Wobblies within
the I.W.W. hall, they had been scattered at strategic spots
which would enable them to lay down a deadly crossfire in
front of the building.

At about one o'clock on the afternoon of November
eleventh, Bert Bland, Loren Roberts, and Ole Hanson had
taken up positions on Seminary Hill—an uninhabited hill rising to a height of about seventy-five feet, and situated about
four hundred yards east of the I.W.W. hall. Each was armed

with a rifle and supplied with ammunition; and from the selected spot each had an unobstructed view of the front of the I.W.W. hall and of a portion of Tower Avenue down which the parade was scheduled to pass.

Davis and Eugene Barnett, also armed, took up positions in Bert Bland's room on the second floor of the Avalon Hotel, where the south front window offered a commanding view of the I.W.W. hall and of the avenue in front of it.

John Lamb, armed with a rifle, and O. C. Bland, armed with a revolver, stationed themselves in an upstairs front room of the Arnold Hotel, thus completing the strategic maneuver by which the Wobblies planned to hold the front of their building under crossfire. The remaining Wobblies were within the I.W.W. hall, and they made no attempt to deny that nearly all of them were armed.

Despite conflicting testimony on many other points, it was conceded that the eight platoons of the Centralia Post of the American Legion were ordered to "halt and close up" when in the immediate vicinity of the I.W.W. hall. The order was given by the Post Commander, Warren O. Grimm, and it was the contention of the State that this was a routine order made necessary by the fact that the distance between the platoons had become more or less unsettled in making a turn at Third Street and crossing from the east to the west side of the avenue. It was the testimony of defense witnesses that the troops broke rank and stormed the front of the I.W.W. hall, and that the Wobblies fired only in defense of their lives and of their property.

By incessant and often savage cross-examination, Vanderveer was able to create a substantial shadow of doubt that the Wobblies had opened fire without provocation. Numerous witnesses testified that the shooting did not start until a number of the Centralia Legionnaires had dashed to the front of the I.W.W. hall and commenced to force an entrance through the doorway. Inversely, there was nothing to refute the State's convincing evidence that the Legionnaires were

totally unarmed, except for the small arms carried by the
color guard in accordance with military rule. Thousands of
people had watched the parade in its long march from the
city park, down Main Street, and back on Tower Avenue,
and the presence of arms carried by the Centralia Post hardly
could have gone undetected.

The court ruled out evidence which Vanderveer had assembled, intending to prove the existence of a conspiracy to
assault the hall; and upon this point he argued bitterly but
without success. He used it, also, as one of the main points
in his appeal to the Supreme Court, charging judicial error.
However, by casual remarks of witnesses and by inference
and innuendo, he was able to offer provocative suggestions
to the jurors; and he repeatedly brought out the testimony
of I.W.W. defendants that they *feared* such an attack.

The principal conflict of the trial, then, settled down to
the question of exactly what happened on Tower Avenue
before the first shots were fired—whether the members of
Centralia Post of the American Legion were merely straight-
ening their ranks in order to continue with the parade, or
whether some of the men actually rushed to the front of the
I.W.W. hall. Upon this point hinged the question of whether
the Wobblies were guilty of unprovoked attack, or whether
they were fighting to defend themselves and their property.
That question became almost irrelevant, however, as the trial
ended and the court issued instructions to the jury.

Judge John M. Wilson informed the jurors that men are
permitted to arm themselves in defense of their persons or
their property, and that such defense in the face of actual
or threatened attack is proper and lawful. He pointed out,
however, that men stationed on Seminary Hill, in the Avalon
Hotel, or in the Arnold Hotel were not in a position to be
threatened by violence in a raid upon the I.W.W. hall; that
they were not in the presence or company of those defending
the hall from within, and they were not in close contact with
their property that was being placed in jeopardy. The as-

sembling of arms and the use of arms in these outside positions
therefore would be unlawful, and if the evidence showed
that Warren O. Grimm had been shot and killed as a result of
these unlawful acts, the killing would be murder. If the
evidence showed that those stationed within the hall had
participated in the conspiracy to assemble arms at such outside positions, then they would be equally guilty of murder.

Thus, by his instruction number 50 to the jury, Judge
Wilson ruled, in effect, that it was immaterial whether the
members of the Legion post had stormed the I.W.W. hall or
not. Because of their strategy in posting armed men outside
the I.W.W. hall, the Wobblies were declared ineligible to
come under the statutory rule of justifiable homicide, and
they would stand equally guilty of murder even if it had
been incontestably proved that the hall was under attack.

Earlier in the trial, at the conclusion of the State's case in
chief, Vanderveer had moved for the release of Bert Faulkner,
against whom the prosecution had failed to establish a case;
and Faulkner had been discharged by order of the court.
The jury, in returning its verdict, found Loren Roberts not
guilty by reason of insanity. It acquitted Elmer Smith, the
attorney who had advised the Wobblies that they could arm
themselves for purposes of defense, and it acquitted Mike
Sheehan—a very old but very ardent Wobbly who was the
father of Vanderveer's special investigator and who had employed defensive strategy of his own. Unarmed and unafraid,
he had attempted to shield Wesley Everest with his own body
at the time when the mob began moving in on the younger
man. The seven remaining defendants in custody were found
guilty of murder in the second degree, and Vanderveer immediately filed notice of appeal.

In a broad sense, the history of the I.W.W. in the Northwest ended with that trial. Its demise was written, not in the
decision of the court, but in the temper of the people on the
street. Its obituary was written between the lines of the front

page editorials. In the courtroom at Montesano the spectators and the jurors had come to realize that there were two sides to the story—or at least there were extenuating circumstances. To the great masses of the people throughout the area, there were no extenuating circumstances. To them, the story of the Centralia Massacre remained as it first had been reported: the story of armed Wobblies firing from ambush and without provocation, into the marching ranks of ex-servicemen who were taking part in an Armistice Day parade. Neither time nor circumstance could ever erase the bitterness or the horror of it. For the I.W.W. there remained no road back.

As an organization it continued. On Seattle's Skid Road the I.W.W. hall remained with its doors open, and with copies of the Little Red Song Book selling for a dime. There were few visitors and few customers. For the hard-core Wobblies, the long, lonely years were starting; and what remained of the I.W.W. as a union could be classified as hardly more than a dust-covered monument marking the resting place of a shattered dream.

The seeds of opposition to the capitalist system, sown among the ranks of dissatisfied laboring men in the logging camps and in the mills and in the harvest fields, continued to yield results; but now there was a new group beginning to harvest the crops. The anti-Communist, anti-political, and sometimes anti-social Wobblies had been all but driven from the field, and the budding Communist party in the United States found fertile fields for growth and expansion. They claimed no part of the poor-but-proud heritage of the I.W.W. They had no aversion to political agitation. They were capable of compromise on matters of principle or practice so long as they moved in the general direction of ultimate goals. And yet, with all of that I.W.W. history spread out before them, the Communists were destined to repeat and to multiply all of the errors that had gone before, and to com-

pound a distrust and a public loathing sufficient to wipe out
any advantages they may have inherited.

Following the trial at Montesano, George Vanderveer returned to Seattle and began preparing his briefs for the appeal
to the State Supreme Court. The Centralia episode had
touched off renewed fervor in the prosecution of Wobblies
throughout the Northwest, and Vanderveer was kept frantically busy attempting to defend them. Attorney Ralph
Pierce was equally busy, but the cases were too numerous
for them to handle.

In Spokane, Judge R. M. Webster had hit upon a unique
and efficient method of consigning Wobblies to jail without
the expense of a prolonged trial on a charge of criminal
syndicalism. He issued a blanket injunction against the whole
wide world, in which he enjoined anybody and everybody
from joining the I.W.W., or associating with the organization
or aiding it in any way. Thus, accused Wobblies who were
brought before Judge Webster did not require the formal
charge of criminal syndicalism and the lengthy trial which
almost invariably resulted. In effect, little was necessary except for the judge to survey the defendant, listen to evidence
identifying him as an active Wobbly, and then sentence him
to six months in jail. It was streamlined judicial efficiency
and Judge Webster generally disregarded the affidavits of
prejudice filed by defense attorneys seeking his disqualification.

Meanwhile in western Montana the young attorney, Leslie
B. Sulgrove, had joined in the battle to defend Wobblies being jailed throughout the Northwest, and he and Vanderveer
met in Spokane to test the very neat question of law raised
by Judge Webster's injunction, and to carry an appeal to the
State Supreme Court in behalf of a Wobbly whom Judge
Webster had sentenced for contempt.

In his appeal, Vandeveer charged that the disputed injunction was unconstitutional; that it was legislative rather than

judicial. He pointed out that a blanket injunction issued against anybody and everybody becomes, in fact, a law of the land; and that Judge Webster, in issuing such an injunction, had assumed powers restricted by the Constitution to the legislative branch of the government. The State Supreme Court, however, skillfully avoided meeting the issue head-on by finding Judge Webster in error for not recognizing the affidavit of prejudice and for not disqualifying himself. Thus the controversial injunction was nullified, Vanderveer's and Sulgrove's Wobbly clients were spared from conviction, and the short-cut method of assigning men to jail had been proved unworkable, because no other judge in the Northwest would enforce it. But the Supreme Court had avoided ruling on the legality of an injunction restraining the whole wide world.

Such legal victories, however, did little to endear George Vanderveer to the people of his state, and there were many in organized labor who shared in the general bitterness toward him. Anti-I.W.W. sentiment was as prevalent among the members of various A.F. of L. craft unions as it was among any group in the Northwest. In the outlying districts, particularly, a great amount of bitterness toward Vanderveer was shared by judges, sheriffs, police officers, prosecuting attorneys, and others connected with law enforcement.

On one occasion when he had finished trying a case in Portland, Oregon, Vanderveer stopped at Vancouver, Washington, on his way home, to see a client who was lodged in the Clarke County jail. It was after six o'clock and he walked through the halls of the Courthouse, unable to find anyone connected with the Sheriff's office. Finally he walked around behind the building and talked to his client through the barred windows. Some minutes later when he was again driving north toward Seattle, he was overtaken and flagged down by a deputy sheriff who told him that he was under arrest.

"On what charge?" Vanderveer demanded.

"Communicating with a prisoner without the consent of the jailer," he was informed.

When Vanderveer demanded to see the warrant, the embarrassed deputy admitted that there hadn't been time to get one made out. After an angry exchange of words, Vanderveer drove on; and the warrant was later served on him in Seattle. He promptly filed an affidavit of prejudice against the trial judge, which the judge ignored. The case of the State vs. Vanderveer was noted for trial.

Before his own case came to trial, Vanderveer defended the client who had been in the Clarke County jail and won an acquittal. When his own case came up, Vanderveer calmly informed the court that his client already had been acquitted of the crime charged against him; that the client therefor had been imprisoned wrongfully, and that the State had no right to restrict the conversation or the communication of an innocent man. His arguments were denied by the court. He was found guilty as charged, and he filed notice of appeal.

Surely it is seldom that a state supreme court has reviewed a more unusual brief than that submitted by George F. Vanderveer in his own behalf. A large portion of the brief consisted of an original poem of dubious meter and encompassing a vast amount of poetic license, written by a newspaperman, Eugene F. Ware, in 1878, while covering the trial of State vs. Lewis.

Vanderveer wrote: "Upon this phase of the case we cannot forbear to quote in full the case of the State vs. Lewis as reported by Eugene F. Ware. A man named Lewis while awaiting trial on a charge of burglary escaped jail, was recaptured, tried on the original charge and acquitted. He was then tried on the charge of jail breaking and convicted."

His brief then presented the poem in its entirety:

> This defendant, while at large,
> Was arrested on a charge
> Of burglarious intent.
> And direct to jail he went.
> But he somehow felt misused

And through prison walls he oozed.
And in some unheard of shape
He effected his escape.

Mark you now! Again the law
On Defendant placed its paw,
Like a hand of iron mail
And resocked him into jail—
Which said jail, while so corralled
He by sockage tenure held.

Then the court met and they tried
Lewis up and down each side,
On the good old-fashioned plan
But the jury cleared the man.

Now, you think that this strange case
Ends at just about this place.
Nay, not so! Again the law
On the Defendant placed its paw.
This time takes him round the Cape
For effecting his escape:
He, unable to give bail,
Goes reluctantly to jail.

Lewis, tried for this last act,
Makes a special plea of fact:
"Wrongly did they me arrest,
And while rightfully at large,
Taken on a wrongful charge,
I took back from them what they
From me wrongly took away."

When this special plea was heard,
Thereupon the State demurred.
The Defendant then was pained
When the Court was heard to say
In a cold impassive way:
"The demurrer is sustained."

Back to jail did Lewis go,
But Liberty is dear.
He appealed and now is here
To reverse the Judge below.

The opinion will contain
All the statements that remain.

Argument and Brief of Appellant.
As a matter, Sir, of fact,
Who was injured by our act?
Point it out, Sir, if you can.

Can you seize us when at large
On a baseless, trumped-up charge;
And if we escape, then say
It is a crime to get away—
When we rightfully regained
What was wrongfully obtained?

Please the Court, Sir,
What is crime?
What is right and what is wrong?
Is our freedom but a song
Or the subject of a rhyme?

*Argument and Brief of Attorney
For the State.*
When the State, that is to say,
We take Liberty away—
When the padlock and the hasp
Leave one helpless in our grasp,
It's unlawful then that he
Even dreams of liberty—
Wicked dreams that may in time
Grow and ripen into crime.
Crime of dark and damning shape;
Then if he perchance escape
Ever more, remorse will roll
O'er his shattered, sin-sick soul.

Please the Court, Sir,
How can we
Manage people who go free?

Reply of Appellant.
Please the Court, Sir, if it's sin,
Where does turpitude begin?

OPINION OF THE COURT. *Per Curiam.*
We don't make law. We are bound
To interpret it as found.

The defendant broke away;
When arrested he should stay.
This appeal can't be maintained,
For the record does not show
Error in the Court below,
And we nothing can infer.
Let the judgment be sustained—
All the Justices concur.

NOTE BY THE REPORTER:
"Of the Sheriff—rise and sing,
Glory to our earthly King!"

Never in an appeal in behalf of a client did Vanderveer
indulge such whimsy, and if the Justices of the Supreme
Court found it either amusing or enlightening, they failed to
make mention of it in rendering their decision. In somber
prose, they ruled that the trial court was in error in failing to
disqualify the Judge upon the filing of the affidavit of prejudice (State vs. Vanderveer 115 Wash. 184). Vanderveer was
free, but there was no applause.

Despite the widespread animosity toward him, respect for
Vanderveer's ability as a lawyer had not diminished. State
officials from Olympia frequently called upon him for legal
advice and, because of his notable work in revising the state's
penal code, he often was asked to help in the framing of
proposed legislation. On more than one occasion he hurried

from his dingy office in the Collins Building to keep a dinner engagement with the Governor in the dining room of the Butler Hotel.

Usually on such occasions he would call Ellinor in advance and ask her to join him, and act as hostess.

"It's the only thing I ask of you," he told her when she questioned the propriety of it. "You're still my wife, and there are times when a man wants his wife at his side."

With apparent pride he would introduce her to his guests, and all through the meal he would enact the role of the attentive and solicitous husband. Taunted and despised throughout the entire Northwest, banished from his place in society, berated and ridiculed in the public press, contemptuous of nearly all tradition, George Vanderveer, nevertheless, and for some peculiar reason, displayed an awesome dread of the scandal of divorce.

Even as Kitty Beck remained upstairs in her room, he stood in the lobby of the Butler Hotel and whispered earnestly to Ellinor: "There's no sense in deliberately inviting scandal."

CHAPTER EIGHTEEN

It will be lonely to be dead, but it cannot be much more lonely than to be alive.—AXEL MUNTHE

A DRIZZLE OF RAIN was falling when Ellinor Vanderveer awakened on the morning of May 22, 1922. She dressed hurriedly, grabbed a bit of breakfast, and waited for Bruce Shorts to stop by and pick her up in his car. Exactly fifteen years earlier, she recalled, she had dressed with similar haste, for it had been her wedding day and there had been many last-minute details to be attended to. Today would be something like that other day, she told herself—except that everything would be exactly in reverse.

Some few months earlier she had informed George Vanderveer that she could no longer tolerate the peculiar relationship that existed between them, and she had demanded a divorce. Because of his dread of publicity connected with such an action, she had permitted him to make the arrangements and he had waited for an opportunity to set the suit in some outlying court where it was more apt to be overlooked by the reporters from larger metropolitan dailies. Taking advantage of the confusion connected with a temporary shift of judicial duties in Kitsap County, he had managed to get the case scheduled for Judge French's court in Bremerton, Washington, across the Sound from Seattle, and not a word of the impending proceedings had found its way into Seattle newspapers. Coincidence had placed the date of the suit on their fifteenth wedding anniversary.

The drizzle of rain had developed into a steady downpour by the time Bruce Shorts reached the house, and they drove slowly through the drenched streets. Hesitantly, almost awkwardly, Shorts attempted to express his sympathy and his regrets but Ellinor preferred not to talk, and they drove on in silence. At the Butler Hotel they stopped to pick up George Vanderveer, and the three of them rode down to the dock together.

It was a trip Ellinor was destined never to forget. Rain beat against the window of the ship's cabin, and the wind whipped up whitecaps across the cold gray face of the Sound. Passengers—most of them wet and miserable—sat huddled in their seats and, all in all, it was a morbid and depressing sight.

George Vanderveer, however, seemed more like a school-boy on an excursion. He produced a deck of cards and invited Ellinor and Bruce to join him in a game of rummy. He smiled often, and he gazed at Ellinor with the half-bashful boyish grin that once had been so familiar. He spoke casually of the earlier days at Eagle Harbor and of the card games that had gone on almost endlessly; and he mentioned them as if nothing had changed except for those inevitable changes wrought by the normal passage of time.

Ellinor and Bruce Shorts attempted to match his mood, and all three of them laughed a little too eagerly and a little too often. The trip from the Bremerton dock to the Kitsap County Courthouse was like a slightly giddy nightmare to Ellinor. The sideflaps of the open touring car trembled in the face of uneven gusts of wind, and blasts of cold, drenched air swooped in from the gaping holes above the doors. Bruce Shorts was kept constantly busy operating the windshield-wiper with his right hand, but he joined in the frivolous chatter. To the casual observer it might easily have appeared as a happy excursion to celebrate a fifteenth wedding anniversary.

The legal proceedings went off smoothly with Bruce Shorts representing Ellinor and George Vanderveer representing himself. There were no reporters and no casual spectators in the courtroom, and news of the divorce never reached the Seattle papers.

When it was over, Bruce Shorts glanced at Ellinor and slowly shook his head. "There goes the loneliest man I have ever known in my life."

With the decreasing demands upon his time for the defense of the Wobblies, Vanderveer spent more and more of his time prosecuting personal injury cases against steamship, stevedore and street railway companies of the Northwest, and his financial situation improved rapidly as he won a succession of large suits in behalf of his clients. Simultaneously, the increasing automobile traffic on streets and highways was beginning to jam the courts with the first great boom of litigation, and he found an unexpected bonanza in prosecuting personal injury suits that resulted from automobile accidents.

Together, he and Kitty Beck built a beautiful home on Lake Burien, south of Seattle, and here they entertained some of the progressives and liberals who visited the city. Once again hospitality became the keynote, as in those earlier days at Eagle Harbor; but it was not the same. Vanderveer had his own close circle of friends in the legal profession who called occasionally at his insistent bidding. His private bar was stocked with the finest of imported liquors, many of which were seldom seen in those days of prohibition, and he poured generously. Kitty Beck—small, petite, attractive, intelligent, and cultured—fitted perfectly into the well-appointed setting as the hostess, and Vanderveer referred to her always as the Kitten. Somehow, visitors often arrived late and left early.

The vast majority of Vanderveer's clients were laboring men; and the few of them who ever visited at his home

usually stood awkwardly and self-consciously as they partook
of his hospitality, and then began edging quickly toward the
door. It was not the type of home in which they could feel
at ease. A number of Vanderveer's old friends still respected
him and admired him as a lawyer, but demonstrated no desire
to enter into his social life. The luxurious home on Lake
Burien, like the man who lived in it, stood like a symbol of
almost pathetic loneliness.

More and more, Vanderveer seemed reluctant to return to
the large and lonely house. He concentrated his energies and
his interests upon his legal practice, and often when he worked
late at night he didn't bother to go home at all.

As the outgrowth of belated inspiration, he established a
Legal Aid Bureau, associated with the Central Labor Council.
All members of organized labor in Seattle were urged to buy
a membership card for a dollar a year, entitling them to free
consultation upon any legal matter.

"Actually, it didn't entitle a man to anything he couldn't
get free in the office of any attorney in Seattle," one of
Vanderveer's associates admitted ruefully in later years. "It
sounded good, though, and it enabled Van to handle a lot
of cases where he never even hoped to get paid." The establishment of the Legal Aid Bureau had one other effect: it
practically guaranteed that cardholders would seek Vanderveer's services whenever they needed legal help of any kind.
With business booming at the old office in the Collins Building, Vanderveer later established similar bureaus in Everett
and Tacoma, Washington; and in Portland, Oregon.

No longer able to handle all of the legal matters personally,
he began building up his staff; and he displayed the same type
of individualism he had displayed in selecting his staff for the
Prosecuting Attorney's office years before. His methods of
selection were unorthodox in the extreme. He sought out
Will Beardslee, a young law student at the University of
Washington, and informed him that a job would be waiting
for him as soon as he was admitted to the bar. His interest

in Beardslee had been kindled when he watched the lad fighting in the prize ring. It was almost parallel to his earlier selection of Al Lundin as a deputy prosecutor. He was ridiculed on many occasions for his methods of selection, but there can be little doubt that he had a peculiar genius for picking men.

Sam Bassett had been a young, liberal, and distraught student of sociology in Washington, D. C., at the time of the Centralia tragedy; alarmed by injustice in a world of mounting prejudice, and struggling to reaffirm his own faith that all men are created equal. He followed the progress of the trial from day to day, and in some of the more radical papers he read the frequent tributes to George Vanderveer —the fighting lawyer of the Northwest who had turned down a profitable practice to defend the rights of the underdogs. During the course of that trial, Sam Bassett discovered that he had found a pattern for his own life and a worthy use for his talents. He dropped out of school and made arrangements to transfer his credits to the University of Washington, in Seattle, where he planned to take up the study of law and to help fight similar battles in the future.

He called upon George Vanderveer several times before he graduated from law school, and he told him how the defense of the Centralia I.W.W. had influenced his life. After he had passed his bar examinations, and after several desperate months of delay, Bassett was taken into Vanderveer's office, where he remained for the rest of Vanderveer's life.

Small of stature, unsure of himself at the outset, overawed by Vanderveer's dominating personality, Sam Bassett offered a strange contrast to most of the other men in the office. He was a quiet, soft-spoken idealist; and to the casual observer, Vanderveer and Bassett might have appeared as the opposite extremes at every point of comparison. Actually, they had a great deal in common, and between them there developed a mutual respect and understanding which Vanderveer had shared with no other man in his life. With Sam Bassett, as with Ellinor during the early years of his marriage, he was willing to relinquish the cold mask of cynicism which he presented to the world, and to reveal his otherwise guarded thoughts and deeper philosophies.

Seldom even with Ellinor had he referred to earlier recollections from his childhood. Almost never had he mentioned his mother. And yet there were times when he would sit with Sam Bassett and indulge in idle reverie. In rambling reminiscence, he described the rebellion which had caused him to turn down the job with the Great Northern Railway—the reluctance to sell his services in a job lot to a single client. He told Bassett how his mother's death had destroyed his simple faith in the orthodox conception of a just God who would selfishly take her for His own. He recalled incidents from his boyhood in Ames, and he speculated as to how much those things may have affected the forming of his admittedly unusual personality.

With the single exception of Sam Bassett, he presented to his intimate friends a cynical attitude toward his own past, and a practised contempt for anything that might appear sentimental. When Leslie Sulgrove was leaving on an airplane trip to the East, Vanderveer grinned at him as they shook hands. "You might flush the privy as you fly over Ames, Iowa. That's where I used to live."

Not even with Sam Bassett, however, did Vanderveer share the secret of the loneliness he must have felt. He was a crusader without a crusade; a fighter without a worthy opponent. He turned more and more of the legal work over to his associates, and he attempted to fill the loneliness of his life from the bottles of Skid Road speakeasies. He became involved in frequent brawls and, because his reflexes were not so quick as they had been, he took many severe beatings.

Will Beardslee, who lived at the Butler Hotel, was awakened one night in the final week of October, 1924, by the sound of pounding on his door. When he opened the door he found Kitty Beck almost hysterical. She told him that she knew that Vanderveer was in the building with another woman, and that she intended to find him. She flung herself away from him as he tried to console her, and she pounded against the wall with her tiny fists. "I can't stand it! I can't stand it!" she sobbed. "It can't go on this way!"

She eluded him again and ran through the halls screaming Vanderveer's name hysterically. Beardslee had thrown a robe around himself before answering the pounding on his door, and now he followed her through the hallway, talking quietly and urging her to be calm. The soothing tone of his voice eventually took effect and the hysteria departed. She continued crying softly, but she promised Beardslee that she would go home and forget about it.

The following day Vanderveer went to Tacoma to try a case with Leslie Sulgrove, and when he returned to the house that evening he found Kitty Beck's lifeless body in the bed. She had secured herself between the blankets with safety pins and taken chloroform. On the wall above the bed she had written with lipstick: "Kitty Beck—sometimes known as Kitty Vanderveer."

He called the police and he was up most of the night answering questions. The morning papers played up the story, but by the time court convened in Tacoma the following morning, he was at his place at the counsel's table, beside Leslie Sulgrove.

"I guess you've already heard about the Kitten," he whispered to Sulgrove. "It's a damn shame." However, with no display of emotion he carried on through the trial, and to the world he presented an unshaken countenance. The Wobblies of Skid Road who had learned to worship Kitty Beck appeared to take her death with deeper regret than did George Vanderveer.

He left the Lake Burien home and moved into the Butler Hotel, sharing a room with Will Beardslee. Night after night Beardslee heard Vanderveer pacing the floor, and he watched him grow progressively more haggard from lack of sleep.

COUNSEL FOR THE DAMNED

Often in the early morning hours Vanderveer would sit pale
and shaken on the side of his bed, his hair disheveled and his
face twisted with emotion, while he conceded that he hadn't
had a moment's sleep throughout the night. "My God! I
keep hearing the Kitten crying!" To the public, however,
and even to other intimate friends, he offered no hint of the
emotion he was keeping bottled up inside himself.

Following the death of Kitty Beck, Vanderveer hurled
himself into his law practice with an unrelenting drive that
left him little time for meditation. In his idle moments he
was seldom sober, and he practised profanity with an almost
fanatical fervor. He was cynical, unyielding, and at times
he was purposely uncouth; but he was still the master of the
courtroom and an outstanding lawyer of his day.

On January 19, 1925, less than three months after the death
of Kitty Beck, a Federal grand jury in Seattle presented an
indictment against Roy Olmstead and ninety other defendants
for conspiracy to violate the National Prohibition Act.
Olmstead, widely recognized as king of the Northwest bootleggers following the forced abdication of the Billingsleys
and the Marquett gang, had been for months playing an
international game of hide-and-seek across the waters of
Puget Sound; operating a fleet of chartered boats and numerous trucks and automobiles while smuggling some two
hundred cases of liquor each day from Canada into Seattle.
It was a multi-million-dollar business, and the so-called Olmstead gang included scouts, transfer men, office workers,
salesmen, telephone operators, dispatchers, checkers, collectors, three full-time bookkeepers, and an attorney. It was
big business.

The ninety-one members of the gang reacted in many
different ways when the indictment was presented. Some of
them struck out for the far horizon and kept right on going.
Some of them descended upon the organization's full-time
attorney, Jerry L. Finch; but an even dozen of them discarded their previous organizational ties and headed for the

office of George Vanderveer in the Collins Building. The
chips were down, their liberty was at stake, and they were
no longer interested in the fine points of organizational
loyalty or honor among thieves. They were convinced that
their one hope for acquittal lay in securing Vanderveer to
defend them. This was the case in which Felix Crane, whom
Vanderveer had defended a decade earlier, declined his
services.

To Vanderveer, at the outset, it represented little more
than another routine case; and to Seattle newspaper readers,
a prompt conviction seemed inevitable. Many of the defendants had been caught red-handed, with liquor in their
possession. The gas boat *Eva B.* had been seized with seven
hundred and eighty-four cases of liquor and three of the
defendants aboard. Voluminous records of the organization
had been seized at the home of Roy Olmstead. Sales of
liquor had been made to Federal agents, who had been working on the case for a great many months prior to the grand
jury presentation of the indictment.

However, when the case opened in the courtroom of Judge
Jeremiah Neterer, it quickly took on a new complexion. The
prosecution introduced evidence gathered by Federal agents,
gained by tapping the telephone wires of the organization;
and Vanderveer opened a bitter and prolonged battle with
Judge Neterer over the admissibility of such evidence.
Attorneys for the other defendants generally were content
to sit back and let him carry the ball.

Vanderveer pointed out that the tapping of telephone
wires was prohibited by state law, and he argued that it was
unthinkable to sanction a violation of the law in order to
enforce the law. Upon this point he was overruled.

Day by day, as the trial progressed, he continued to
hammer away at the question of admissibility, and his objections were renewed with each new witness and with each
new point of evidence. Gradually, in the public mind and
in the public press, interest shifted to the new issue, and the

charge of violating the Prohibition Act became almost incidental. The case became known across the nation as Seattle's
celebrated "wire-tapping case," and George Vanderveer once
again was on the offensive. The jury in Judge Neterer's
courtroom was pondering the guilt or innocence of Roy
Olmstead and his associates; but the nation was pondering
the moral guilt or innocence of Federal agents who tap telephone wires in order to gather evidence.

To Vanderveer, it was a new and timely crusade; and by
throwing himself whole-heartedly into the legal battle, he
had less time to sit and brood. By staying up most of the
night and riffling through law books in search of precedents,
he could free himself of the haunting hallucinations in which
he heard the Kitten crying. By the time he was well into the
case, there can be little doubt that he had convinced himself
that the basic liberties of Americans yet unborn rested
squarely upon his shoulders.

Any hope for the acquittal of his clients in Judge Neterer's
court had disappeared with the Judge's ruling that evidence
gained by wire-tapping would be accepted, and Vanderveer
used his time in court to build the foundation for an appeal,
seeking every opportunity to invite judicial error. His technique was not unlike that of a legal toreador, taunting and
tormenting the able jurist in an attempt to promote some
injudicious charge, while never permitting himself to get
beyond the borderline of contempt.

Judge Neterer, with equal skill, pondered his judicial rul-
ings and took occasion to place his own substantiating arguments in the record; and professors and law students from
the University of Washington converged upon the courtroom
to watch one of the classic legal battles of Northwest history.

It came as no particular surprise to anyone when the
defendants were found guilty in the lower court and were
sentenced to terms of eighteen months to two years at hard
labor; but Vanderveer carried his appeal to the Circuit Court
and on to the United States Supreme Court. By now, the

fate of the original defendants was almost incidental, for this was a fight on a matter of principle; a crusade in the name of Justice.

In neither the Circuit Court nor in the Supreme Court (Consolidated for trial: Olmstead vs. U. S. 72 L. Ed. 944 and Green vs. U. S. 277 vs. 438) was Vanderveer able to win a reversal of the lower court decision, although it was a 5 to 4 split court in the top tribunal; but as a result of his prolonged battle, a great deal of public feeling was building up. The dissenting opinions of Justice Holmes and Justice Brandeis in the Supreme Court and of Judge D. J. Rudkin in the Circuit Court, all added fuel to the flames; and the Congress of the United States hurriedly passed a bill prohibiting the use of evidence gathered by tapping telephone wires.

George Vanderveer's clients were serving time at the United States penitentiary at McNeil's Island, and their terms were not one day shorter than those of their co-defendants. However—if it was any consolation to them as they went about their duties at hard labor—they had helped to shape the new law of the land and a new conception of the people's rights before the court.

Despite his courtroom loss, George Vanderveer had won his crusade.

CHAPTER NINETEEN

He was a man, take him for all in all, I shall not look upon his like again.—SHAKESPEARE

WITH HIS FIRST real taste of financial success from an increasingly profitable law practice, George Vanderveer developed a sudden gambler's urge to break the bank. He invested wildly in an assortment of get-rich-quick endeavors, sinking thousands of dollars in wildcat oil wells, unproven gold mines, and similar ventures. He bought a large filbert orchard in California, convinced that nuts would soon become the staple food of a meatless diet for a nation that had exhausted its grazing land. Under the terms of his divorce, he assigned to Ellinor several hundred acres of unirrigated land at Hanford, in south-central Washington—land upon which she was unable to pay taxes, and which the Federal government used in later years as a heavily guarded site of operations for the Atomic Energy Commission.

He scorned conservative investments in insurance, and he told Sam Bassett: "I'll buy term insurance—on *my* terms!" He taunted his younger associate for his financial conservatism when Bassett urged him to invest in sound securities, and on at least one occasion he interceded on Bassett's behalf to make sure he "got in on a good thing." This was when Vanderveer was promoting stock in a mine in Idaho.

"Sam," he explained, "I've invested five hundred dollars

of your money in this stock. You'll find it charged against
you on the books."

Bassett was somewhat taken aback, but he did not protest.

"You're so damned conservative!" Vanderveer grinned.
"This is going to be the biggest thing that ever happened;
and, by God, I just couldn't stand to see you left out of it,
when the rest of us are raking in money hand over fist!"

There could be no doubt of Vanderveer's sincerity; and
although Bassett had no faith in the mine or in any other of
Vanderveer's promotions, he accepted the stock and he paid
each of the eight successive assessments until he had invested
some $1,300. Years later, after Vanderveer's death, he re-
ceived two small dividends.

On another occasion Vanderveer became interested in a
soft-spoken old gentleman who informed him, after a few
drinks, that there was a vast fortune in oil beneath the ground,
near Redding, California. Supposedly, it was a guarded
secret; and it had some connection with a vast conspiracy
among the major oil companies. But if the old man could
just raise private capital and move in there and start drilling,
it would be a sure bonanza; the biggest thing that ever
happened. Vanderveer organized and promoted the Redhead
Oil Company, and he succeeded in getting a number of his
friends to invest heavily in the venture.

It was but another of many of Vanderveer's frantic
gambles to hit the jackpot and to become fantastically
wealthy overnight. Eventually, however, in the face of
Bassett's persistent and logical arguments in favor of conservative investments, fortified by the mounting evidence of
his own folly, George Vanderveer began buying real estate.

In the final years of his life he acquired a sizable fortune,
representing organized labor during an era when unions had
vast operating funds. In association with his old friend, John
Savage, he made numerous other investments that served to
compound his spiraling income. Together, they owned the
money-making Trianon Ballroom, and Vanderveer, as a self-

discovered patron of the arts, invested thousands of dollars in fine oil paintings which decorated such unlikely places as the women's powder room. The walls of his Lake Burien home were covered with splendid examples of art, including two Remingtons and a Renoir.

He became personally acquainted with Oscar Strobel, the desert artist, and he bought, in all, some ten of Strobel's water colors. Strobel recalled, later, that two of the paintings had been ordered by a long distance telephone call to his studio at Scottsdale, Arizona. It was midnight, and undoubtedly Vanderveer had been drinking, but he was exacting and explicit, and he knew what he wanted. He ordered two water colors of the Arizona desert. Strobel described Vanderveer as a two-fisted drinker, but he insisted that he had never seen him or spoken to him when Vanderveer failed to appear alert, or failed to know exactly what he was saying and doing.

Both Vanderveer and John Savage owned large blocks of stock in the Seattle Baseball Club, which proved at that time to be somewhat less than a bonanza. Vanderveer, alone, bought a hotel for seventy-five thousand dollars; and he paid advertising rates to place the notice in the leading newspapers when he discovered that he was still receiving a journalistic cold shoulder from the Seattle press.

Belatedly in his life he developed an interest in acquiring wealth, and an almost sadistic delight in flaunting it in the face of any person who ever had questioned his ability to do so.

On a trip to California he visited Ellinor, who was living in a small apartment in Hollywood. Ellinor was earning her own living as a movie extra, and making her own way, and she was completely out of debt for almost the first time in her adult life; and yet it was a rather precarious existence. The day of George's visit was the day before Thanksgiving. During his short visit, he mentioned that in recent years he had been in the habit of buying several hundred turkeys each Thanksgiving and having them delivered to the homes of the poor. He also extracted a one-thousand-dollar bill from his wallet and handed it to Ellinor.

"Ever see one of these, Gus?" he asked.

Ellinor smoothed out the bill on the top of the table and drew her hands away. If he intended the money for her, he could leave it there. If he intended to take it back, he could pick it up without embarrassment. There had been no indication of what he had meant by it.

"I don't think I've ever seen one before in my life," she told him.

He picked up the bill and slipped it back into his wallet, still grinning. "Well, at least you can say you've had a thousand-dollar bill in your hands. It's not everybody who can say that."

To Ellinor, there appeared little resemblance between this hard, cynical, and strangely conceited man, and the man she had loved and respected and admired and married. She was not entirely alone in that, for nearly all of Vanderveer's early friends insisted that there existed hardly a basis for honest comparison between the man he had been, and the man he had become.

In the final years of his life, George Vanderveer was in almost endless clashes with the police. He had learned to drive a car some years earlier, and now he drove with a wild abandon that seemed to defy his personal gods of Fate. He was arrested for speeding, for reckless driving, for driving while drunk. He was involved in numerous traffic accidents, but he continued to live a charmed life.

He sat at the bedside of his friend, Bruce Shorts, who was slowly dying, and in the presence of Bruce Shorts, Jr., he cursed the injustice of the world. "God damn it, it isn't right!" he protested. "You've been a fine and decent man, and you've done everything that's right and good, all of your life. I'm a no-good bastard; I've messed up my life and the life of everybody who's been close to me! I should be lying there, and you should be sitting here—but how in hell do you appeal the decision?"

On July 3, 1927, George Vanderveer married Ethel Hoover in Tacoma, Washington, and once again opened up the Lake Burien home. The welcome mat was out, and the aura of loneliness left the big house. Chin Suey, a highly efficient houseboy who had worked for Will Beardslee, became a servant in the Lake Burien house when Beardslee left Seattle to take a position with the Justice Department in Washington, D.C., and Chin Suey became respected as an institution. On one occasion a visitor to the house, unaccustomed to such hospitality, attempted to pay Chin Suey for a drink and was promptly thrown out of the house by the irate George Vanderveer who took it as an insult.

Sam Bassett, meanwhile, had started a quiet search for larger and better offices. He found many vacant suites in many different buildings; but each time the bargaining over the proposed lease had bogged down when he had explained that George Vanderveer would be one of the occupants. Eventually he had located a suite of offices in the Alaska Building, and the building manager had assured him that Vanderveer would be welcome—that any tenants would be welcomed so long as they paid their rent and obeyed the rules of the building.

Vanderveer found the news difficult to accept. "Did you tell them about me?" he asked. "Are you sure they knew who you were talking about?"

Bassett assured him that there was no misunderstanding, and the two men walked to the Alaska Building and inspected the vacant offices. For a long time Vanderveer stood at the window, looking out over the city.

"This is where I started, Sam," he said at last. "We moved in here just after I took office as Prosecuting Attorney . . . right here in this same building. It's something like coming back home. . . ."

From somewhere, a few days later, he produced a framed

picture of his father and hung it on the wall of his private
office. It was an informal picture of the old man, sitting on
a log and whittling; and it was the only picture Vanderveer
ever hung in his office. It was his one public admission of a
sentimental attachment and, on several occasions, Bassett
entered the office to find Vanderveer studying the picture.

The return to the Alaska Building appeared to have a
sobering effect upon George Vanderveer, as if he had been
granted reprieve and had returned to the folds of respectability. He showed Sam Bassett the offices he had occupied
as Prosecuting Attorney and he spoke almost fondly of his
earlier days in the building and of his earlier associates in the
practice of law.

However, when President Herbert Hoover nominated
Kenneth Mackintosh for the Circuit Court of Appeals,
Vanderveer immediately began communicating with labor
attorneys all over the country, demanding that they use their
influence to block Mackintosh's appointment by the United
States Senate.

Judge Campbell hurried to Seattle to protest. "What in
the name of heaven are you up to?" he demanded of Vanderveer. "Who got you your first job in Seattle, in Judge
Burke's office? It was Mac! Who gave you your appointment as a deputy prosecutor? It was Mac! Who gave you
the endorsement to become Prosecutor? It was Mac! After
all he's done for you, how can you try to mess up his appointment to the Federal bench? That's what he's dreamed of,
for years!"

Vanderveer shook his head. "Personal feelings don't enter
into it, Bill. Mac is too conservative, especially on labor
cases. He doesn't have organized labor's point of view."

Campbell stared at him. "Don't you feel that you owe
him anything at all?"

Vanderveer shrugged. "Who knows? Maybe I owe him
a hell of a lot—but I'm not going to let these poor God damn
laboring people pay my debts for me! I'm not going to let

some poor bastard lose his appeal, just because I'm obligated, personally."

"You're not even being reasonable," Campbell protested. "You know as well as I do that there wasn't ever a more fair-minded man than Kenneth Mackintosh! There isn't a better qualified man in the whole damn country! You could at least be reasonable about it."

"I'm not a judge, I'm a labor attorney," Vanderveer reminded him. "You can talk about a man being fair-minded and impartial and qualified; but what I'm interested in is to get a man on that bench who's a friend of organized labor!"

Despite Campbell's protests, Vanderveer continued his frenzied campaign. He was able to arouse sufficient protests from organized labor across the country to block the necessary confirmation by the United States Senate. It proved to be a hard blow to Kenneth Mackintosh, and it served to alienate some of the lingering respect a number of old friends held for Vanderveer.

Respect for his legal ability never diminished, however, and there is no evidence that he ever took a drink before going into court. At times he was blunt and outspoken in the courtroom, but never profane.

At one time he represented a girl sixteen years old, who had been severely injured by coming into contact with twenty-two thousand volts of electricity. She had been on an outing with her parents and had crawled under the barbed wire fence that enclosed a high voltage transformer. Her hair had touched the open wires and the twenty-two thousand volts had leaped through her skull and made a hole in the earth about ten feet behind her. Beyond a doubt, if there had been only two thousand volts, the discharge of electricity would have grounded down through her body and killed her instantly. As it was, she lived; but the entire top of her skull had been burned away.

In court, the defense offered to prove that the transformer produced an ominous humming sound, like a hive of bees;

that the enclosure was clearly marked with a metal sign warning people to stay back: "22,000 VOLTS"; and that the sturdy fence surrounding it had obviously been erected for the sole purpose of keeping people out. Unfortunately, the transformer house and box had been built on a fill, and some of the earth had sloughed away leaving an opening large enough for a person to crawl under the wire. Unfortunately, also, the metal warning signs were on the front of the enclosure and not visible from the rear, where the hole had opened up.

Vanderveer brought out the fact that the girl had left her family, seeking some secluded spot to "answer a call of nature."

He turned to face the jury, shrugged his heavy shoulders, and announced blithely: "When you've got to go, you've got to go." There was a titter in the courtroom, and that bit of blunt vulgarity was due, in time, to become fairly familiar across the nation.

After building his case patiently, Vanderveer called the girl to the stand. She was young, attractive, and seemed to possess a luxuriant head of dark hair. However, as Vanderveer questioned her, the girl reached up and removed the wig almost as casually as a man might remove his hat. The jurors gasped and somewhere in the back of the courtroom, a woman cried out. A woman juror became ill after one look at the horribly seamed and ridged tissue spanning the flat top of the head, and a recess had to be taken. The jury could hardly wait to go out and bring in a verdict of twenty-five thousand dollars for the plaintiff.

Called to Ellensburg, Washington, to defend the accused rioters in the wake of the so-called "Ellensburg Riots," Vanderveer indulged in a bit of courtroom legerdemain which undoubtedly turned the tide of the legal battle.

Upon first reaching the courtroom, he discovered that the prosecution had assembled a great variety of weapons which it intended to introduce into evidence and to have various

witnesses identify as the weapons used by the accused rioters.
There were clubs, blackjacks, pick-handles, pool cues, and
similar items, all stacked on the floor of the witness stand.

Together with his young associate counsel, John Geisness,
Vanderveer assembled a stockpile of similar weapons. He
bought a pick-handle from a hardware store, picked up a
length of pipe from a plumbing shop, and bought a short
length of wood from a lumberyard. Upon each he had John
Geisness make some inconspicuous identifying mark and
then, unobserved, he added these to the prosecution's stockpile.

He watched and listened, expressionless, as prosecution witnesses identified these items along with the others. On
cross-examination, he forced the witnesses to amplify their
identifications and then, at the proper time, he placed John
Geisness on the stand.

Geisness identified the various items Vanderveer had added
to the stockpile, told where each had been secured, and
pointed out the identifying marks he had placed upon each.
It was sufficient to counteract the effectiveness of the State's
other exhibits, and to undermine the credibility of its witnesses—and yet there could be no possible charge of tampering
with evidence. He had made his addition to the stockpile
prior to the admission of any of the objects into evidence,
and he had not altered the State's exhibits in any way.

Following Vanderveer's victory, there were those who
charged that he had thwarted justice through trickery and
that in this case, as in many others, he had made a mockery
of the cherished right of trial by jury.

To his associates, Vanderveer made it plain that he did
not agree with these charges in any way; and there can be
little doubt that, in his own mind, he had prevented rather
than induced a miscarriage of justice.

Despite his courtroom wizardry and often-unorthodox pro-
cedures, there was hardly a judge or an attorney in the Pacific
Northwest who ever questioned Vanderveer's integrity. Even

when he was banished from uptown Seattle, socially scorned and publicly condemned for his defense of the Wobblies, his oral word was accepted as unquestioned surety. The senior member of one of Seattle's most conservative law firms announced later that he knew of no single instance when any member of his firm had ever asked Vanderveer to back up an oral agreement with a written agreement, unless it were for a matter of record. "I don't think it ever occurred to any of us to doubt his word."

At approximately the time of his move to the Alaska Building and for a number of years thereafter, Vanderveer's law practice was so extensive that most of his daytime hours were spent in the courtroom, and he depended more and more upon his associates to do the preliminary work and the investigation. It was not uncommon for jurors returned to the courtroom with a verdict, to find Vanderveer in the midst of examining jurors for his next case. To many thousands of persons, the services of George Vanderveer represented the unfailing antidote for any type of legal difficulty, or the safe and sure road to generous compensation in event of injury.

In such a wholesale type of practice, there were occasions when Vanderveer first met his client, personally, in the courtroom as the trial was about to begin; and there can be no reasonable doubt that his reputation was sustained, also, by his legal associates who prepared the groundwork and provided the ammunition for his devastating cross-examinations. Those associates, over the years, included Frank Pierce, Will Beardslee, Roy DeGrief, Roscoe R. Smith, Maurice Cooperman, Sam Bassett, Sam L. Levinson and John Geisness; in addition to Leslie Sulgrove in Tacoma and Douglas Ballinger in Everett. No longer did Vanderveer have time to use his feet as well as his head in the practice of law, as Judge Burke once had recommended; but he had associates of exceptional caliber to do the footwork, and most of them were excellent trial lawyers as well. They knew what was needed to win each case, and they seldom let Vanderveer go into court without it.

With the tremendous volume of legal business pouring constantly through the office, there were bound to be occasions when Vanderveer and his associates were caught off balance; for a client is not always entirely truthful with his attorney and he may exaggerate the extent of his injuries, hoping to win a larger judgment.

On one occasion, Vanderveer agreed to represent a seaman confined to a Seattle hospital who, according to his story, had stepped on a round metallic object at the head of the stairway after entering the Pantages Theatre in Seattle. He had fallen down the stairway and, screaming with pain, had been rushed to the hospital by ambulance. X-ray pictures taken at the hospital showed the shadowy line of a fracture across the ball of the ball-and-socket joint of the hip—a particularly painful type of injury. Hospital attendants had placed the man in a Bradford frame to ease his suffering; and his first request, after that, had been: "Send for Vanderveer!"

It appeared to be an open-and-shut case. An usher at the theatre had seen the fall, and the injured man had demonstrated remarkable presence-of-mind even while screaming with pain, for he had demanded that the round metallic object on the stairway be retained as evidence. Without more than feeling it under foot he identified it as the round head of a curtain rod.

Vanderveer was in an affable mood when he was called upon by Attorney Ralph Potts, serving as attorney for a client insurance company. "We've got you over a barrel," Vanderveer announced, grinning, "and there isn't a damned thing you can do about it."

"All I want is your agreement to let our doctor examine the patient," Potts explained, and Vanderveer agreed readily.

Two days later he practically leaped out of his chair when Potts called him and informed him that new X-rays had been taken and they showed no fracture at all. Together the two attorneys went to the hospital and questioned the technician and the hospital doctor in charge.

"How is this possible?" Vanderveer demanded. "You take
an X-ray one day and it shows a severe fracture; then you
take an X-ray some days later and it doesn't show any fracture at all!"

The doctor shook his head. "I don't know. Off hand, I'd
say that it *isn't* possible—but there it is. I can't explain it."
He was obviously baffled.

Through their questioning of the X-ray technician, the two
attorneys learned that there was only one difference in the
method of taking both pictures. Because the patient obviously
was in severe pain when the first X-ray was taken, there had
been no attempt to strap him to the table; he had merely been
asked to lie as quietly as possible. For the second X-ray, the
patient had been strapped securely to the table, despite his
very strenuous objections.

The two attorneys took the X-ray pictures into the ward
and confronted the seaman with them. "How in hell do you
explain this?" Vanderveer demanded.

The seaman groaned, and shook his head, and insisted that
he didn't know anything about it; and he couldn't understand
it. However, Vanderveer questioned the man as relentlessly
as if he were cross-examining him upon the witness stand, and
he finally brought forth an amazing story.

During World War I, the seaman had been a corpsman on
a Navy hospital ship. Somehow he had discovered that by
twisting his leg around, almost throwing it out of joint, he
could cause the ragged top of the femur to cast a shadow
over the ball—producing a line upon the X-ray plate which any
physician would instantly classify as a fracture. In the intervening years he had traveled around the country having a
succession of "accidents" and winning a series of judgments;
each time, of course, using a different name.

"You dirty little bastard!" Vanderveer shouted at him, "I'll
give you just ten minutes to get your clothes on and get out
of this hospital—or by God, you won't be able to leave!"

The theatre management had previously agreed to pay all

medical and hospital expenses, convinced that it would be liable; and Attorney Ralph Potts now suggested to Vanderveer that he dismiss his action with prejudice. "You do that, and my client will take care of any expenses that have been run up to date."

Vanderveer shook his head. "To hell with that! You send all the bills to my office and by God, I'll pay them myself!" And he did.

Riding back downtown together in a taxi, Vanderveer stared thoughtfully at the younger attorney. "How did you get wise to this fellow?" he asked at last. "What made you think it wasn't legitimate, when an impartial man took the X-ray and a qualified doctor offered the diagnosis?"

Ralph Potts shook his head and grinned. "Actually, I was just fishing in the dark. I know that when you step on a round metal object in a soft carpet that you can't ordinarily identify what you stepped on, particularly to the threads inside the ball. And then, if you're actually screaming with pain, you don't take time right then to think about gathering evidence for a lawsuit. To me, the whole thing just didn't seem quite right."

For some time Vanderveer continued studying the younger man before replying. "You know, when I was your age I would have wondered about those things, too; I would have had time to wonder about them," he said at last. "By God, you lose something when you start handling too many cases and just run them through like clockwork. Hell! You lose everything!"

Apparently, in the later years of his life, Vanderveer was unable to find the excitement and the satisfaction in his practice of law which he had known as a younger man, and he was no longer content with the courtroom as his entire world. He began groping for new worlds to conquer.

Annoyed with his minor role as a stockholder in many of John Savage's enterprises, he finally offered to trade his stock in the Trianon Ballroom for Savage's stock in the Seattle

Baseball Club. "Damn it, I want to manage something my-self," he argued. "I'm getting God damn sick of being just the guy who sits in the back seat while somebody else drives!"

Savage shook his head. "You can't swing it, Van. You don't have enough money behind you to handle a deal like that. You don't realize how much it takes, especially if the club has a bad season."

Apparently, however, Vanderveer had become obsessed with the dream of personally guiding the destiny of the Seat-tle Indians through their Coast League schedule—of sitting in the dugout and inspiring an unconquerable team spirit that would guide them to a pennant. To him, no doubt, it prom-ised a duplication of those exciting days long ago when he had served as Prosecuting Attorney, with his "team" gathered about him, and all of the men working together toward a common goal. Once again he would slap his men on the back and tell them to get in there and fight! He would stand be-hind his men when they were criticized by the sports writers, and they would go out on the field and play their hearts out for him. There would be tense, gripping, exciting days; and once again, life would have its old zest and sparkle. Reluc-tantly he conceded that he lacked Savage's experience in busi-ness management, but he clung doggedly to his contention that he knew one hell of a lot more about baseball.

He signed over to John Savage his stock in the Trianon Ballroom, and he took Savage's stock in the ball club; and he discovered that running a baseball club was altogether dif-ferent from running the office of Prosecuting Attorney. For a time he attended every game and he sat moodily pounding his fist into the palm of his hand as he watched errors and weaknesses he could neither prevent nor cure. He argued frantically with deputy sheriffs and Internal Revenue agents who showed up periodically to impound the gate receipts; and a favorite story around the ball park concerned the man-ager of the Sacramento ball club who pulled an extempora-neous switch on the old cry: "Is there a doctor in the house?"

Internal Revenue agents had impounded all of the receipts shortly after the start of the game, including Sacramento's share of the gate. After arguing frantically and getting nowhere, the distraught manager stormed out onto the playing field between innings and bellowed up at the stands: "Is there a lawyer in the house? I want a lawyer!"

In order to finance a spring training camp in 1937, Vanderveer was forced to hypothecate large blocks of tickets to various ticket-selling agencies, and he stood on the brink of complete financial disaster when Dave Beck came to his rescue and promoted the sale of Vanderveer's stock to Emil Sick, a Seattle brewer, who changed the name of the team to the Seattle Rainiers and produced a winning ball club.

The cynicism of Vanderveer in his later years is difficult to appraise. He was chief counsel for a great many labor unions, and he served them well. And yet Attorney Ford Smith later recalled a story that had become a widely quoted classic in Spokane, Washington:

Vanderveer had been called to Spokane to represent the Laundry Workers in a court action, at a time when that union was feuding with the management of the Davenport Hotel. He was met at the train by union representatives, who drove him to the Spokane Hotel. There they parked the car, got out, and opened the door; but Vanderveer stared out in amazement. "What in hell are you stopping here for? I always stay at the Davenport."

The union leaders explained that they were in litigation with management of the Davenport Hotel, that the place was being picketed, and that it would seem hardly proper for Vanderveer to stay there when he was in the city as a representative of their union.

"To hell with that!" he snorted. "The way I represent your union in court in the daytime, that's your business; but where I sleep at night, that's my business!" And in the face of his demands, they drove him to the Davenport Hotel, where he stayed throughout his visit to the city.

Vanderveer not only served as attorney for the Teamsters' Union but also served Dave Beck, international representative of the union, as his personal attorney. He represented Beck in three suits for libel and slander filed against Seattle newspapers and radio stations. These suits were settled all together in 1937. Vanderveer refused to accept the proffered fee for his services.

"Hell, I wasn't the one who was slandered," he protested, but he finally accept the fee in the face of Beck's threat to cancel professional relationships.

He received substantial retainers from the unions he represented, and he gave them full measure in return. His mastery of the courtroom had not diminished, and he continued to fight labor's battles with the zeal of a crusader, backed up by all of the cunning he had acquired through his years of experience. His sympathy and compassion for the laboring class could not be seriously questioned, and yet a certain bitter cynicism had become ingrained in his nature.

His clashes with the police continued, and on one occasion he was fined for contempt of court. Twice he nearly demolished an automobile when it skidded and rolled over while he was traveling at high speed. Miraculously, he escaped both times alive; but in the second accident, a broken rib punctured a lung.

His doctors advised him to quit smoking and quit drinking, but he would do neither. However, he did reduce his smoking because it irritated the injured lung, and, as a grudging concession, he switched back to tailor-made cigarettes.

In October, 1942, George Vanderveer was admitted to Providence Hospital for an operation made necessary by the lung condition. Before he was scheduled to be wheeled into the operating room he sent for Sam Bassett and together they reviewed the brief of a case pending east of the mountains.

"You'll have to carry on now, Sam; I'm leaving it all in your hands."

"I'll take care of it."

Vanderveer shook his head. "It's not just this case, Sam. I mean—everything."

The two men shook hands soberly, and Sam Bassett walked quickly out of the room to hide the tears that were welling up in his eyes. Never before had the two of them shaken hands upon departure, and he knew that he would never see George Vanderveer alive again.

The funeral for George Vanderveer was impressive and well attended. Professional, civic, and business leaders of Seattle stood with bowed heads as a Justice of the State Supreme Court delivered the major oration and suggested a fitting inscription for his tomb: "True to his oath, he never rejected, from any consideration personal to himself, the cause of the poor, the defenseless, the oppressed. . . ." Belatedly but in generous measure, Seattle offered its tribute to a great lawyer.

However, a more suitable epitaph for George Vanderveer may have been a statement he made before the court, in a trial conducted some years before his death. A young Indian deck hand on one of the Puget Sound steamers had been convicted of the rape of a white woman and sentenced to death. Believing that the young man had lacked adequate legal representation in the lower court, practically an entire tribe had descended upon Vanderveer's office and demanded that he carry the appeal to the Circuit Court of Appeals in San Francisco. Vanderveer accepted the assignment and in his arguments in San Francisco he attempted to show that improper evidence had been admitted in the original trial.

One of the Justices on the Circuit bench halted Vanderveer in the midst of his arguments and pointed out that there had been no exception requested by the defense attorneys to a court ruling when the case was being tried in the lower court and that thus there could be no charge of judicial error upon the point in question.

White with anger, Vanderveer demanded of the court:

"Would you hang a man because his lawyer failed to except to a ruling?"

Chief Judge Rudkin roared with laughter at the pointed irony of the barb, and a new trial subsequently was ordered. In the new trial, Vanderveer defended the young Indian and he was acquitted.

In his summation before the case went to the jury, Vanderveer pleaded for understanding of the plight of the American Indians. He charged that they were among those of this earth who are damned by fact and circumstance.

And in his final words, in a rare outburst of bitterness and personal humility, he offered the key to his own unhappy life as he stood with bowed head before the jury:

"I speak with feeling of such men, for I know what life can do to them. I speak with feeling because I am one of them . . . because there is something undeniable within me that compels me without mercy to my inescapable destiny . . . to serve as counsel for the damned. . . ."